INTERROGATIONS

Author Interviews
By
Jon Jordan

Published by:
Mystery One Books
2109 Prospect Ave
Milwaukee Wi
53202

First Edition October 2003

10 9 8 7 6 5 4 3 2 1

This book is for

Karen Jordan for giving me my passion for books and Armand Jordan for indulging it

Dick and Kathy Flannery for Ruth

In memory of Grandma Jean

Acknowledgments : Many people helped me with this, whether they know it or not. All the authors who took time out of their work to let me pick their brains, Doug Aanes who does such a great job with the Mystery One website, Vicki and David Ball who likewise do a great job with the Booksnbytes. com website. Richard, and he knows why. Annie Chernow and Thalia Proctor for editing and proof-reading. And my Uncle Douglas for keeping me grounded. Thanks to Rob Zombie, Andy Part-tridge, and U2. And also to everyone else who has encouraged me over the years. And my family and friends for letting me bounce ideas off them, often at odd hours of the night.

And of course my wife Ruth, for putting up with falling asleep while I'm still banging away at the keyboard late into the night, and letting me keep the light on so I can read.

Table of Contents

Forward by Jon
Introduction by Deborah Morgan

Forward

This book grew out of an idea hatched right after Bouchercon 1999. It was originally intended to add content to the Mystery One Bookstore's website to help increase traffic. Not long after, they started to appear on booksnbytes.com as well.

A major goal of the interviews has been to ask questions that haven't been asked before. I also like to give readers enough information to determine if this is an author they might want to read. I was pleased to find this was actually working when two ladies drove to Milwaukee from southern Illinois. They came up just to meet Sparkle Hayter after reading her interview on the Mystery One site.

I pick which authors to interview somewhat randomly. Sometimes I stumble across an email address and contact an author cold. Sometimes I meet an author and set it up in advance. And there are still many, many authors I would love to interview. If there's an author I haven't interviewed, it's just because I haven't gotten to them yet.

The interviews in this book are from the last four years. Katy Munger's was my first and Warren Murphey is from this spring. If some of the questions towards the end of the interviews seem a little out of place it's because I've asked some new questions to update the interview for this book. For instance, the Brian Wiprud interview was originally done last fall. The update was done after he got a contract with a major publisher, almost a year later.

I hope you enjoy reading these as much as I enjoyed doing them. If the mix is right, you'll see a few old favorites and find a some new authors you'd like to try.

Jon Jordan

Three Dimensions

Jon Jordan loves mysteries. He consumes crime fiction in its many forms. He's a film *noir* buff. Likely, he knows more about more mystery writers than any other reader buying crime fiction today. Why? Because he interrogates.

Fortunately, he's decided to share what he's learned.

Alfred Hitchcock once wrote, "Crime is the stone thrown into a quiet pool. . .. The detective is the diagnostician. It is his business to study the ripples on the surface of the pool and to find the disturbing stone."

The writer sends his fictional detective out to study those ripples, solve those crimes, and make sense of the worlds he creates--knowing full well that the real world often doesn't make sense.

Jon Jordan studies the ripples made upon the lives of those writers, and asks: Why? Where? When? How? Who? What?

Why vampires? (Charlaine Harris)

Where do the darker ideas come from? (Jeffery Deaver)

When were you attacked by a wrestler? (Val McDermid)

How did you end up on screen in The Wire? (George Pelecanos)

Who has given you the best writing advice? (S. J. Rozan)

What about the music? (Peter Robinson)

And he asks everyone: "What's the one thing that's always in your refrigerator?"

Things to ponder, for sure.

Of course, those queries were couched in Jordan's conversational banter. He knows there are questions that must be asked, questions that have been asked by every other interviewer worth his salt. Even those have an individual spin, are framed with Jordan inquisitiveness, thus making them more interesting, for both his subject and his audience. His approach invites humor, reflection, revelation. How does he achieve this? By reading. He's walked the mean streets with our protagonists, he's solved his share of fictional crimes, and he's come away both satisfied and wanting more.

He's been there, but he hasn't *stopped* there.

Question. Answer. Explore. Interrogate. All things that we, as writers, do of our psyches, ultimately of those characters who live in our minds, thus bringing them to life, working with smoke and mirrors in order to turn one dimension into three between our thoughts and the page.

With these interviews, Jon Jordan takes the *writer* from one-dimensional, if you will, to three--providing you with a glimpse into the life behind the page and what influences the characters and the stories that result.

Jordan is a champion of mysteries, and his passion--not only for crime fiction, but also for a glimpse into the lives of those who write it--is evident in his unique approach. Thanks to his efforts, you can look inside the world, the psyche and, yes, even the refrigerators of many of the top-notch mystery writers working today.

Enjoy!
Deborah Morgan

Deborah Morgan is the author of the Jeff Talbot series

Colin Bateman

Once upon a time, a punk rock journalist, aspirations shining through clouds of newspaper writing like sunbeams of hope, wrote a wonderful book. In a self-deprecating style common of Irish writers, he had little regard for it until his judicious girlfriend Andrea advised him of its greatness and encouraged him to follow his dreams. He did. The book languished in the dungeons of Harper Collins until plucked by a book troll. The book was dusted off, examined, loved and published. The punk rock journalist made good on his dream of writing greatness and won the Betty Trask prize. Oh, how the people liked him. For love of writing, the journalist began to write screenplays for movies and television, eventually having a series called Murphy's Law on the BBC. His courage grew and directing a short film joined his lists of achievements. Those lucky enough to read his books revered him for his dark humor, twisted plots and fallible heroes. They felt blessed by his prolific writing habits and cherished every release as manna from heaven. "We want more Divorcing Jack!" they'd say. "We want more "Chapter & Verse!" And the punk rocker smirkily obliged.
    --Jennifer Jordan

Jon: After reading Chapter and Verse, I feel that you might have a few issues with the world of publishing. Have you had some less than happy experiences?

Colin: Well, I think every author probably feels hard done by; I'm sure even JK Rowling has gripes from time to time - 'What, only ten thousand people at my last reading?' - and, judging from the reaction of people I meet, I think I should be selling a lot more books, but I'm doing okay. Chapter & Verse is just a story at the end of the day and has more to do with the ego a writer has than anything. I mean we're all just typists until one day someone decides you're an author, and then you get all these airs and graces and fantastic excuses not to do any real work because you're an artist. Although, that said, I should point out that what I think of as my best book, Mohammed Maguire, has been cruelly overlooked everywhere apart from in my own house.

Jon: Is there anything readers of this interview can do to help you get an American publisher?

Colin: I believe hunger strikes are quite effective. I think American publishers are a lot more conservative than British ones - the swearing and what is perceived as political incorrectness probably puts them off. I just happen to think they`re wrong. I think the humour works internationally, although probably not in German.

Jon: Was is a good experience writing the screenplay for Divorcing Jack based on your own book?

Colin: It was a fantastic experience - you always hear stories of writers having horrible times, but the people involved couldn't have been more supportive. Basically, they loved the book, and every time I started to veer away from it they hauled me back in. They also helped me solve a few holes in the plot, which weren't that noticeable in the book but would have been quite glaring up on screen.

Jon: What other type of things have you done before writing?

Colin: I was always jealous of those writers who listed their fantastically adventurous other lives at the front of their books - you know, cowboy, lumberjack, international terrorist... Obviously I've been all three, but I prefer not to talk about it. I have also been a journalist, managed several punk rock bands, and proved myself to be the worst businessman on this side of the Atlantic. Thank God I've finally found something I'm reasonably good at.

Jon: How did you meet John Connolly and has your sanity suffered for knowing him?

Colin: My home town of Bangor, Northern Ireland, has a literary festival every year, and as I'm the home town boy I get lumped in with whatever rising star is on tour but who might not draw a crowd. So John came to town and we did a good show together and hit it off; he's very easy to like, as long as he keeps taking his medication.

Jon: How much of yourself do you put into your books? Does reading them give us some insight into you?

Colin: Well I think I'm probably a bit of a Jekyll & Hyde character (as opposed to John, who's just a Hyde) in that I'm very shy and retiring until about the eighth drink and then I go a bit mental. The Dan Starkey sense of humour and approach to life is very much mine, although probably more a reflection of my single days than my current married state. These days as an author doing the publicity circuit, which again Chapter & Verse deals with, you have to be a bit of a performer and I find that I quite enjoy that. Luckily I can do readings from the books which are good fun, a lot of authors can't or won't read their stuff because it doesn't work in an audience setting, and when they do it can be like watching paint dry. John doesn't do readings - but then he can talk the leg off a stool.

Jon: You were sued by the boys brigade? What was that all about?

Colin: I don't think you have the BB in America, but they're basically like the Scouts (you have them don't you?) but slightly more religious, I like to think of them as the military wing of the Presbyterian Church. (And I'm an ex-BB boy myself.) However, way back when I was a journalist, and looking for an intro to a travel piece, I wrote that I'd just been to America buying guns for the BB, and, attempting to send up the nice quiet middle class town where I live, I said that the BB would host paramilitary coffee mornings `with an Armalite in one hand, and a packet of Jaffa Cakes in the other`, which is an adaptation of a very well known phrase used here by the Irish Republican Army, `an Armalite in one hand and the ballot box in the other`. I thought this was reasonably funny and satirical and the sort of thing I was popular for in the paper I worked on. However, between me writing it and it being published, there was a sudden upsurge in the Troubles here, things got very tense and dangerous and suddenly what had seemed funny wasn't quite so funny to a lot of people, especially the mothers of all the BB boys who besieged the paper with complaints crying that `their little Jimmy` was going to get murdered because of my article. Ludicrous, of course, but the BB took three separate libel actions against me; they would never have won, but libel is really expensive in the UK, so my publisher chickened out and published all kinds of apologies and retractions. I remain defiant!

Jon: I think part of what makes Dan Starkey such a great character is that he is so real. He has faults that many people try not to admit they have. And as a recovering alcoholic some of the scenes in the books make me cringe! Do you think that's part of his appeal?

Colin: Absolutely. I tend to think of Dan in terms of what I would do in any given dangerous situation, i.e. cry and run away, which he does a lot of. We see a lot of films with so-called ordinary people in extraordinary situations, like North by Northwest for example. Well, imagine Dan in it instead of Cary Grant and you might have had a very different movie. And much shorter. Dan just opens his mouth and says things without thinking about them, as we all do; he doesn't have much of an editing facility. But I think his heart is in the right place.

Jon: Do you think there is anything that would be too outrageous to put into a book?

Colin: No. I thought I might get into trouble with the IRA here for taking the piss out of the hunger strikes in Mohammed Maguire, which is quite close to blasphemy in certain parts, but the book was so badly promoted I doubt they even read it!

Jon: What are some of the books and authors you enjoy reading?

Colin: I don't read much when I'm writing, usually saving up a lot of `worthies` for when I go on holiday. Then I invariably chuck them in the bin and go and buy the latest Robert B. Parker. Actually, I have to pay tribute to old Robert B, because when I was a callow youth and de-spairing of ever being able to write, I read all the Spenser books and loved them and they absolutely inspired me to start writing: so simply written, yet great fun. Divorcing Jack started out just copying Robert B; before very long I developed my own style and went back and started that book again, but he absolutely got me going. I'll shake his hand if I ever meet him, but judging from all his work out routines, he'd probably break my hand. John Connolly`s a bit like that as well.

Jon: How do you react to reviews of your work, good and bad?

Colin: All my life my reviews have been very good until quite re-cently. I don't know, I think critics (over here anyway) are just getting harder. I think they have to justify their existence in some of the papers here by being nasty; this is especially true of TV and movie critics. They should be put up against a wall and shot (with film, of course). Of course, it might be that my writing's crap now.

Jon: What is a typical work week like for you?

Colin: Hectic. I have a pulp fiction approach to my work. I don't think spending any longer on it would necessarily make it any better. I used to be a journalist and nobody would say to a journalist - 'You wrote two stories this week? Well done! Take a few days off you must be exhausted.' I write quickly, I get bored easily and I like working on lots of different projects. I never expected to become a writer, so its a dream come true, and I grab every opportunity that comes along with both hands.

Jon: What is it about politicians that makes them so easy to make fun of?

Colin: Everything. The art of not answering questions mostly.

Jon: Where does the throwing potatoes at windows come from? Is this something you've done, a local custom or just something you came up with?

Colin: Oh, just a little something I came up with. Coming from a country where the national sport at one time seemed to be throwing petrol bombs, I thought it would be nice to throw the national dish as well.

Jon: I think it's safe to say that Dan and Patricia haven't always had the best relationship. After the events in The Horse With My Name, will we be seeing her again?

Colin: Oh Patricia and Dan are going to go on for ever because they love each other really. As the saying goes, can't live with them, can't live with them.

Jon: If someone decided to go to Belfast on Holiday and asked you what to see and do, what would you suggest?

Colin: Dublin? To us Belfast is just a small fairly boring city. But if you were a wide eyed American, you would probably want to take one of the terror tours to show you the war murals and the army posts, plus the one which takes you to all the pubs Dan Starkey`s been drunk in, although it takes a couple of weeks.

Jon: Is Murphy's Law the first crime fiction you've done with an actual detective?

Colin: Yes it is. I'm not sure if you've seen the TV series that goes with it yet, but even though he's a detective Murphy is quite like Dan Starkey in that he doesn't actually do a lot of detecting - he just gets thrown into an unusual situation and makes such a nuisance of himself that the bad guys give themselves away. There will be several other Murphy's Law novels. The first TV series has just been shown on the BBC and I'm currently writing the second series.

Jon: I notice that a lot of things written about you seem to compare you to other authors. Does this make you a little nuts at times?

Colin: Yes, I suppose I'll have arrived when Carl Hiaasen's books boast the legend `the new Colin Bateman` It is a bit annoying. I get Tarantino references as well because I think what I do is very different from Hiaasen`s and Tarantino`s. But I understand it as well, because I used to be a journalist and when you're not sure how to describe something, you naturally compare it to something else that's out there but better known.

Jon: What are some of your favorite movies?

Colin: I'm a real movie buff and am fascinated by the whole business end of it as well and the chance to work in the business has been a dream come true for me. Unfortunately the UK film business is in a pretty terrible state (i.e. my movies haven't done that well) so I'm doing a lot more TV work. My Murphy's Law series has just been shown on BBC 1 prime time and there's a second series on the way. As for what movies I watch, sometimes it's Hollywood blockbusters, sometimes it's Art House, sometimes its the old classics. A bit of everything really.

Jon: What are some of your favorite albums?

Colin: Afraid I'm stuck in a rut from the late 70's, all the punk stuff that never really took off in America - the Clash, the Pistols. I like Springsteen. And the Paul McCartney live album out at the moment is kind of nice, but mostly just to hear the old Beatles stuff done live.

Jon: I've heard a few people who love your work say that Empire State is their favorite book. What's that one about? I haven't gotten it yet.

Colin: Empire State is about the President of the United States being held hostage at the top of the Empire State building by a young Irish kid, who does it by mistake, thus foiling a mad Southern racist who really was intending to take him hostage. I thought I'd sell it for millions and have Bruce Willis in it, but it is so politically incorrect that the studios ran a mile. I did write a screenplay for it which nearly got made by a small British company, it was cast, the money was apparently there, sets were being designed, but they never thought to actually ask the Empire State people about it. They didn't realize that the building was actually copyrighted. You can't reproduce its likeness without their permission. So they had to go meet them. First question was: `Is there any violence in this movie?` I think it was a very short meeting. Never did get made, but yes, it's a lot of people's favourite. Ironically, it became the first of my books not to be published in America!

Jon: What's the biggest difference in how you spend your weekends now that you are married with children?

Colin: Weekends? What are they? At weekends I get my only exercise, which is five-a-side football with my friends. I work in Dublin during the week, and then travel up to my family at weekends, which is nice. You may not know about the Irish Republic and its bizarre tax laws i.e., writers don't pay any tax - ANY TAX. Which makes a big difference to your life. That's why I work in the South of Ireland and my family home is in the North. It's hard, but it's not for ever.

Jon: Would you say that writing for you is more of a calling or more of a job?

Colin: Well it used to be a hobby, but then your hobby becomes your job, and its not always so much fun. But its much better than working down a coal mine.

Jon: What's the strangest thing you saw as a reporter?

Colin: I'm from Northern Ireland - guns, bombs, etc., but the only time I dealt directly with terrorists was with the Animal Liberation Front! They called my paper to make a statement about something they'd done and to prove they were who they said they were they said, `The code word is.....` you know, badger or something. And I said, don't you have to advise us in advance what the codewords are so that we'll recognize it, at which point they got very embarrassed and hung up. Such was reporting on a small weekly newspaper.

Jon: Your titles are really great. They are image provoking and they make readers want to grab the book to see what they are about. Do you decide on them before or after you do the book? And how important are the titles?

Colin: The titles are very important to me, they set the whole tone of the book. For instance, the next Dan Starkey, which I'm currently writing, is called `Driving Big Davie`. And as for the children's book....

Jon: Is it true you are working on a kid's book?

Colin: I have a contract to write three children's books for my publisher, they're a series about teenage gangs in Belfast. And the first one is called `Reservoir Pups`.

Jon: Are there ever times when you sit down to write and your mind goes blank?

Colin: Very rarely. I used to be a journalist and nobody says to a journalist, hey, you've written six paragraphs there, take a rest, go out for a walk. I love writing, it was a hobby, but its now my job, so I work office hours and beyond and rarely have a problem. If I do get `blocked` its usually just for an afternoon. Then I usually take myself off to the movies - and if its a good movie it inspires, and funnily enough, if its bad it inspires as well, because you think, I can do better than that. Only problem is if you go to see something like `Crouching Tiger/Hidden Dragon` you come back and start writing this Belfast gangster story, and it starts to get all Eastern mystical. So you have to be careful.

Jon: What advice would you give to aspiring authors?

Colin: Don't - I don't need the competition. Go make hats. No - I would say go for it because I was stuck in a dead end job going nowhere, and suddenly my life changed completely - money, sex, drugs, and all before breakfast. No - I mean, all my dreams came true. Literally. I would say switch off the TV, spend at least an hour every night at the start just writing what you want to write. Some people dismiss the `write what you know` idea, but I think at the start, when you lack confidence, its best to write what you know just make it more interesting. And if what you really want to do is write novels, then don't bother with short stories or poetry because they're the easy option, you can do them in one night or a couple of nights. Novels are for the long haul, but at least you might get paid in the end.

Jon: What's the most embarrassing thing you've ever done?

Colin: At my first ever awards dinner, which was a very plush affair with the leading lights of publishing and at which I was one of the honoured guests, I got so drunk I fell asleep in my first course, and then had to be carried out, down three flights of steps by my six months pregnant wife. I was put to bed and she ended up in McDonalds. I was not very popular the next day.

Jon: You've just done a short film? What is it and where can we see it?

Colin: It was called 'The Devil You Know' and I adapted it from a short story I wrote for a crime anthology. It was great fun to do, and no you can't see it! It wasn't very good, but a great learning experience. I'm hoping to direct another in September, but they're so time consuming they`re difficult to justify. But I`m a big movie buff, and the thought of one day going up for that Oscar.....

Jon: If you decided to commit a crime, what crime would you commit? And could you get away with it?

Colin: Oh I think you would have to go for the big one. And the key would be disposing of the body. I like those films were the heroine opens the fridge and there's a head in it but she doesn't see it.

Jon: What's the one thing always in your refrigerator?

Colin: Diet Pepsi - because my wife and I are hopeless addicts.

<u>Colin Bateman's website :</u>
http://authorpages.hoddersystems.com/ColinBateman

<u>Colin Bateman's books :</u>
Babysnatchers 1 (children's book) (2003)
The Horse With My Name(2003)
Chapter and Verse(2003)
Murphy's Law(2002)
Wild About Harry (2001)
Mohammed Maguire (2001)
Shooting Sean (2001)
Crossmaheart -Paperback - (1999)
Turbulent Priests (1999)
Maid of the Mist (1999)
Divorcing Jack: The Screenplay Paperback - (1998)
Empire State (1997)
Of Wee Sweetie Mice and Men (1996)
Cycle of Violence (1995)
Divorcing Jack (1995)

Mark Billingham

Mark and I became friendly a couple of years ago when he came to interview me for Shots magazine about my books. As we talked, we realised a strange set of parallels in our lives. We're both huge Elvis Costello fans. Our favourite play is Trevor Griffiths' Comedians. Our wives both work in the entertainment business (TV director and theatre costume designer respectively). Our kids are the same age and same sex as each other. We were freeloading in the same flat at the same time during the Edinburgh festival in the Eighties, with the cast of a cubist interpretation of The Government Inspector (don't ask). We've both worked as stand up comics (although Mark has been much more successful at it than me). And, of course, we have a huge interest in crime fiction. As Elvis Costello said, 'In time we can turn these obsessions into careers.'

*And he has. Mark has had three books published now – **Sleepyhead**, **Scaredy Cat** and **Lazy Bones**. With them he has swiftly defined and cornered the market in North London serial killer noir, with hard bitten, cynical, loner cop, Tom Thorne, tracking down man (and woman)-created monsters in a world instantly recognisable as our own. Told with whiplash, diamond-hard prose, they're all deservedly critically and commercially acclaimed. If you haven't read them yet, do so straight away. You'll be in for a treat.- Martyn Waites (author of Born Under Punches)*

Jon: What can you tell us about your first book? Is it the start of a series?

Mark: Yes it is. SLEEPYHEAD is the first in a series of books featuring Detective Inspector Tom Thorne and a cast of supporting characters! In this first novel, Thorne is on the trail of a man who deliberately induces strokes in his victims and has left three women dead and a fourth in a coma. The police think that in leaving this woman alive, the killer has made his first mistake. The horrifying discovery Thorne makes early on is that it is the dead women that are the killer's mistakes. The fourth victim, Alison Willetts, is his one success. Alison lies in a hospital bed suffering from a hideous condition called "locked-in syndrome". She can see, hear, feel but she is completely and utterly unable to move. Thorne is hunting a man who for reasons he cannot fathom has a unique agenda - to leave his victims at the mercy of machines, neither alive nor dead but somewhere in between. Thorne has got to find the killer before he "succeeds" again and Alison, the one person who holds the key to his identity, is unable to tell anyone.

Jon: You have also written for television right? What kind of stuff did you write?

Mark: Oddly, considering the dark stuff in the books, I used to write a lot of children's comedy and drama. I began writing as part of the creative team behind a show called "Maid Marian And Her Merry Men" which I was also in. It was a comic version of the Robin Hood story created by a great writer called Tony Robinson, who you may know as Baldrick from "Blackadder". Since then I've written both my own shows and as part of a team on other peoples shows for the BBC. I think writing comedy for kids is hard. They're so much more picky about what they laugh about. I truly believe that it's actually tougher to get an honest to goodness laugh out of a twelve year old than it is to get one from a drunk at half past Midnight at the Comedy Store. Plus, the kids are rarely bigger than me and they don't throw glasses.

Jon: As a new author, what is your take on the whole publishing industry? Was it hard to get the first book published? Is there anything about that surprised you?

Mark: The publishing business in the UK seems to be quite an old-fashioned one in many ways. Deals are made on trust and a certain level of professional etiquette tends to be observed. It may be the same in the US but I was astonished that when various publishers were bidding for SLEEPYHEAD, they never checked the figures in the auction that they were being given by my agent, and at no time do they know who they are bidding against. It's all done on trust, and I think that's amazing and very refreshing. I think I got very lucky in terms of getting the book published. I'd written about one-third of it when it got sent to publishers and I suppose the manuscript landed on the right desks at the right time. It jumped through the necessary hoops quite quickly and the publisher did a phenomenal job in helping get the book into the top ten bestsellers here. I'm still hugely excited about the whole process, and having gone through the euphoria of publication and so on in the UK, I'm now gearing up for the huge thrill of publication in the US which is one book behind. I find the whole process of checking proofs, looking at jacket designs - all of it- immensely exciting. Maybe I won't in a few years time, but at the moment I'm still pinching myself...

Jon: What other jobs have you had?

Mark: I'm also a stand-up comic and I was a jobbing actor, so it would be true to say that I've never done a proper day's work in my life. Hang on, I did work as a cleaner at a holiday camp one summer just before I went to University but I got scared after a few weeks and came home. I was working on the night shift with some very rough characters. One guy was a punk rocker who was trying to look like Sid Vicious from the Sex Pistols. He worked in the kitchens, and every day after he'd unloaded the meat he would put handfuls of fresh blood from the meat trays into his hair to get just the right amount of spikiness. He also had a padlock on a chain around his neck. It was a nice image, but unfortunately he'd lost the key and his neck was turning green. These were scary people. These were the sort of people who, because I had stayed at school beyond the age of fourteen, called me "professor"...

Jon: Does Thorne have any of you in him?

Mark: Well, he's around the same age and he likes a little of the same music, but aside from that, not really. He's definitely shorter than me! Sometimes if the character is musing about the state of London - the public transport, the health service, whatever, he may voice an opinion or two that I happen to share, but I don't see the point in just putting yourself on the page. It's fiction, not autobiography. I certainly have a much different life from Tom Thorne in domestic terms. Thorne is, to say the least, unsettled, but that of course goes with the territory. Cops have unhappy love lives and dark pasts in the same way that cowboys have six guns and Stetsons. I'm sure there are detectives who have perfectly blissful private lives and go home to their families every night and drink hot chocolate and watch television. I'm just not interested in reading about those characters and certainly not in writing about them.

Jon: Do your friends read this book and wonder about all this dark twisted stuff in your head?

Mark: Yes, there was a certain amount of that, a few odd looks. I think we all have dark, twisted stuff in our heads and, cliche as it is, it's probably therapeutic to get it out of there and into the heads of other people.

Jon: What authors do you like to read?

Mark: Most of my favourite writers are American. We have some great crime writers in the UK, writers I admire hugely - Rankin, McDermid, John Connolly - but the ones I salivate over are definitely American.

 Michael Connelly, James Lee Burke , Daniel Woodrell (who should be far bigger than he is). I am a massive fan of Dennis Lehane. We now share an editor in the US which is a huge thrill for me. She kindly sent me an ARC of "Mystic River" as I was writing my second book, and it was so outrageously good that I couldn't write anything for a month! My very favourite writer is George Pelecanos, whose novels have elegance, grace, and integrity dripping from them. His "DC Quartet" is as fine a piece of writing as anything in the last fifty years, and his next book "Hell To Pay" is truly, truly a masterpiece I think.

Jon: Was there anyone along the way that inspired you to write, or to just keep trying to do what you wanted to do?

Mark: I was inspired to write simply from reading, and all of the people I've mentioned inspired me and continue to do so. The day that I stop reading stuff so great that it makes me want to give up, is the day I will give up.

Jon: Are you going to continue to write for television?

Mark: I haven't really decided. There is other stuff I am still doing, TV work, comedy, the screenplay for an Andrew Lloyd-Webber musical ??!! But increasingly it all feels like an interruption from writing the books, which is where my heart is at the moment.

Jon: There are actually other crime fiction writers who also did stand up comedy. John Ridley also started out doing stand-up, and then moved to writing for television. Do you think a certain amount of humor is important to being able to do this kind of writing?

Mark: Yes, I think humour is pretty crucial in any kind of writing and yes, strangely, the darker the subject matter the more this tends to be true. What is certainly true, and rather odd, is that writing crime fiction and performing comedy both use many of the same techniques. First off, a strong opening is important. That first gag has got to be a cracker if the crowd is to trust you and to relax into your material. Ditto the readers of your book. Most have not got time to give a novel the "benefit of the doubt" or to "persevere" if it doesn't grab them straight away. If the audience/reader is to be engaged, it needs to be done pretty bloody quickly. Whether in a sweaty, smoky club or nestled in a favourite armchair, good money has been paid and the attention has got to be grabbed by the scruff of the neck if you are not to be heckled off the stage or find your novel discarded in favour of another. The same applies to the climax of your act/novel. The big finish is all important. Whether your loose ends are to be tied up or left dangling, whether you leave the audience on a shaggy dog story or a song, a bang is always preferable to a whimper. The most striking similarity between writing comedy and crime fiction is the use of what comics call the reveal. In joke terms, this is the moment when it becomes clear that you have been led down one path only for the punchline to come rushing up the other and smack you in the face. (My grandfather died last week. Audience goes "aaahhh" No, it's OK. He died very peacefully, just sitting there in his chair. He went very quietly. Unlike the passengers on his bus...) Crime or mystery fiction uses reveals like this all the time. The writer chooses the most effective or dramatic moment to reveal key information. This is often a clue, though the biggest reveal of all, of course, is usually the identity of a killer. In the case of whodunnits, it might be said that the whole book is one extended pull back and reveal. I enjoy writing for both these mediums. If either were to cease being enjoyable I should stop doing it but right now that seems unlikely. For the present I get the best of both worlds. Death, blood and terror. And then there's the crime writing...

Jon: Where would you like to see yourself in ten years time?

Mark: Reflected in the silver of the World Cup trophy, which I am holding aloft, accepting the plaudits of 100,000 fans, having been called up (at a somewhat advanced age its true) to play football for England, and captaining them to victory in the final against Germany. Or just happy and healthy, coping with two teenage kids, and with a dozen well-thought-of novels under my belt.

Jon: When you write, do you need solitude, or does having a family close to you make it easier?

Mark: Having a young family around certainly makes it impossible to get too "up oneself". Of course, solitude is necessary for the actual fingers on keyboard stuff, but I often get my best ideas or visualize the most affecting images while doing the most humdrum family things. It would be strange but true to say that some of the nastier moments in SLEEPYHEAD had their birth in the car, on the school run with "The Wheels On The Bus" on the cassette player.

Jon: I guess this is an obvious question, but I'm going to ask anyway. Were you a class clown in school?

Mark: Yes, I was the class clown. However, I was also the class bully. If people didn't laugh at my jokes I would poke them with something sharp...

Jon: In the book, the media is portrayed kind of like sharks circling a body in the water. Do the papers in the UK tend to sensationalize crime to sell papers?

Mark: Yes, they do, but no more than anywhere else I don't suppose. What has become quite repulsive here is the way the media has whipped up quite natural feelings of disgust and repulsion towards pedophiles into something approaching mob rule. A certain ghoulish "shrine" mentality has grown up here that can be traced back to the death of Princess Diana, I think. People will travel the length of the country to lay a bunch of flowers at the side of the road where a child they did not know has disappeared. The media feeds this kind of frenzy, taking advantage of the natural compassion in people until it becomes something ugly. Rumours are fed by the media and flames of bigotry and ignorance are fanned to the point where justice is no longer possible. There was an incident here recently where a woman was hounded out of her home because of a sign on her door that told people what she did for a living. She was a pediatrician. She looked after children! PAED... was however enough for some people, and she was forced to flee after violence. You couldn't make that sort of dark, dark tragic-comedy up.

Jon: Did you have to do any research for the book? And, if so, what kind?

Mark: I had to do a fair amount of medical research for SLEEPY-HEAD, for which I am eternally grateful to one hugely creative doctor friend and the crime writer's very best friend - the internet. Ditto with police procedure. I did enough research to get the basics right. That's all I'm interested in really. As long as there aren't any glaring errors I'm happy. I know (because I am one) how picky crime readers are about mistakes, so I will take every step necessary to avoid them. Crime writers owe it to readers not to insult their intelligence, but they should also honour their imagination. I'm writing fiction and not documentary so I want to take the facts and use them to my own dark and dastardly ends so as, hopefully, to entertain the people that read the books.

Jon: Was the title, Sleepyhead, your idea?

Mark: Yes, and it was a title I came up with very early on. The word itself is highly significant polities as well as being appropriate for a story which in many ways is about a woman who is permanently trapped somewhere between being asleep and awake. The word also has a childlike, innocent quality to it which, in the context of the book becomes something altogether spookier and far from reassuring.

Jon: Minette Walters once said that she sees her books as a chance to play a game with her readers; to see if they can pick up the clues and figure out the ending before they get there. What is your take on this? Do you give the reader a fair chance to figure it out, or do you want them to buckle up and enjoy the ride?

Mark: Both. I want the ride to be enjoyable certainly but it isn't one that's dependent on clues or puzzles. I think (I wait to be corrected!) that a lot of US crime readers have a perception that British writers specialize in these books which stand or fall on solving elaborate puzzles. Some do, of course, but an increasing number of writers here are creating stuff that is character driven, that comes from a concern for certain issues and I would certainly place myself in this camp. Of course I want the reader to be enthralled until the very end and there is, of course, the big reveal in which I have given them, I think, every chance to figure out, but this is not solely what the book is about.

Jon: It seems that a lot of British writers are starting to catch on in the states. Do you think it's important for the books to do well outside of the UK?

Mark: I think my agent thinks it's important! Yes, I certainly hope that the books do OK. I am an enormous Americophile (I may have invented that word). The genre of crime fiction I like was invented over there, and so for my books to be well thought of by US crime readers would be fantastic. It's such an enormous market over there that I think it is quite hard. It's tough enough for any number of brilliant American writers to get a foothold in the States so I am thrilled to have even got a deal over there. Anything else will be a huge bonus and, of course, a good excuse to come to Bouchercon!

Jon: I believe that Death on Deansgate was your first convention as a writer. What was it like to interact with the other authors as one of them?

Mark: It was great. I'd actually done some panels at this year's Crimescene at the National Film Theatre but Deansgate was my first real chance to hang out with some of these writers. Crime writers generally seem a pretty nice crowd - far less bitchy than other groups I've spent time among (notably actors and comedians!!) and very welcoming of new blood. It was great to meet some writers for the first time - John Harvey, Steve Booth and a real treat to get to know George Pelecanos, who I had the honour of interviewing on stage for the convention. He was hugely supportive of my book and very generous. Even though everyone was there to hear him talk about his work I had to keep working very hard to stop him steering the conversation round to mine! That's an absence of ego that you would never encounter among actors or comedians.

Jon: Any thoughts on why UK television does mystery and crime stuff so much better than it's done in the US?

Mark: I don't think it does do it better, it just does it differently. We do those languorous, rather elegiac treatments of stuff like Morse, or Frost, or Dalziel & Pascoe, very well and, in recent years, series like Cracker have developed more of an edge. I don't think any of these shows though can hold a candle to US shows like Homicide, NYPD Blue, The Sopranos, or Oz. Like I said earlier, I'm an Americophile. Perhaps we are all drawn to...otherness.

Jon: What are some of your favorite movies?

Mark: Oh, all sorts of stuff. I'm a huge movie fan. Comedy wise it doesn't get funnier than "Manhattan" or "Spinal Tap" and I've a soft spot for everything from the Ealing comedies to the best of the Carry On series. I love stuff ranging from epics like the Godfather series through to beautifully made self-contained crime stories like "The Usual Suspects" and "One False Move". My top ten, which of course changes all the time, would feature everything from "Blood Simple" to "Its A Wonderful Life".

Jon: And ...what kind of music do you like?

Mark: Like I said, I share some musical passions with Tom Thorne - notably his love of (proper) country music. Cash, Haggard, Williams, Parsons, Earle. Aside from that I'm pretty retro I suppose, still into the singers and bands that I was a fan of at eighteen. The Clash, the Jam, XTC and above all the mighty Elvis Costello, the finest singer-songwriter of his generation. Always easier of course to say what you don't like - folk music, hip-hop and it goes without saying all boy-bands, who should be tortured live on national television.

Jon: Do you have another book in the works now? Can you tell us about it?

Mark: I'm actually working on the third Thorne novel at the moment. The second one is finished and delivered. It's called SCAREDY CAT and will be published here next July, at the same time that SLEEPY-HEAD is published in the US. In SCAREDY CAT, Thorne is investigating a series of killings whose origin dates back to a school playground and the disappearance of a young girl fifteen years before. The book is about is about the nature of fear. How certain individuals can be manipulated by it into the most terrible acts. How those that have the ability, and the lack of conscience to inspire it possess the most powerful weapon there is.

Jon: Are you going to be setting up a website?

Mark: I already have one, though I am about to have it shut down and redesigned. It was set up a while ago, before I got a book deal and so is there solely as a publicity tool for my career as a comic. It is therefore very silly, and somewhat rude, and not representative, as it should be, of my new found and very sombre and arty persona as an (ahem) serious writer.

Jon: With your popularity as an writer growing and you doing more events as an author, is it getting harder to find time to write?

Mark: It's less to do with the number of events and more to do with the traveling involved. I'm spending an increasing amount of time overseas and, though I always think that I'll be able to write while I'm away, I can never really manage to do it. The management of time is definitely becoming a major consideration. Time spent promoting at home and abroad is unquestionably important, not to mention enjoyable - what, you want me to sit around in this five-star hotel all day talking about my books and then take me out for dinner??? How dare you!! - but a book a year, if that's what you want to do, is actually more like a book every nine months, because for the rest of the time you're tarting around. All that said, the events themselves are, for the most part, hugely enjoyable. As someone with a performance background (ie, a shameless attention-seeker) I love reading and interacting with an audience. I especially enjoy events in the US where audiences seem more receptive to showing-off than in some other countries.

Jon: Now that you're working on the fourth book in the series, do you find it going where you thought it would when you started, or has it started to take a life of its own, with you writing down what happens?

Mark: I never really believed any of that "the characters do what they want and I am but a cipher who must bend to their will" bullshit. The story goes where I tell it. There is a degree however to which Thorne forces himself into stories that weren't originally meant to be his at all. He's now done that to me twice. I have what I think is a great idea for a standalone novel and then I turn around and he's somehow wangled his way into it and actually it's become much more exciting.

Jon: What would you consider the perfect breakfast?

Mark: I had corned-beef hash with a poached egg on while I was on tour in the US - that was pretty fabulous, but you have to go a long way to beat last night's leftover curry warmed up.

Jon: If a television show was put together in the style of Survivor, with yourself, John Connolly, Martyn Waites, Paul Johnston, Fidelis Morgan and Lauren Henderson, who would win and why?

Mark: God, I have to be SO careful here. It's a major leap of imagination to picture Lauren roughing it for too long. I would probably follow her back to civilization pretty quickly thereafter, as my practical skills go no further than knowing how to cook a hedgehog. I can't see Paul or Fidelis as King or Queen of the Island either, though I can picture them strolling languidly along the shore clad in banana leaves - Fidelis's decorated with diamante, obviously. I think it would de-generate into a Lord Of the Flies, savagery thing pretty quickly with conch shells and pig-sticking, and I'm very entertained by the idea of Connolly and Waites fighting each other for overall supremacy, daubed in blood and bits of livestock. Waites is bigger, but Connolly is tough and determined and would probably have a dirty trick or two up his sleeve, so my money would be on him. Yes, I think that we would probably all end up as Connolly's bitches...

Jon: What's the last book you read, and what did you think of it?

Mark: THE CUTTING ROOM by Louise Welch and I loved it. Very much touted as literary crime and I have to say that I'm still not sure what that means. If it just means well-written then it is certainly that, but I think that by the same token there are a great many "literary" crime writers out there. If that is the criterion, then aren't we all trying to be literary crime-writers? For my part, I'm trying to tell a good story, but I'm also trying to tell it as well as I possibly can...

Jon: What is the one thing that's always in your refrigerator?

Mark: An electrically powered refrigeration system. If not for this, my refrigerator would just be a big, shiny, white cupboard.

Mark Billingham's website:
www.markbillingham.com

Mark Billingham's books :
Sleepy Head (2001)
Scaredy Cat (2002)

Cara Black

Cara Black reads the same authors I do. It's so nice to know you're not alone in a world of varied reading tastes. Cara Black waxes poetic over Paris. She'd better; her books take place in the 20 Arrondissements that make up the city. Cara Black takes some fantastic pictures. Her photographs of Paris have graced the covers of her mysteries. The cover of her Murder in the Sentier was up for an Anthony award for best cover design. She managed to top this by having this same novel up for an Anthony for best novel

Murder in the Marais introduces us to Aimee Leduc. Aimee does corporate computer security work but as business is slow she decides to help a rabbi get to the bottom of a murder. This story moves from Nazis old and neo to politics French style. Other plots in other books involve murder, immigration, politics again, pearls and loss of vision. As a P.I Aimee moves through all the novels with a sureness that grows from case to case as Cara Black's writing does from book to book. - Dave Biemann

Jon: How would you describe your series with Aimee Leduc?

Cara: Aimee's a thoroughly modern Parisian who works in computer security. Her father was a flic, her grandfather too, giving her a criminal investigative background via osmosis. Raised by her father after her mother abandoned them, Aimee grew up doing homework on the marble Commissariat floor and hearing flic's tales over poker at the kitchen table. When her father left the force, joining the detective agency his father started, she began to help out. She often gets pulled into criminal investigations, against her better judgment.

Jon: What made you decide to set the series in France?

Cara: Sometimes, I think Paris chose me. Many have asked me where I got the idea. The inspiration came from many places but the seed was planted in Paris. In the Marais. My first introduction to the Marais was in 1984 when my friend, a Parisian, invited me to explore a part of the city that not many knew of at that time. We descended from the green open-backed bus down the narrow cobblestone streets and past the 16th century hotel particulars, still as yet ungentrified. Cobblers, Yiddish bookshops and Jewish restaurants with Middle Eastern food lined the rue des Rosiers. And I knew this quartier was special, unique and in a very odd way felt like "home". I saw former aristocrats mansions with plaques commemorating victims of the Gestapo executions shot at that spot.

And then my friend gestured toward an old stone building and told me the story of her mother's life. All afternoon, as we walked in the Marais, she recounted the story of her mother, a young Jewish schoolgirl, who hid from the Germans. And how her sisters, brother and parents were taken by the French police under German orders, and how they never returned.

Her mother's story haunted me as did the Marais with it's layers of history. If only those stones could talk! Ten years later, I re-visited France, staying in the south on a lavendar farm with my husband Jun, and young son, Shusei.

We spent our last few days in Paris, around the corner from Place des Vosges the magnificent square once home to medieval jousting tournaments built by Henri the fourth. At night I walked around and my friends mother's story came back to me, as vivid as if she'd stood next to me on those narrow cobbled streets.

Arriving back in San Francisco, I suffered jet lag, couldn't sleep. So in the middle of the night, I sat down at the computer and Hartmuth's story poured out, then Sarah's. I was in a writing group at the time, and this group process helped me clarify my ideas and thoughts to help weave the characters and their lives in a thread that spans fifty years. Three and a half years later, MURDER IN THE MARAIS emerged.

I visited Paris many times after that, researching and documenting history and daily life from that time. I went to the Jewish Documentation center. It was important to find ration cards, see the uniforms school children wore and many other details so intrinsic to that era. And the most important, to feel those cobbles under my feet again, smell the espresso and scent of Gauloises. I met and interviewed three of the four female French private detectives who had their own firms at the time. One remains a good friend and through her introductions, I've met private investigators and the former police chief of Paris, now retired.

But disturbing to me, were the riots and demonstrations in Paris protesting immigration, so reminiscent of the feeling of the Vichy laws against Jews during the war. It felt as if history repeated itself. I tried to understand modern day France's reactions to new waves of immigrants, the legacy of their colonial empire.

On my last visit to Paris for research on my third book, I had the fantastic opportunity to tour the Quai Des Orfevres, the police headquarters, and see the "office" of Inspector Maigret, Simenon's famous detective.

Jon: Do you put any of yourself in Aimee? Are you as Hip as Aimee?

Cara: I wish. And I wish I had her apartment on Ile St. Louis.

Jon: I noticed that you ride a Moped. And you actually admit it! Is it a safe way to travel?

Cara: Uh..oh. Well no endorsement but in Paris I ride a bike or walk or hit the Metro...but I often wish I had my old moped. Saves those legs on the Montmartre hills!

Jon: What other things have you done besides writing?

Cara: The Mom job...a preschool teacher, running the espresso machine in the Basel (Switzerland) train station, teaching English in Tokyo.

Jon: How much research goes into your books?

Cara: A lot. But never enough, as I tell my husband, when those cheap RT fares to Paris come across my eyes and I feel the need to jump on the plane and really see how that corner looks and would that shop be there, could she really jump over that fence etc. But I really fact check everything, and make sure that all the Metro exits really are where she exits. Geographically you can follow along in the book, via the map and go where she goes. Sometimes the little passages and narrow streets aren't on the map in the book but are on a bigger Paris map.

Jon: The SOHO books all look great. I love the design of them. Are you going to take any of the photos used for the covers?

Cara: Thank you! Yes, they used my photo on the cover of MURDER IN THE SENTIER. The scene you see was taken from the rue St. Denis with several streetwalkers behind me peering into the courtyard with garment sweat shops in historic hotel particulars and a very wonderful one in the back, Hotel St. Chaumond, that unfortunately you can barely make out.

Jon: How does your creative process work? Do you have set writing hours? Do you work from an outline?

Cara: I work in the mornings, during the day, until I pick my son up at school. The outlining I do is with colored post-its...since the plots get complicated and different points of view, it's easy to move them around. I also tape butcher paper on the walls and steal my son's markers and do vague broad notes and what to include.

Jon: Who are some of the authors you enjoy reading?

Cara: There are so many. Right now I'm reading The Piano shop on the Left Bank - wonderful book and a very nice author who I met who lives in Paris. Paretsky, Rendell, PD James, and many others.

Jon: What's the coolest thing about being a writer?

Cara: I get to go to Paris every day with no passport, avoid those long security lines in the airport and the hassle of paying extra for baggage in those Paris taxis! And I'm home by three pm.

Jon: Do you enjoy the signings and Mystery Conventions?

Cara: Sure. I love meeting people who like mysteries and who ask me about Aimee, her dog Miles Davis and Rene' her partner, a dwarf and computer wizard. People always want to know about Rene' and want more of him. After sitting in small room at a keyboard for a year or more, it's great to get out in the world and breath and talk about these characters who've you've lived with for so long.

Jon: Where did the idea for Rene' come from? Not too many mysteries with dwarves in them that I know of except George Chesbro.

Cara: Nice segue. Here's a generalization, but often when people look at a dwarf they see only her or his limitations and diminutive size. Not the possibilities. We had a dwarf apply for a job at the preschool I taught at and this was the case. This short statured person was hired at a neighboring school. Later, we all realized we were the losers as she was an excellent teacher and the children loved and learned so much from her. So, I hope to explore more of Rene's issues in later books.

Jon: Your books have a wonderful feeling of place in them. Having been to France, I get flashbacks reading them. Have you spent much time there?

Cara: Never enough. But I lived in Basel, Switzerland on the French/ German border and often went to Paris and France. I've stayed for long periods of time in France and in Paris and went twice last year. I'm wearing out my friend's couch in Montmartre!

Jon: If you had a week to do what ever you wanted, wherever you wanted, what would you do?

Cara: Only a week? Can I use a Lear jet? Walk the streets of Prague at night, spend a day on Paros, ride the moped to the artesian well in the middle of the island, (my favorite Greek island), eat noodles in the old part of Peking, dive in the corals off Madagascar, see the orangutans in Indonesia, be given the keys to Paris by the mayor who'd allow me peek inside any wonderful building I wanted, hang out with the computer security division of the Brigage Criminelle and do a ride along with the flics, have a night to take all the Paris night photos I want, there's more but I guess with jet lag, this would about take care of it.

Jon: After getting the first book published, I imagine that you are expected to get books out on schedule. Does that make the writing harder?

Cara: My editor is great and says when the book is done then the book is done.

Jon: Is there anything thing about being a published writer that you weren't expecting? Any thing about the whole thing that surprised you? Did it give you any insight having a husband who owns a bookstore?

Cara: My husband encourages me to 'get out there' and talk about my book and says if I don't do it, it won't get done. And I'm surprised that people think I make a lot of money. I have to say most of us don't do it for the money, we have someone else to support us.

Jon: Okay, in the first book you had neo-nazis, in book two you had illegal immigrants and political intrigue, what is in store in book three?

Cara: 70's European terrorists, Senegalese in sweatshop conditions in the Sentier, and clues to Aimee's mothers disappearance.

Jon: Do you have any self-set limits in terms of what you will and won't write about?

Cara: I don't like serial killers and I'm just about to break that rule.

Jon: If people see you at a convention, what could they say to really make your day?

Cara: Take my airplane ticket to Paris...you need it more than I do. Thank you for writing about things that matter.

Jon: In MURDER IN THE BASTILLE. René gets to do a little more actual footwork than in the past. Are we going to see René become more of an investigator as the series progresses?

Cara: Well, René had been demanding page time for awhile. Yet for him, the footwork part turned out more of a challenge than he'd expected. But that's a question I'm wrestling with right now in the next book. Along with the possibility of a love interest and medical issues.

Jon: What's the most challenging part of writing for you?

Cara: Getting my derriere in the chair and the fingers on the keyboard! And having faith the characters will speak to me and, if I'm hospitable enough, stay and take over the page. Rewriting used to make me want to leave the room, but I'm trying to take Voltaire's maxim "WRITING IS REWRITING' " to heart and just do it. I'm also following Balzac's caffeine addiction, the man drank upwards of 30-40 cups a day and look at his output! Of course, he died in middle-age. So far, I'm just up to an espresso and latte in the afternoon.

Jon: Do you have any guilty pleasures? For me it's watching the History Channel with a stack of Twix bars.

Cara: Uhmm...sounds good. But make it dark chocolate and The Third Man DVD with Orson Welles. I secretly watch that every so often and wish I could have been Graham Greene in post war bomb-ravaged Vienna with the director who said...'go for it Graham, write it and we'll film it.' That and Orson Welles!

Jon: Are you an organized person, or disorganized?

Cara: Moi...organized? My plotting techniques consist of jumbled colored post-its with characters names and scene ideas that fly away in a brisk wind and a desk to match.

Jon: What's the one thing always in your refrigerator?

Cara: Good French Champagne and dog sausage...

Cara Black's Website:
www.carablack.com

Cara Black's books :
Murder In Marais (1998)
Murder In The Belleville (2000)
Murder In The Sentier (2002)
Murder In The Bastille (2003)

Stephen Booth

I first met Stephen Booth when he came to the launch of my first book, Only Darkness. He was not, then, published, but the manuscript of his book, Black Dog, was already causing a lot of excitement in publishing circles. The rest, I think, is history. There are not many writers who have made such an impact on the world of crime fiction so immediately. This is hardly surprising, as his books represent the best that modern crime fiction offers: compelling stories convincingly told in a realistic and recognizable context. His characters, Ben Cooper and Diane Fry have entered the consciousness of the readers of crime fiction, and are set to join some of other fictional names that have moved beyond crime fiction into the awareness of the wider reading public.

I have been an enthusiast for Stephen's books since I first read Black Dog shortly after it was published. It isn't just the gripping narrative that attracts me to them, it is the development of the characters as the books continue, the attention to detail in even the minor characters, the ear he has for the spoken word and the touches of humour that enhance the realism of the world he has created.

Stephen is a wordsmith whose success is well deserved.
-Danuta Reah (Author of Only Darkness)

Jon: For people who haven't seen your books yet, how would you describe them?

Stephen: I'm writing a series about a young police detective duo, Ben Cooper and Diane Fry, set in the Peak District area of Derbyshire, England. I consider these to be character-driven novels, although there is a traditional 'whodunit' element, and the setting is very important to me in providing atmosphere. The mood tends to be fairly dark, as I explore the secret lives of ordinary people who are driven to a point where they are capable of committing a violent crime. But there is humour, too, in the interplay between some of my fictional Derbyshire police officers.

Jon: Did you start with the idea of a series? If so, why?

Stephen: It was during the writing of the first book, BLACK DOG, that I realized I had a potential series. I discovered there was far more I wanted to say about the main characters than I could possibly fit into one book, and ideas for future stories just kept popping into my head. This was very lucky, as my publishers wanted a two-book deal and asked for a synopsis of the sequel during the auction for BLACK DOG. I already knew the direction of that second book and produced the synopsis for it overnight. I even had the title ready.

Jon: Are you anything like Cooper? Or for that matter, Fry?

Stephen: Since my characters are born out of my imagination, they must all have something of me in them, I think. For example, Ben Cooper is a country boy and Diane Fry is a city girl, and they have contrasting viewpoints. I'm a country dweller myself now, but I was raised in cities, so I've seen both viewpoints.

Jon: Does research play a big part of your writing?

Stephen: I research certain specific subjects for each book. For example, for the next one I've done research into Polish customs and World War Two aircraft. But one of the most important aspects is the location research. When I'm describing a place, I want it to be a real place, so I take a lot of trouble finding the right locations for the scenes in my books.

Jon: Why did you pick the locations you use?

Stephen: The Peak District is a beautiful area, but it has a lot of inherent tensions and conflicts. It was the UK's first national park and it attracts nearly 30 million visitors a year - making it the second most visited national park in the world. Yet it is a small area and much of it is populated in small towns, villages and farms, where the local people face a constant influx of visitors and everything that goes with them, like traffic and crime. There are big cities nearby, and there is always that old antagonism between the villagers and 'incomers' from the city.

Some of the remoter areas are favourite places for dumping murder victims, and people die in all sorts of mysterious ways out there. I also love the vast store of history (all 2,000 years of it), legends and folklore that is there in the Peak District for a writer to call on. And there is even an irresistible symbolism for me in the fact that the Peak District is divided into two contrasting geological areas called the White Peak and the Dark

Peak. Good and evil, of course.

Jon: Do you write full time? If not, what else do you do?

Stephen: I'm a full-time writer now, having given up the day job as a newspaper journalist earlier this year. This is not the same as writing full time, as I spend a lot of my time on promotion, including events such as conventions, book festivals, signings, talks - and interviews.

Jon: And you really breed goats?

Stephen: Yes! Well, I did for many years, but am left now with just three non-breeding pet goats. I was also a judge and am still very well-known in the UK among goat breeders. I'm president of one of the national breed societies.

Jon: BLACK DOG is your first published novel. Were you surprised by the response to it?

Stephen: Very surprised. In fact, I've continued to be surprised almost every week for the last 18 months! When I finished the second book, DANCING WITH THE VIRGINS, I really didn't know if it was any good, because I was too close to it by the end to be able to see it properly. So I was completely amazed when it was nominated for the Macallan Gold Dagger, the UK's top crime writing award, for best novel of the year. I still haven't come to terms with that one.

Jon: Who do you like to read?

Stephen: When I have time, I try to catch up on the latest books from people like Reginald Hill, Minette Walters, Laurie King and Michael Connelly. But I also like to read some of the most promising new authors as they come along.

Jon: Do you think it's important, sales wise, to be selling in the US as learn it's now 1923 or whatever, Rutledge is completely healed and getting married in May. That works well with any types of characters, don't get me wrong. But here what is happening within this man is a gradual process of discovery.

All the same, if readers want him to go on, he's going to be there in his late fifties (looking quite distinguished with that graying dark hair) and probably still battling with Hamish. We've got November in the computer and a glimmer of an idea for December, so he's going to get to the 1920's before long.

Jon: Aside from the fact that I have to wait until next fall for the next book, what can you tell us about A FEARSOME DOUBT?

Charles: A FEARSOME DOUBT is something we thought would be interesting to try. It's November, Rutledge is having troubles with the Armistice celebrations that everybody is talking about--it has revived too many of his own memories of the war. He doesn't see himself as a hero welcomed home, he doesn't believe he belongs with the honorably wounded, and he's got too many dead on his own conscience after four years of fighting to stand and listen to political speeches about the meaning of dying for one's country. At this very difficult time, he's thrown into two investigations--one from his past, pre-war, pre-Hamish, and another present day one that inadvertently drags him back into an experience he had wiped out of his mind in the last day of the war. It's a challenge to write! If you can't wait, pick up the paperback of WATCHERS, when that comes out, and you'll find a preview of DOUBT.

Jon: Your series seems to have very wide appeal. I know people who read almost nothing but hard-boiled who love them, and the same is true of historical readers and cozy readers. Also, they seem to attract a broad age range. Why do you think this is?

Charles: At first we were completely unprepared for this. We expected to reach readers who wanted to walk through an interesting case with someone like Rutledge. Instead, there are thousands of people who are drawn to this man. Romantic Times has given us an award for SEARCH THE DARK, best historical for that year. Vietnam vets have told us that they see a lot of their own suffering in Rutledge's. We hear from readers who would never dream of getting hooked on this genre, telling us that they rushed out to buy the only Rutledge short story.

ers, readers, book sellers?

Stephen: I've found them an incredibly friendly, helpful and supportive bunch of people. It was quite a surprise to me how willing a lot of the big-name, successful authors were to help someone new to the business. Many book sellers are themselves avid readers and fans. And, of course, the readers are wonderful!

Jon: I've always been curious where authors get the names they use? Do you scour newspapers? Go through old classmates names?

Stephen: With some of the main characters, the name just comes into my head with the character and seems to fit naturally. Where possible, though, I like to use local names that are common in the area I'm writing about. So if I need to find a name, I sometimes hang around in village churchyards looking at the names on gravestones! For a very minor character, I might just pick a name out of a newspaper or a phone directory.

Jon: What kinds of movies do you like? And..... best Bond?

Stephen: Something moody and dark, which makes you think a bit. 'Blade Runner' springs to mind. The Best Bond? Sean Connery (are there any others?)

Jon: How do you relax?

Stephen: Walking is my main relaxation and exercise. I walk a lot in the hills of the Peak District.

to meet these people at conventions--to reach out and touch authors you admire. We also make an effort to try new writers, because you never have enough favorites.

Charles: I discovered a lot of new writers when I did the best first novel judging. speaking of favorites, Peter Lovesey was at Bouchercon, and he's a great guy. I remember watching his Sergeant Cribb series on Mystery. Little did I guess that I'd actually wind up knowing him as a person. I'd second Caroline's list an give you another half an hour.

Jon: When you began writing the first book, did you have any idea that it would be so wildly popular?

Charles: No. We weren't even going to send it in to an agent. Nobody would be interested, we weren't sure of that. Then we decided to send it to Ruth Cavin, just to find out if it was really a novel--we only wanted her to say something like, "I have enjoyed reading this manuscript, but--" and it would in a way give us a sense that we hadn't done too badly after all. Sort of that last flourish before putting the book away and looking for something else to work on together. I'd seen this neat video on building your own helicopter... but it's also why we just used the one name--didn't most collaborators?

Look at Emma Lathen or Maan Myers. And we intend to keep it that way, one name. Before you feel too sorry for Caroline, remember that Charles and Caroline have the same root. I told you she was clever.

Jon: How would you describe Rutledge?

Charles: I don't think we ever have. He's tall, to begin with, that's come out. And he has dark eyes, probably dark hair. The Celtic background, we think. He has an aquiline nose, like one of our ancestors, and he has a compassionate nature. And when he smiles, and it touches eyes, you see something other than the thin haunted ex-soldier trying to survive. A glimpse into the man who lived before the war. Everyone tells us he's a very attractive man, and even sexy. But that wasn't what we were setting out to write. It's what others see in him.

More importantly, he cares about people and is interested in them. He can empathize while standing back to judge someone's involvement in a murder. He's attracted to interesting women, and that comes through spent a fair amount of time in the states. How do you find the driving over here?

Stephen: I was amazed that so many American drivers obey the speed limit, which took some getting used to after the UK. The interstate highways are great, and I've found most US cities pretty easy to get around. Except Boston, obviously.

Jon: I heard you tell this story at a signing, but I'd love you to tell it again here - your wife thought you might have been the Yorkshire Ripper?

Stephen: Well, it was a combination of circumstances, and a result of the paranoia that was around in the north of England while the Yorkshire Ripper was at large.

It started with one of the Ripper's victims being killed in a cemetery about two miles from our home in Manchester, which was scary enough in itself. This was in 1978, just about the time Lesley and I got married. Shortly afterwards, we moved to live near Huddersfield in Yorkshire, and the Ripper killed his next victim right there, in Huddersfield. But that was a coincidence, okay?

Of course, the police hadn't a clue how to catch the Yorkshire Ripper, so they were constantly putting out appeals aimed at local women, stressing that the killer had to be someone's husband, boyfriend, father, son or whatever. At the time, I was working night shifts on a newspaper in Manchester in addition to my day job, and sometimes I wasn't getting home until 3 o'clock in the morning. After one night shift, I discovered that Lesley had been listening to the appeals on the radio and had put two and two together. She pointed out that she had no idea where I really went to when I was out all night. She was always asleep when I came home, so she
didn't know what condition I was in when I got back at 3 in the morning. And given the fact that the last two victims had been killed close to where we lived, in two entirely different locations.... Well, you can see her point.

A few weeks later, my car was pulled over by the Ripper Squad late one night. But Lesley was with me that night, and a police officer leaned in the window and asked her if she knew who I was. She said: "Yes, he's my husband." I was convinced that she was going to add:

"But I think he might be the Yorkshire Ripper." Fortunately she didn't, so I got away with it that time!

The scariest bit is that when they eventually caught the real Yorkshire Ripper, Peter Sutcliffe, it turned out that he lived not very far from me - and he looked an awful lot like me, too. I've always thought that if Lesley had ever seen a photofit picture of him, I'd have been dead meat.

Jon: I know you're a Tom Petty fan. What other music do you enjoy?

Stephen: I always like to say I have eclectic tastes in music - mostly because I like the sound of the word 'eclectic'. But I compile my own CDs to play in the car, and the names that feature most often are Tom Petty, U2, Bob Dylan, Bob Marley, Mike Scott and the Waterboys. And if I don't hear Lynyrd Skynyrd's 'Free Bird' every day or two, I start getting withdrawal symptoms.

Jon: And..... What is the one thing always in the Booth refrigerator?

Stephen: Mayonnaise. Oh, and goat's milk.

- Stephen Booth's Website:
www.stephen-booth.com

Stephen Booth's books:
Black Dog (2000)
Dancing With The Virgins (2001)
Blood On The Tongue (2002)
Blind To The Bones (2003)

Max Allan Collins

The fact that Max Allan Collins is such an obvious fan of the genre he writes shows in everything he does. What he does is write; and write a lot. The first books of his that I read were in the Nate Heller series. I love the research that goes into them and the attention to details. They are everything a PI story should be. After reading everything that was available in the series I started tracking down his other work. And from Dick Tracy to Quarry and Nolan; Mallory and the disaster books

Barbara and Max Allan Collins

and his books with Elliot Ness, he has a body of work that helps explain my love of reading.

Max himself is also a bit of a character. Every time I've seen him he's happy. And you can't help but think that his inner child is in control. And I think that is a wonderful thing. His enthusiasm for everything he does just makes him glow. I think he is truly a renaissance man of entertainment; working on movies, books, playing with his band, he covers all the bases. Hopefully I was able to capture some of that energy in this interview.
Jon

Jon: You write a lot. The Heller series, along with a few others, movie tie-ins, you do stand alones, and you have written comics as well. Let's start with your series with Heller. How would you describe them to a potential reader?

Max: The Heller novels are designed to be traditional private eye stories in the Hammett/Chandler/Spillane manner, using this style and voice to explore crimes and mysteries of the twentieth century. Nate Heller is a "private eye witness" to major events (and particularly crimes) that take place during the period of history when Sam Spade, Phillip Marlowe and Mike Hammer were operating.

Jon: Do you plan to keep on writing Nate? It seems to me the possibilities are endless.

Max: As long as I can find a publisher who will allow me, I'll continue to do Heller. Right now I have another eight or nine books I want to do, and -- if I live long enough -- I want to follow Heller's son through cases starting in the '70s. (Heller's final cases -- if I get to write them -- will be JFK and possibly RFK assassinations...somewhere in there, maybe Martin Luther King, the ball would get passed to his son. But this all assumes somebody wants to publish these, plus I'll have to still be alive.)

Jon: Looking at the back of the Heller books one can see how much research goes into the books. Do you get caught up in it?

Max: Research -- in the sense of gathering material, and considering possible subjects -- is ongoing. George Hagenauer has helped me from the start, and is VITAL to the process. Lynn Myers is a big help, as well. Sometimes I enlist an expert on a specific case. My writing schedule has gotten busier and busier, and I don't really get to enjoy the research as much as I used to.

Jon: How many books do you average a year?

Max: For some ungodly reason, I'm busier now than ever -- I'd say it's usually around 3 books; but this year it's way over that. I'm doing 4 books in less than four months -- about mid-way through that schedule right now. This crunch happened because I lobbied to get the ROAD TO PERDITION novelization, but couldn't count on it and had to take on other assignments...then when ROAD came through,

I had to bite the bullet and do all four books right in a row. One of them is the first novel from the CSI TV show, and my writer friend Matt Clemens helped me by handling the research and pitching in with the plotting.

Jon: When you write film adaptations, do you see the film, or work from a script? And is the editing process a little different?

Max: Strictly script -- I almost never see any of the movie. The trickiest part is dealing with point of view...movie scripts bounce all over the place...and this drives me crazy, because I much prefer to stay with one POV on a character, say, through an entire chapter. Movie scripts require a lot of reorganization to make them play properly as a novel. I add lots of backstory, flesh out short scenes into longer, richer ones; and usually throw out most of the dialogue and create my own.

Jon: You also have different movie projects as well. Are you planning to do that more , in addition to the books?

Max: We're planning the fourth independent film, to be shot in Iowa next March. I'm also working on a documentary with Steve Henke (who has worked with me on all three prior indie features) on V.T. Hamlin, the Iowa cartoonist who created Alley Oop. That's in progress now.

In addition, I hope to write several "spec" screenplays for Hollywood consideration. I've done several already, which are being shown around now -- some have had options, like the JOHNNY DYNAMITE screenplay. A SPREE/Nolan screenplay exists, as does a MIKE HAMMER script.

Jon: The disaster books are great fun (that seems like a weird thing to say). Are you going to do more?

Max: I'm just about to start THE LUSITANIA MURDERS. I'll do at least one more, and -- if the readers and publishers want more -- I have ideas for another two or three.

Jon: Could you see any point down the road when you may write comics again, even if briefly?

Max: I'm talking to DC about doing a major BATMAN project right now.

Jon: You have done some work with Mickey Spillane, including a comic series, 'Mike Danger'. When did you meet Mr. Spillane?

Max: I met Mickey at the 1981 Bouchercon, where I was the convention's liaison with this special guest. We became friends, and have visited each other's homes. Mickey is my son Nate's godfather.

Jon: Do you enjoy doing the signing tours and meeting fans?

Max: I love doing bookstore appearances, and convention appearances; love meeting fans. Praise rocks.

Jon: What's the strangest experience you've had with a fan?

Max: Can't think of one--everything's been pretty positive. It did freak me out when one comics fan had a Wild Dog tattoo (the little cartoony logo from the comic book Terry Beatty and I did, some time ago).

Jon: The Ms. Tree comic is a wonderful format for short mysteries. Is there any chance of a Ms. Tree novel at some point?

Max: MS. TREE keeps getting optioned for TV and/or movies. If anything ever comes of that, I can almost guarantee you I'll do some novels. Problem in the past is, for a time DC held co-control of the property; we had a publisher wanting to do Ms. Tree novels, and DC wanted half of the take...so I said no. My movie REAL TIME: SIEGE AT LUCAS STREET MARKET (which will be out on DVD from Troma any time now) is based on the Ms. Tree prose story, "Inconvenience Store." Ms. Tree is not in the movie, but Brinke Stevens plays the Ms. Tree-like character I substituted. (REAL TIME is in a documentary format, so using a comic book character as the lead was out of the question.)

Jon: Do we really want to hear the Three Bean Salad story?

Max: No -- but one day, you may have to. It works best -- at it's most disgusting -- when delivered in a buffet line, when the individual just ahead of me is considering helping him- or herself to a generous serving of Three Bean Salad.

Jon: What authors do you like to read when you have the time?

Max: The only mystery writers I still read regularly are Ed McBain (87th Precinct only) and Don Westlake. And Mickey, when he publishes his occasional book. I try to read my friends -- some of whom are terrific, like John Lutz and Ed Gorman and Bob Randisi and Larry Block and a number of others -- but can't get to everything. Just don't have time with all the research stuff I read.

I do on occasion return to the classics -- Hammett, Chandler, Spillane, Cain, Horace McCoy, Erle Stanley Gardner, Jim Thompson, Agatha Christie, Jonathan Latimer, W.R. Burnett. My favorite mainstream authors are William March and Mark Harris.

I read a lot of stuff on movies -- on directors, in particular Hitchcock, and film noir books.

Jon: What advice would you give to someone thinking about writing as a career?

Max: Start young -- write as a hobby and find ways to get school credit for it.   Read voraciously.   Influences are fine, but try not to imitate (I'd have been in print three or four years sooner if I hadn't been trying so hard to be Mickey).

Jon: When you aren't writing or making movies, what do you do with your time?

Max: Time?

I watch a lot of DVDs and laser discs, and Barb and I (and sometimes Nate, though he's off at college now) go to lots of movies; we like a nice meal out, love to shop for books and CDs and DVDs. Now and then a concert. Always have been a pop culture junkie. This, however, is a mostly dreadful era...as would be any era largely characterized by rap, piercings and cell phones. I still play with my rock band Crusin' a few times a year -- four or five gigs. Not real pressing. Poker with friends now and then.

Jon: You have a wonderful website. www.muscanet.com/~phoenix/ Do you find that it helps promotion? Is it a lot of work?

Max: My son Nate maintains it, but we both get kind of lazy. I should do more updates. We haven't sent a newsletter out in well over a year... just too busy. This has been a crazy, frantic year.

Jon: If you could collaborate with someone living or dead, on a project, who would it be and what would the project be?

Max: I would love to write a movie for/with Alfred Hitchcock.
I hope to continue collaborating with my wife Barb. I enjoy collaborating with Matt Clemens, too. I wish I could get Mickey to do something with me, but he's too much of a loner...not surprising, as personal as his writing is.

Jon: Are the CSI books going to be original? And is this the first time you've really dealt with the forensics side of detection?

Max: I'll be doing at least two CSI novels, and this is in fact my first foray into forensics and science...and that's not my long suit. My assistant on the books, Matt Clemens, has written true-crime material and he contributed almost all of the forensics stuff in CSI: DOUBLE DEALER, working with a Bettendorf, Iowa, police criminalist.

Jon: ROAD TO PERDITION has been turned into a major motion picture. Are you happy with the results?

Max: Haven't seen it yet. (this question was asked before the movie was released) Today I finished the novelization of the screenplay, which is very good and quite faithful. The cast and director and producer are all the best the movie industry has to offer.

I do wish I could have written the script. Their take on the story differs from mine slightly -- my vision is more violent, wilder, a John Woo kind of American samurai thing...whereas this movie will fall more in the GODFATHER area...which is a nice area. I'm cool with the fact that it's not my movie -- it's my STORY, but as a movie director myself, I understand that the vision needs to be the director's. That's the nature of the medium. If it's not a terrific movie, I'll be very surprised.

Jon: Do you have anything else that we might see on the big screen?

Max: JOHNNY DYNAMITE may happen. MS. TREE has been optioned for TV. And I have several screenplays in mind that -- in the wake of PERDITION -- should get looked at seriously...if I can find to time to write 'em.

Jon: What are some of your favorite films?

Max: Top three (pretty much a tie): KISS ME DEADLY, CHINATOWN, VERTIGO.

Also in the top ten: THE SEARCHERS, PHANTOM OF THE PARADISE, GUN CRAZY, RIO BRAVO, THE BAD SEED, MIRACLE ON 34th STREET, IT'S A WONDERFUL LIFE.

I love Peter Jackson's movies -- THE FRIGHTENERS, MEET THE FEEBLES, DEAD ALIVE. Big John Woo fan. Don Siegel. Jack Webb. Howard Hawks.

Hitchcock, Hitchcock, Hitchcock.

HOW TO SUCCEED IN BUSINESS WITHOUT REALLY TRYING, THE PRODUCERS, DAMN YANKEES, Shemp Stooges. I own thousands of movies on DVD and laserdisc.

There is no question here to cover this, but my biggest enthusiasm of all is probably Bobby Darin. I have followed the late, great singer's work and collected him since I was in the fifth grade. Great movie actor: PRESSURE POINT is his best performance -- he plays an American nazi! He was better than Sinatra -- and I also love Sinatra!

Jon: If you could talk to yourself at an earlier age, like around 16-17, what would you say to yourself?

Max: This assumes I've progressed from that age. I am still sixteen. But I'd guess I say: hang in there, it's gonna happen.

Jon: Being a pop culture junkie, what would be your favorite era?

Barbara and Max Allan Collins

Max: I would have a hard time choosing between the '30s, '40s and '50s. The '60s, until they go to shit with drugs and hippies, is a worthwhile era. No other period in the 20th century (or after) is as rich in popular arts as '30 thru, say, '68. Oddly, the '50s -- repressed as they were -- gave birth to great pop culture; rock 'n' roll and arguably the very best movies.

Jon: What's the one thing that's always in your fridge?

Max: Coca-Cola.

Max Allan Collins' Website:
www.muscanet.com/~phoenix/

Max Allan Collins' Books:

The Nate Heller Series
Chicago Confidential (2002)
Angel in Black (2001)
Majic Man (1999)
Flying Blind (1998)

Damned in Paradise (1996)
Blood and Thunder (1995)
Carnal Hours (1994)
Stolen Away (1991)
Neon Mirage (1988)
The Million-Dollar Wound (1986)
True Crime (1984)
True Detective (1983)

Media Tie-In Novels
Windtalkers (2001)
The Mummy Returns (2001)
U-571 (2000)
The Mummy (1999)
Mommy's Day (1998)
Saving Private Ryan (1998)
U.S. Marshals (1998)
Air Force One (1997)
Mommy (1997)
NYPD Blue: Blue Blood (1997)
Daylight (1996)
NYPD Blue: Blue Beginning (1995)
Waterworld (1995)
I Love Trouble (1994)
Maverick (1994)
 Dick Tracy Meets his Match (1992)
Dick Tracy Goes to War (1991)
Dick Tracy (1990)

Disaster Series
The Pearl Harbor Murders (2001)
The Hindenburg Murders (2000)
The Titanic Murders (1999)

The Quarry Series
Primary Target (1987)
The Slasher / Quarry's Cut (1977)
The Dealer / Quarry's Deal (1976)
The Broker's Wife / Quarry's List 1976)
The Broker / Quarry (1976)

The Nolan Series

Mourn the Living (1999)
Spree (1987)
Scratch Fever (1982)
Hard Cash (1981)
Hush Money (1981)
Fly Paper (1981)
Blood Money (1981)
Bait Money (1981)

The Elliot Ness Series
Murder by the Numbers (1993)
Bullet Proof (1989)
Butcher's Dozen (1988)
The Dark City (1987)

The Mallory Series
Nice Weekend for a Murder (1986)
A Shroud for Aquarius (1985)
Kill Your Darlings (1984)

Miscellaneous
Regeneration (1999) (with Barbara Collins)
Protect and Defend (1992)
Midnight Haul (1986)
Road to Perdition (1998) (graphic novel)

Critical/Biographical Works
No Cure for Death (1983)
For the Boys: The Racy Pin-Ups of World War II (2000)
The Baby Blue Rip-Off (1983) Elvgren: His Life and Art (1998)
The Best of Crime and Detective TV (1988)
Jim Thompson: The Killers Inside Him (1983)

Short Story Collections
One Lonely Knight: Mickey Spillane's Mike Hammer (1984)
Dying in the Post-War World (1991)
In the Line of Fire (1993)
Kisses of Death (2001)
Murder--His and Hers (2001) with Barbara Collins
Blue Christmas and other Holiday Homicides (2001)

John Connolly

If human existence were a heavily wooded forest, John Connolly would be writing about the very center of it. That place among the tallest trees that has you looking around wondering how to get out and forgetting how you got in. Very little light reaches this place and every sound will have your heart pumping as the unknown creeps up behind you. His Bad Men are the shadows you see out of the corner of your eye and that snap of a twig in the midnight hour. What your mind conjures up doesn't live up to the reality of this forests beasts. His Charlie Parker is the guide that stands back to back with you, fending off the evil that men do as his own internal struggle darkens his eyes. As the night turns to dawn, and the dappled light finally reaches you again, you look down and see what the darkness has done to you. And you know you'll never be the same.
- Jennifer Jordan

Jon: Right off, I need to ask, as an Irish author - why an American protagonist?

John C: Short question, but a very long answer. Firstly, it was very much a reaction against what I felt Irish writers were expected to write about: famine, religion, sexual repression, Britain, terrorism, how often it rains in Limerick. When I was growing up, Irish fiction - although sometimes superbly crafted - was pretty miserable stuff. In school, I once had to read 'Men Withering', in which an old man dies, and dies long and hard. I'm sure it's a fine book, but it put me off reading for six months. Also, we didn't really do crime writing in Ireland, crime writers tending to be the exception. It's not a tradition we've really had,

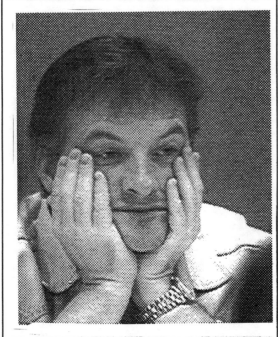

and a number of writers who might be considered to be writing crime have ended up using some of its structures to write about terrorism, which was our worst form of crime for so long. Again, that wasn't an area I was interested in exploring.

Secondly, I was curious both about the United States - a place about which I have mixed feelings, finding it both welcoming and threatening -and American crime fiction, which seemed more concerned with empathy and compassion than its British counterparts. (I was particularly influenced by Ross Macdonald.) I didn't feel like those structures necessarily transferred terribly well to other cultures or societies, so I decided to work with them in their original setting.

And, as an Irishman, I thought I could bring something slightly different to the US crime novel. After all, there was no point in simply slavishly imitating, since American writers do crime rather well. I suppose I bring an outsider's point of view, as well as the influence of a slightly different European tradition. My writing style isn't really similar to what would be considered "classic" American crime writing - the prose isn't stripped down at all; the opposite in fact - and there are strong elements of the Gothic, which is something Irish writers (Bram Stoker, Sheridan Le Fanu) did very well.

Jon: Your books are a bit dark. Does it have an effect on you, or does it stay with the book?

John C: A bit dark! There are those who might regard that as understatement. I suppose they are dark, but it's balanced throughout with a promise, if not the actuality, of hope and redemption. And there's a certain amount of humor, too.

But, yes, it does affect me at time. DARK HOLLOW was particularly difficult. I'm not sure why, to be honest: I suppose it deals with a man teetering on the brink of hope or salvation, and uncertain of which way he's going to fall. And I feel that if, as a writer, you're dealing with dark material, with death and suffering, then it should affect you, otherwise you're just a dabbler and there's no truth to what you're writing. I think it should affect the reader too: I'm not sure that crime fiction should always be an "easy read" for the reader; otherwise it becomes voyeuristic, almost pornographic.

Jon: The books have a real feeling for the locations. Have you been to these places or is it just damn good writing?

John C: I go to a lot of trouble to get the locations right. I stay in the places I use, talk to local people, find out about their history and the history of the area, take notes when I eat, walk the streets, drive. It's like scouting locations for a movie. I suppose there are probably easier ways to do it, but this is the only way I know how to work. It's very time-consuming, but worth it at the end if the reader feels he or she inhabits a real world. And because I don't write "realist" crime fiction, insofar as any crime writing is truly realist, it is important that the world of the novels is as real and believable as possible, so that when the strange or supernatural begins to infect it the reader is prepared to go along with it.

Jon: The British covers are beautiful, and even the American covers are pretty cool. Do you have any input on the art?

John C: I have very little input on the American covers, although I hope that's going to change with the third book. In Britain, it's been very collaborative, particularly for THE KILLING KIND and the forthcoming WHITE ROAD. Hodder allows me to go off and find the illustrations that I like and then suggest the color schemes. After that, it's up to Hodder's art department, who has been brilliant right from the beginning.

Jon: The name Charlie "Bird" Parker is an obvious jazz reference. Are you a big jazz fan? What other kinds of music do you enjoy?

John C: It's funny, I chose the name mainly for the nickname, since I liked the idea of a character so mired in mortality having a name associated with flight and freedom. It irritates some people, but it's too late now. Also, it's kind of a small joke, since Parker hates jazz and his parents named him without realizing that he would be sharing his name with a jazz musician. He listens to a lot of the music that I listen to: alternative country, indie rock, classic eighties. I mean, he's only a year or two older than I am, although one of my friends was very distressed to think of a former policeman turned potentially violent private eye listening to The Blue Nile, who my friend regarded as kind of weedy. I prefer sensitive.

Jon: In the first book, one of the killers is getting ideas from anatomy drawings? Do these really exist?

John C: Absolutely. That whole tradition of anatomical drawing and modeling, of the obsession with the workings of the human body and the intimations of mortality that could be drawn from it, is factual. I make up very little of what is in the books. In THE KILLING KIND, the strange history of religious obsession in the state of Maine that forms the novel's backdrop is all true.

I tend to be a bit prickly about EVERY DEAD THING, at times. I never really set out to write a standard serial killer novel, much as I've enjoyed some of them. I wanted the Traveling Man to be one part of a larger web of corruption, from the level of city government right down to the individual human soul. Maybe I didn't succeed, but I tried. That whole anatomical tradition is linked to something much stranger: the idea that this world is merely a passing thing, something to be endured, while the next world will provide the reward. The idea crops up again in THE KILLING KIND: that idea of suffering being an integral part of the human experience.

Jon: Do write you novels full time, or are you still doing some journalism work?

John C: I still do occasional journalism: author interviews, mainly. I remain a fan of good writing.

Jon: I think Angel and Louis are great characters, are they going to stay a feature of the books?

John C: I've been working toward something with Angel and Louis, and it kind of comes to fruition in the fourth book, THE WHITE ROAD. They become far more ambiguous characters, colder, more violent, and estranged from both Parker and each other. In the beginning, I used them to show aspects of Parker that might otherwise have been hidden: his sense of humor, his  capacity to inspire love and loyalty in others, and also his first faltering steps toward redemption. But as he has progressed, I think Louis and Angel have begun to find that his struggle with morality is different from their own, that he is genuinely, deeply tormented by the choices that he is forced to make. In THE WHITE ROAD, some of the consequences of that struggle become clearer. We also learn a bit more about Angel and Louis, and why they are the way they are. Louis's story does, I think, have a blackly comic element to it, while Angel's does not.

Jon: People being the strange creatures that they are, do you get any flak about having gay characters in your books?

John C: No, I'm sure that there are some complete rednecks that won't read a book with gay characters in it, but they're in the minority. The fact that they are gay is largely incidental. It doesn't define them, any more than Parker's heterosexuality defines him. Love is love.

Some gay readers have written to me to say how much they like them. In fact, one confessed that he was a bit in love with both of them: not sure that you could actually love both of them, since they are, in some ways, polar opposites.

Jon: Any thoughts on having Parker travel out of the US?

John C: I suppose it's a possibility, but only as part of a larger plot set within the US. I'm not a huge fan of blockbuster globetrotting thrillers. In fact, I think one of the stand-alones may be set almost entirely in a very isolated, self-contained community, which is the exact opposite of the globetrotter model, really.

Jon: Is there anything happening with film or television options?

John C: I'm very cautious when it comes to film. I just think a lot of film adaptations of thrillers tend to be average at best, and generally poor.

Also, I get depressed when I see writers obsessively chasing the movie dollar or, worse, tailoring novels for film. I write books, not movie treatments. In fact, I was kind of perversely proud that EVERY DEAD THING is probably unfilmable. I would have fewer difficulties with the later books, but it's still something I'm cautious about.

Jon: With the new trend in publishing for authors to do stand-alone books, do you have any plans in that direction? And also, would you want to keep the series going in addition to stand-alones?

John C: Mystery readers are very loyal, but also very demanding. I know, for myself, how much I look forward to the next Robicheaux or the new Kenzie and Gennaro, so I sympathize. It's nice to get a kind of "fix" of your favorite characters, to keep up with what's happening in their lives. But that can be a kind of trap for writers, and can lead them to be unambitious. Sometimes, what readers, editors, publishers or agents might want may not be best for you as a writer.

I think, after THE WHITE ROAD, there may be a non-crime novel: still genre, and still quite dark, but probably not what people would expect. Then, probably one or two out of the next three may be Parkers, but there will be a stand-alone somewhere along the line: either very traditional crime, or a book that takes the supernatural/ crime hybrid as far as it can go, from my point of view. I love doing the Parker books, but I'm very anxious not to short-change readers or myself.

It's why I don't take an advance for books any more: an advance means that you commit to a date of publication, possibly for a novel that isn't ready yet but which you may have to give up, or to a novel that you may not want to write, but now you've taken the money and have to accede. Each Parker novel has been quite different from the next, and has tried to push the envelope a little. I'd like to continue to do that. I will always return to him, I think. I'll be curious to see what he's like when he's sixty.

Jon: Who are some of your favorite authors, and who would you consider influences?

John C: Macdonald, because of his compassion; Burke, for the quality of his writing; Lehane, because he's just so good and Mystic River is a superb novel; Harlan Coben, for being damn funny; Julia Wallis Martin, for the darkness and beauty of the novels; and Paul Johnston, for trying to do something a little different in creating futuristic, satirical crime novels. Oh, and Colin Batemen, who is Ireland's Carl Hiaasen.

Jon: You have a wonderful website. Do you feel that the internet plays an important role for authors?

John C: I wanted the website so that people could contact me if they chose, could get to read other things I'd done (the BBC ghost stories, for example, or the author interviews) for free, could feel that I was as interested in them as, I hope, they are in me. It's really a way of staying in touch with people.

Jon: What are some of your favorite movies?

John C: Oh, that varies from day to day. I've just been taking my videos out of boxes to shelve in my house, so let's see: pretty much the whole Laurel & Hardy collection is there, early Steve Martin, Carpenter's 'The Thing', 'Southern Comfort' (a great action movie), Michael Mann's 'Last of the Mohicans', 'Chinatown', 'Annie Hall', 'Manhattan', 'Love and Death'. Surprisingly, maybe, a lot of comedy, but very few crime movies.

Jon: As a fairly new author, how do you like doing store appearances? Is it a weird feeling to become a celebrity?

John C: I love doing them. Well, I do as long as people show up, otherwise it gets a bit sad. I'm always flattered when people show up, and I try to talk to them individually if they want to chat. To be honest, I put quite a bit of effort into the store appearances: I hate writers who feel that it's enough just to read some chunk of their latest opus to a captive audience. Most aren't good enough at reading their own work to hold an audience. I tend to just talk - about the books, about crime fiction, about whatever comes to mind at the time. I love what I do, and realize I'm very lucky to be doing it, but that's down to readers and booksellers. I owe them a lot, and when I do bookstore appearances I try to pay it back in some small way.

Jon: So, is there anything about you that would surprise people to know?

John C: Er, I'm not tormented, at least, not all the time. And I have a Bob Wilson drawing in my kitchen, depicting a bunch of teddy bears loaded down with food and lemonade with the lead bear saying: "This looks like a nice spot..."

Jon: When you write, do you have the book laid out in advance, or do you let the book show you where it needs to go?

John C: Half and half, really. I've never plotted a book out in advance, but I tend to have an idea of where it's going to go. That usually changes, though: characters assume greater importance, plot lines assume more significance. It's an interesting experience, both at once within and outside your control.

Jon: How important are is an editor to the writing process?

John C: Hmmmm. I think I'm pretty open to editorial suggestions, but so far I haven't had any that were terribly controversial. I think American editors are more hands-on: they tend to give detailed notes, while my British editor adopts a more softly, softly approach. Most of the editorial stuff I've received has been very minor. Funnily enough, I tend to be much harsher on my books than my editors, and keep making changes right up to the wire. For example, my agent saw one ending to DARK HOLLOW my editor a second, and the readers a third.

Jon: Would you care to give an insight to the other two endings for DARK HOLLOW?

John C: Um, one was just a complete misfire, so I'll let it lie. The other just involved a slightly brighter ray of happiness for Parker at the end, with Rachel arriving on his doorstep. It was a nice scene (actually, someone who read it in proof burst into tears, but I think she may have been oversensitive) but just felt a bit premature.

Jon: Does your reading audience seem to be more male or female?

John C:I think I have a nice balance but, by and large, I think it's probably more women than men. But that reflects the patterns within mystery fiction as a whole, I think, and readers in general. Women read more than men.

Jon: Do you put any of yourself in to your books? Are you at all like Bird?

John C: There's a lot of me in Parker: I share his sense of humor, his view of the world. I'm interested in the ideas of morality and compassion that infuse the books. I think, like a great many people, I wish I was a better person than I am. In Parker, I get to explore how one might apply that wish to life.

Jon: What other things occupy your time besides writing?

John C: I cook. I go to the gym. I travel a lot. And I read.

Jon: If you could go back in time and speak to a younger John Connolly, what would you tell him?

John C: Don't take yourself so seriously. Be nicer to people. And when you have the opportunity to have a pint with your dad, take it, because when you'll want to do it later, he won't be there.

Jon: You do some relentless touring, almost non stop it seems. Does it take its toll on you?

John C: I think it was Henry Rollins who said that you're only 75 per cent as interesting as you think you are. After eight or nine weeks of non-stop touring, you begin to feel that 75 percent is a vast overestimation of your capacity to interest other people.

I like touring. It's deeply flattering when people come along to a store and let you know that they enjoy your books, because writing is such a solitary pursuit for much of the time. The downside, apart from being a bit tiring, is that it's really hard for me to write when I'm on the road. I need to be at home, with a certain routine in place. In the end, there are only a limited number of outcomes to the that situation: either you curtail touring so you can write, or you begin rushing the books to fit the time available to you, or the books simply start to take longer to produce. I'm going for a combination of the first and third options. That, or death.

Jon: I really enjoyed BAD MEN. Are you going to be writing more in this direction?

John C: I'm a genre writer, but I'm curious about experimenting in a number of genres. I've always been interested in supernatural fiction, and there's a strong element of that in the Parker novels. In part, it's because I have a pretty flexible definition of what "mystery" means to me, stretching from its use to describe crime novels right back to a much older definition of the word, which has religious/ supernatural origins. A mystery, as the word was originally understood, is a revelation - usually divine in origin - which cannot be understood by human reasoning alone. So I suppose that I don't see any conflict between crime and the supernatural. Rather, one seems to me to be a natural from the other.

Jon: What are you working on right now?

John C: I've more or less finished a collection of ghost stories, the centerpiece of which
is a long Parker novella currently entitled THE REFLECT-
ING EYE, although that may
change. That book will be followed pretty soon after by the
next full-length Parker novel,
if I'm spared.

Jon: What's the last book you
read and what did you think
of it?

John C: The last book I read was Louise Welsh's THE CUTTING
ROOM. I liked it a lot, although it told me a little more about certain
types of sexual activity than I really needed to know.

Jon: Steve Martin. Why does he make you laugh?

John C: Happy Feet. Bunny rabbit ears. "The Absent-Minded Waiter."
Attempting to seduce Kathleen Turner in "The Man With Two Brains"
while seated with his hat on his lap, then being rebuffed and, massively
frustrated, walking toward the window, his hat still dangling from his
groin. The camera focuses on his face as, from below, we hear glass
breaking...

Jon: What's the one thing that's always in your refrigerator ?

John C: Skimmed milk. I'm a healthy boy.

John Connolly's Website:
www.johnconnolly.co.uk

John Connolly's Books:
Every Dead Thing (1999)
Dark Hollow(2000)
The Killing Kind(2001)
The White Road(2002)
Bad Men (2003)

Jeffery Deaver

According to his official biography, Jeffery Deaver was born outside of Chicago in 1950. Poet, journalist, performer, and attorney; all these provide a wealth of background information and experience than lend a believability to his novels. Four Edgars, an Anthony, and three short story awards give you a good indication that this author's scope is not limited to one format or characterization. His list of best-sellers will confirm that for you. Movie credits can be very "iffy" for some authors, but "The Bone Collector" was magnificent and Denzel Washington's portrayal of Lincoln Rhyme was superb.

My favorites are the Lincoln Rhyme novels, but the standalones and the Rune series [quirky, 60's style heroine] have appeal, too.
-Vicki Ball (booksnbytes.com)

Jon: In the books with Lincoln Rhyme, the dynamic between him and Amelia really makes the books work great. When you first wrote about these two, did you plan on writing more than one book with them?

Jeffery: No, I never did. Frankly I never thought that a book featuring Rhyme would be as popular as it was. The issue wasn't that he was a quadriplegic. I thought that there wouldn't be a continuing market for the technical forensics-oriented type of police work that he's involved in. But his popularity has soared around the world.

Jon: I've heard that a television show may be in the works. Is this true?

Jeffery: I was involved in the Murder in Small Town X show for Fox and have been talking to other networks about a purely fictional crime-based show.

Jon: Your books all have a wonderful thrill ride quality to them. Is it hard to keep up that kind of pace book after book? Or even within a single book?

Jeffery: Thanks for the comment. I try hard to keep up the roller-coaster element. And, yes, I have to say it's challenging. But it's part of the job and we authors just have to roll up our sleeves and give our readers what they
want.

Jon: With the amount of detail in your books I would imagine that you really do your homework. Do you like researching for the books?

Jeffery: Oh, research is great fun. It's one of the best parts of writing fiction--to be able to learn something new with every book. Readers too (speaking from personal experience), enjoy learning facts that they haven't been exposed to in novels--provided, however, that they move the story along. You can't let the research pull your story down through digression.

Jon: Have you thought about bring back Rune from MANHATTAN IS MY BEAT, HARD NEWS, and DEATH OF A BLUE MOVIE STAR?

Jeffery: I love Rune, as do many readers. For your readers not familiar with her, she's a waif-like, bundle of feisty energy living in Manhattan--a young amateur detective sort. But there's a lightness about her--and about the situations she gets involved in--that's very different from stories in my current books. I enjoy the bigger, faster paced stories I'm writing now, and my readers seem to as well.

Jon: Any chance of VOODOO being reprinted?

Jeffery: Hmmm. Let me think. No. Never. Not a terrible book, by any means, but an occult book, and that's a genre I'm not comfortable writing in.

Jon: Hollywood seems to have a reputation for really mangling books when turning them into films. But your books have been portrayed very nicely. Is there a trick to it, or did you get lucky? And what's it like seeing your characters come to life on the screen?

Jeffery: I have been lucky, having had two books turned into films, 'Dead Silence' (my book was A MAIDEN'S GRAVE) and The BONE COLLECTOR, and I was pleased with the results in both cases. I have to say it was largely luck; I had no involvement in the actual production of the films. Making movies is a very arduous process--I have great respect for everyone involved in the industry--and one that I wouldn't have the patience for.

Jon: You also write quite a few short stories. What do you like about writing them?

Jeffery: I love short stories. Since I love twists and turns and surprises in my novels, of course, I do the same in my short stories. Nothing is quite what it seems to be. The best part of short stories, though, is that since we have no emotional investment in any of the characters (because of the brevity of the story) I can do terrible things to the good guys and make the bad guys successful in all their evil doings. Great fun.

Jon: As your work gains in popularity, people seem to compare other work to yours. I would also imagine that you get asked to read a lot more books so you can blurb them. Are there downsides to being a successful writer?

Jeffery: My goal has always been to be a working, professional novelist, nothing more than that. Success to me is being able to make a living by telling stories. I don't think it gets any better than that. I just wish there were more hours in the day--to write as much as I'd like and still do the public appearances, blurbing, and author touring around the world that I'd like to do to meet fans and my publishers and editors.

About downsides, there are some people--critics and readers--who feel a need to take potshots at the books. You'd be surprised at some of the criticisms I've read. On the one hand, we authors invite that by putting our words out for millions of people to peruse and we have to remain thick skinned. On the other hand, come on, folks, it's only a suspense novel ...

Jon: And what would be the upside to being a best seller?

Jeffery: You become a best seller by--hold on--selling more books, rather than fewer books. This means that you must be doing something that appeals to a large number of readers. As a result, your editors and publishers tend to listen to you and respect your opinion about editorial changes and publishing strategies.

Jon: When my mother heard I was going to interview you she asked me to ask a question. Where do some of the darker ideas for the books come from, and do they linger after you finish writing them?

Jeffery: I'm very calculating. The darker ideas are solely products of an imagination that's always looking for ideas to thrill a large audience with a commercial thriller. I myself have no emotional involvement in the sick-and-twisted ideas I come up with. (It takes a lot to scare me!) After the book is over (actually before the book is over) I'm already thinking about new ways to give my readers the next roller coaster ride.

Jon: What kind of control do you have on the finished product? Do you decide on art and titles?

Jeffery: At this stage, I have pretty good control over the finished product--but largely because I know what my readers want. If I were to write a romance novel and try to shove it down the throat of my publisher, I'd hope they'd come after me with big sticks and force me to go back to what I do best. I write my own titles, though I've certainly had initial ideas rejected. I consult on art but that's ultimately the publisher's call.

Jon: What kind of movies do you enjoy watching?

Jeffery: Any kind of movie, as long as it's got some substance to it. Recent favorites: 'Saving Private Ryan', 'Chocolat', 'Amelie', 'Spy Game'.

Jon: Who are some of your favorite authors?

Jeffery: John LeCarre, Thomas Harris, James Patterson, Ian Rankin, P. D. James, John Gilstrap, Barbara Vine (Ruth Rendell), and literary writers like Saul Bellow, John Updike, John Cheever. Oh, yeah, that guy from England--Bill Shakespeare--he's okay too.

Jon: One of your bios mentioned that you used to be a folksinger. Do you still play?

Jeffery: No. Did that for a few years. Loved it. But it was time to move on.

Jon: Between writing and the stuff with Hollywood, you must be awfully busy. What do you do to relax?

Jeffery: Mostly I entertain. Wine and cooking for friends, traveling. Living alone and working alone, it's important to have human contact, so I have a very busy social life.

Jon: Readers being the way they are, I would imagine you get asked for certain things from the books. things like " Will Lincoln and Amelia get married?" . Do you let these type of things influence your writing ?

Jeffery: Well, let me say this: I always listen to readers. Their interest and desires for the books are very important. On, the other hand, just because a passenger says he'd like the pilot of an airliner to fly at three hundred feet off the ground, so he can wave to his friends, the pilot knows better than to do so. I'm the pilot of my books and I think I know how best to handle the story for the reader's optimum enjoyment.

Jon: Setting plays a big part in your work. How important is the right location?

Jeffery: Important to some extent. But my books are first about plot. Setting enhances the story but it doesn't become a point of the book itself. Essentially the setting must be in harmony with the story.

Jon: Walter Mosley has written some Sci Fi books. Have you ever thought about writing outside the mystery/thriller genre?

Jeffery: No, I'm happy writing what I'm writing.

Jon: If you hadn't made it as a writer, what do you think you would be doing instead?

Jeffery: Hmmm, hard to answer that. I've always had in mind being a writer. I guess my answer is I'd still be trying.

Jon: If you were able to talk to a young Jeffery Deaver, what advice would you pass along? And would he have listened?

Jeffrey:
1. Stay focused on your goal of being a writer.

2. No way in hell.

Jon: Do you work according to a schedule, or do you write in spurts as it comes to you?

Jeffery: I don't have a schedule as such, but I work 8 to 10 hours a day. In this business, if you want to be a working writer, you can't wait for inspiration. You have to out and trap it.

Jon: What is the one thing that is always in your refrigerator?

Jeffery: An empty jar of blackberry jam that I've been meaning to throw out for six years.

Jeffery Deaver's Books:

The Vanished Man (2003)
The Stone Monkey (2002)
The Empty Chair(2000)
The Blue Nowhere (2001)
Speaking In Tongues(2000)
The Devil's Teardrop(1999)
The Coffin Dancer(1998)
The Bone Collector(1997)
A Maiden's Grave(1995)
Praying For Sleep(1994)
The Lesson Of Her Death(1993)
Mistress Of Justice(1992)
Hard News(1991)
Death Of A Blue Movie Star(1990)
Manhattan Is My Beat(1988)
Hell's Kitchen(2001)
Bloody River Blues(1993)
Shallow Graves(1992)

Collections including a short story by Jeffery Deaver:

A Hot And Sultry Night For Crime, edited By Jeffery Deaver (2003)

Much Ado About Murder, edited By Anne Perry (2002)

The World's Finest Mystery And Crime Stories:Third Annual Collection, edited by Ed Gorman and Martin H. Greenberg (2002)

The First Day Of School (2002)

A Century Of Great Suspense Stories, edited By Jeffery Deaver (2001)

A Century Of Great Suspense Stories, edited By Jeffery Deaver (2001)

A Confederacy of Crime, edited By Sarah Shankman (2000)

The World's Finest Mystery And Crime Stories, edited by Edward Gorman (2000)

Irreconcilable Differences, edited By Lia Matera (1999)

The Best Of The Best, edited By Elaine Koster and Joseph Pittman (1997)

Crimes Of The Heart, edited By Carolyn Hart (1995)

Sean Doolittle

"The trouble didn't seem to start so much as it simply landed, like a hunk of blazing debris."

Sean Doolittle's success didn't simply land either. It is based on years of writing short stories that appear in various anthologies and crime magazines. He is among a group of neo-noir writers that are slowly creeping up the crime writing ranks, earning respect and a satisfied reading audience wherever they roam. His work will draw you in like a Hoover in overdrive and it won't let you go. He's that damn good. He has an incisive writing style and a wit drier than the Mojave in the noonday sun. When I finished reading his first book Dirt, I had a grin on my face that was gone the minute I realized I'd have to wait for Burn. Not bad for a boy from Nebraska.
* - Jennifer Jordan*

Jon: Can you tell us about your first book, DIRT?

Sean: I generally describe DIRT as a crime novel set in and around a crooked funeral home. How's that for 25-words-or-less?

Jon: Why did you pick funeral homes as the setting?

Sean: It started when I read a magazine article written by a freelance reporter   who went out on assignment to cover this annual trade show for funeral industry professionals. A mortician's convention. I remember being both fascinated and entertained by the idea that somewhere in the world, there's a sales rep whose job is to stand in a booth at a trade show and convince people why his company's brand of embalming fluid is superior to the   competitors' brands.

That article led me to a book called 'The American Way of Death' by Jessica Mitford. For those who aren't familiar, this is a book first published in the sixties, long considered by many to be kind of a seminal modern expose of some of the shadier business practices consumers might find in certain corners of the so-called "grim trade." By the time I finished Mitford's book, the basic seed for DIRT was beginning to germinate.

I think what initially intrigued me the most, on a symbolic level, was the nuts-and-bolts aspect of the mortician's job. So much of what we've come to recognize as typical American funerary custom has to do with sanitizing and cloaking the unpleasant physical aspects of death for the emotional benefit of the bereaved. I can certainly appreciate the intent behind the practice, as I think anyone who has ever mourned a loved one probably can.

But as a writer, I also found kind of an interesting metaphoric potential in the idea that all the cosmetic aspects of the typical funeral are essentially a decorative curtain draped over life's greasy machinery.

Of course, somewhere in there, there's also just another make and model of the same engine that powers so many crime and mystery stories: that things aren't always as they are made to appear, and there is often an ugly truth behind the surface presentation.

On the whole, I believe that the business of caring for the dead is a noble and necessary profession populated by many honest, hard-working folks. But it's also a business. It's subject to the same market pressures and competition and bottom-dollar concerns as any other. On top of that, it has a uniquely vulnerable consumer demographic: the grief-stricken. On top of THAT, the funeral industry, like many other industries, is now dominated by a small handful of mega-corporation. For every small family funeral parlor, there are three ultra-efficient chain outlets who tilt the playing field.

It just seemed like a good setting for a crime novel.

Jon: As this is your first book, it's probably still fresh in your mind. What did you have to go through to get published?

Sean: I'd been publishing short stories for awhile before attempting something novel-length. Like many writers, I've collected my share of rejection letters along the way. I had an agent in New York for a previous novel that didn't sell; while I was writing DIRT, that agent left publishing altogether and moved to the West Coast to work in film. Her eventual replacement was so unenthusiastic about DIRT's "breakout potential" in a market that was supposedly soft for crime fiction that we parted ways before the book ever darkened an editor's desk.

So I found myself faced with a brand new manuscript and a decision to make: start over with the long process of finding a reputable new agent, and hope for the best in a market where first novels always have a tough row and many talented midlist authors were being unceremoniously dropped from their publishers, or find a good, supportive small press myself and get on with it already.

So I turned to the Internet and put together a short list of independent presses who I thought were putting out quality books. At the top of the list was a new mystery publisher in Los Angeles calling itself Ugly-Town. I queried them cold, they responded by asking to see sample chapters, and things went from there. I think it was apparent fairly early on that we were sending and receiving on many of the same frequencies, and I was extremely appreciative when they offered to put Dirt on the shelves.

Jon: So who is UglyTown books? Yours is the first I've seen from them. They are beautiful books.

Sean: I really can't say enough about UglyTown. In my opinion, they're everything a small specialty press ought to be. They do spend a great deal of time and energy on the physical design of the books they release, but more than that, they're committed to staking a claim in publishing and they back their authors 100%.

UglyTown puts out around four books a year. DIRT was their second quarter release for 2001. The first book they released this year was an excellent young adult mystery called 'The Secret of Dead Man's Mine' by another first-time novelist named Rodney Johnson. They just released a dead-on 40's-era noir called 'Rat City' by Curt Colbert. And as I write this, they're gearing up to release what promises to be a high-test thriller called 'Gun Monkeys' by Victor Gischler.

The company itself is owned by a couple of guys named Tom Fassbender and Jim Pascoe. They are memorable and unapologetic in style, and I've grown to consider them friends. Hard cold market realities aside, that's not something everybody I've talked to can say about their publishers.

Jon: Quince Bishop is a cool character. Are you thinking about doing a series?

Sean: Quince Bishop thanks you for the compliment, but he really doesn't get what you're talking about.

Actually, quite a few readers have asked me if he'll be a recurring series character, and I'm really gratified that they'd want to read another book about him. . .but I honestly can't imagine what Quince would DO in another book. He just doesn't strike me as the adventure-seeking type, you know? And as much as I like having the guy around, I think it would strain credibility if he stumbled his way into caper after caper.

I think that must be why so many mystery series novels feature PI's, cops, and reporters. Most "regular" people just don't find themselves in the middle of many dangerous and exciting mysteries.

Or maybe that's just me. But on the subject of cops, I'll say that Detective Timms has showed up to play a larger role in the book I'm working on now. It's not a series entry per se, but it's set in the same general L. A. area, this time during fire season. It's called BURN.

Jon: How much of yourself do you put into your books?

Sean: A friend of mine submitted the opinion that Quince Bishop is me without the day job. I think that's putting it a bit broadly, but I'll admit to certain personality overlaps.

I think it's just about impossible to write a book that means something to you without putting something of yourself into it. How much varies from character to character, but I think if most writers are completely honest, they can probably identify some of their own personal traits in even the not-so-nice characters they come up with. Amplified or muted, perhaps, but present, whether in abundance or only in trace elements. And even if you're cutting some character out of whole cloth, or basing a character very specifically on somebody you've known, or some combination of people, the way you choose to portray that character is still based on your own perceptions of the character's prevailing qualities.

Beyond that, I think just about everything feeds into the work in one way or another. I'd never met a mortician before I began researching DIRT, but I've been to funerals. Arlen Maxwell looks an awful lot like my next door neighbor, but my neighbor and I don't have long back-yard conversations. My parents are alive and well, I'm grateful to say, but I own a Swiss Army pocketknife very similar to the one. . .well, I don't want to give too much away, but you get the idea.

Jon: Have you done many signings or conventions yet? What are your impressions?

Sean: When you're just starting out, like I am, I think signings can be a mixed bag. The range? From surprisingly nice turnouts all the way to me at a table in the middle of a big store somewhere with the sound of crickets   chirping in the distant background. And everything in be-tween. But that's all part of the game, and I think you need to learn to play it. I'm completely grateful to any store who is willing to make room on their shelves for one of my books, and if they're willing to host a signing event on top of that, I consider myself in their debt. We had a great time at Mystery One this past September.

I think conventions are huge fun. I've been to a few outside the mys-tery genre over the years, and a few of the people I've met through these events have become some of my very closest friends. I think con-ventions can get to be an extremely expensive way to socialize, but I do enjoy them.

Jon: Who do you like to read?

Sean: I know I'll forget ten people if I try to list my faves, so instead I'll list the books I've read lately. Let's see. 'Mystic River' by Dennis Le-hane. 'Land of Laughs' by Jonathan Carroll. 'Fake Liar Cheat' by Tod Goldberg. 'Captains Outrageous' by Joe R. Lansdale. At the moment I'm revisiting 'The Shining" by Stephen King, because it's Halloween time and I'm in the mood. Currently waiting on my nightstand: 'White Teeth' by Zadie Smith, 'A Heartbreaking Work of Staggering Genius' by Dave Eggers, 'A Prayer for Owen Meany' by John Irving, a nonfiction book about the health care industry whose title I can't recall. About thirty others that are equally scattered around the map.

Jon: I'm guessing you don't write full time yet, so what is your regular job?

Sean: I write software manuals. For more information, see question #6, Line 1.

Jon: How do you approach your writing? Do you work from an outline? Do you do a lot of research?

Sean: I used to write between the hours of about 10 pm. and about 2 am. Recently I've inverted my schedule: early to bed, up before dawn to write before the rest of the house-

Sean Doolittle and Victor Gischler

hold begins to stir. This program is still in the experimental stages, and it goes against my nocturnal inclinations, but it seems to be getting more productive all the time, so I'm hanging with it. The other way just wasn't working anymore.

I generally need to have at least some kind of rough outline. Maybe an opening, a few ideas for mileposts along the way, maybe some vague idea of an end point. The course often changes as things develop, and I try to stay flexible enough to let that happen. But I've learned that if I start with nothing and just try to wing it, the way some writers say they do, I'm in the weeds in no time. Often, after a book makes it past the first handful of chapters and really begins to assert itself, I'll sit down and try to sketch out two or three chapters in advance, just to try and avoid coming to the computer with absolutely no idea where to go next. I'll write up to that point, take stock of things, and try to rough out a couple chapters ahead again.

As for research, I tend to approach it on an as-needed basis. Quite a lot went into DIRT just because I knew so little about the day-to-day aspects of the funeral business going in. Often, I find that general research for its own sake can help to get the juices flowing. On the other hand, I'll sometimes find myself wasting an hour hunting for some brand name of metal detector for some throwaway line simply to avoid getting to work. Usually that's when I know I'm spinning my wheels.

Jon: What do you like to do with your free time?

Sean: Spend it with my wife, Jessica, and our six-month-old daughter, Kate. Go to movies (or, for the past six months, watch 'em on DVD). I have a small digital home recording setup in my office; I'm an extremely amateur musician, but a total gearhead, and the two together make for a nice method of creative crop rotation. A couple of years ago, a good friend of mine named Brian Hodge--if you haven't read his crime novel 'Wild Horses', I
recommend treating yourself to it post haste--turned me on to playing the didgeridoo. If you don't know, this is the Australian aboriginal wind instrument that produces the low, distinctive, growling drone you've heard in Australia documentaries and Subaru Outback commercials. You have to develop this circular breathing technique to play it properly, and it's just damned addictive and relaxing. The cat hates it.

Jon: Does having a family make it harder to find time to write?

Sean: Yeah, but I love 'em. Actually, in terms of total hours per day, the day job is the real obstacle. It occurred to me recently that a life of crime could free up my schedule AND count as a tax-deductible research expense. But I go to bed too early for that now.

Jon: Can me tell us a little about writing your next book, BURN? You said earlier that Detective Timms from DIRT is in it.

Sean: BURN is a rewrite--actually a demolition, redesign, and rebuild--of a failed early manuscript. Even though that first version had its share of problems, the characters always stayed with me, so I decided to give them another go. This one fought me tooth and claw to the bitter end, but I finally muzzled it. Eudora Welty said, "Each story teaches me how to write it, but not the one afterwards." In some ways, BURN is the story that resisted the telling. But I feel like I've told it, warts and all, and I'm glad the characters got a second chance at life.

Detective Timms actually existed in the first version of BURN. In fact, he existed in trunk stuff even earlier than that. I recycled him for DIRT, not knowing that I would later rewrite the former book. It seemed pretty natural for BURN, then, to overlap the character, and to give Timms a somewhat larger role than he'd had in either of his previous incarnations. At this point, Timms probably deserves his own book one day. We'll see...

Jon: If your daughter came home from school and told you she wanted to become a writer, what would you tell her?

Sean: I'd be interested to ask James Lee Burke what he told his. I guess I'd tell her to go for it. I'd tell her to never doubt her ability, because there will be plenty of other people more than willing to do that for her. I'd tell her to keep working at all costs, but to take care of herself if the costs start to grow larger than she can afford. And I'd tell her to remember her folks when the first big advance check comes in.

Jon: Any thoughts on book three? Have you started it yet?

Sean: Book three is called Book Three until I come up with a title. This one is a bit of a departure from DIRT and BURN, at least in setting and overall tone. The story takes place in the Sandhills of western Nebraska, my home state--specifically in Cherry County, which is, according to the latest statistics I've seen, the largest, least-populated county in the United States. Call it middle-of-nowhere noir. I'm just in the first 100 pages at this point, so I don't want to talk about it too much. I'll say that it's a more personal book in many ways than I've done so far, and I'm liking how it's going. Plot elements include methamphetamine production and recreational canoeing.

Jon: What bands or artists make you want to stop what you are doing, and just enjoy the music?

Sean: Man, I have a two-year-old and a day job. You want me to stop what I'm doing and enjoy the music? Next you'll be telling me to smell flowers!

Jon: What's the last book you read and what did you think of it?

Sean: As of this minute, the last book I read was 'A WILD SHEEP CHASE' by Haruki Murakami. The book before that was Steve Hamilton's 'BLOOD IS THE SKY'. I admired both of them a great deal.

Jon: What's the coolest thing you've heard from a reader?

Sean: A young, single woman once expressed what seemed like genuine disappointment that Quince Bishop was fictional. I don't know if that qualifies as the coolest thing ever, but I took it as a high compliment. Characters are everything to me. I want them to be everything to everybody.

Jon: What kind of car do you drive, and what kind of car would you like to be driving?

Sean: I drive a 1989 Geo Prism with 230,00 miles on the odometer, rust holes in the fenders, a leaky radiator, and bad tires. I would like to be driving my wife's 1996 Honda Accord. Or maybe one of those small SUV's. I hear the Jeep Liberty tows 5000 pounds and still gets okay gas mileage.

Jon: Anything I can do to facilitate you writing faster?

Sean: Is this an offer? Does it include funding? I'd settle for a decent family health insurance policy. Let me know.

Jon: You actually started writing in a different genre. Care to elaborate on that?

Sean: Most of the early short stories I published appeared in horror magazines and anthologies. I was a big fan of Robert Bloch and Stephen King in high school, through them discovered writers like Joe Lansdale, David J. Schow, and Brian Hodge. For a while, all I wanted to be in life was a horror writer. Eventually, I noticed that I was trying to shoehorn ideas into a mold that didn't really fit, so I decided to just try to keep writing stuff I'd actually want to read and let the work be what it wanted to be. I see now that Bloch, King, Lansdale, (David) Schow, and Hodge have always done the same. It's one of the things I admired immediately about writers like
Dennis Lehane and John Connolly, and a host of others I won't even attempt to list here. It's what all good writers do, whatever label they choose or acquire.

For me, the natural progression seemed to be stuff that generally fits into the crime/mystery category, and so far the fit seems right. Of those earlier stories, I'd say about half had ideas but an undeveloped voice. A few had some good ideas but a prose style still in that awkward braces-and-acne adolescent phase. And a few just flat-out sucked. In general, I'm happy to let most of them stay obscure. But for better or worse, they do represent my growth as a writer. As a human being. I wouldn't want to stop growing in either category.

Jon: A lot of books seem to pick up on hot topics of the day. Do you think novels need to be socially conscious or are they still essentially entertainment?

Sean: don't know that these two qualities need to be mutually exclusive. Social consciousness shows intelligence, and I prefer intelligent entertainment. At least most of the time.

Having said that, I'm always leery of a novel that has an obvious political agenda or an armload of axes to grind. And as a reader, nothing shuts me down faster than a didactic tone.

But I don't think social consciousness necessarily requires dealing with a specific topic from the headlines, or cramming a particular viewpoint down a reader's throat. I think there's a level of social consciousness in something as simple as a realistic portrayal of a character dealing in a real way with a real problem. Which often turns out to be not so simple at all. Very few things are black and white in life. And most of the interesting stuff is in the gray areas.

Jon: What's the one thing always in your fridge?

Sean: Speaking of gray areas. . . .
Oh, I don't know. You can usually find a beer or baby formula. They both come in bottles; one has the nipple. I'm not saying which.

Sean Doolittle's website :
www.seandoolittle.com

<u>Sean Doolittle's books are :</u>
Dirt 2001
Burn 2003

Short Stories:
"Worth" appears in the March/April issue of Plots With Guns
"A Kick in the Lunchbucket" - appears in Crimewave 5
"Summa Mathematica" - appears in The Best American Mystery Stories 2002

Loren D. Estleman

I tell a lot of people to read Loren D. Estleman. So far everyone who has taken my advice on this has been very happy with whichever of his books they read. However they are also unhappy with me. Why? Because now they are hooked and have to buy all his books, and there are a lot of them to buy. Loren writes PI books, westerns, crime oriented history, and has even written some Sherlock Holmes.

He is very prolific. This makes me happy because every time I'm caught up, he has a new book for me. Loren is also very knowledgeable about his field. Because of him I started reading Bill Pronzini. When I first met Loren I was just diving into the genre with the gusto I give everything else I do. I was familiar enough with the bestsellers, but just starting to scratch the surface of great writers out there. He was right, and I love Pronzini's work. So now, when Loren mentions books and movies, I take notes. And while I know a whole lot more than when I first met him, he always has new leads for me.

Loren D. Estleman personifies everything that is right with the mystery genre, and writing in general. He is truly one of the greatest, and this is not something I say lightly. -Jon

Jon: You have a lot of books out. How many books do you write a year on the average?

Loren: I average two books per year. It's a metabolic condition; one would leave me with too much time on my hands and the disturbing conviction that without writing I'd be just a bum. Three, and my work would suffer from haste. I write on a manual typewriter, which allows me to work steadily, rather than fast. Unlike computers, manual typewriters never break down. My
output doubled when I abandoned electrics.

Jon: A lot of your books take place in Detroit. And it seems as though you know enough about Detroit to be considered a historian of the city. Throughout the books we get a historical look at the city. Have you thought about doing a non-fiction book of Detroit? Maybe even "Amos Walker's Detroit" ?

Loren: AMOS WALKER'S DETROIT is the very title I chose for a book coupling Walker's descriptions of various neighborhoods and land-marks with photographs. It's still just in my head, and there's been no interest. I am the author of the Detroit entry in the forthcoming Ency-clopedia Britannica, but I effectively and with great relief gave up non-fiction when I left my last newspaper job. Writing from the imagination is a lot more fun.

Jon: I had heard rumors about the possibility of another Peter Macklin Novel. Any truth to that?

Loren: SOMETHING BORROWED, SOMETHING BLACK, the first Peter Macklin book in 15 years, will be published by Forge in April 2001. In it, Macklin has a new young wife who has no idea what he does for a living, and much of the narrative is from her point of view.

Jon: Earlier in your career you wrote two Holmes novels ('Sherlock Holmes vs. Dracula' and 'Dr. Jekyll and Mr. Holmes') Was this your first foray into mystery/crime novels?

Loren: My very first novel, THE OKLAHOMA PUNK (not my title; these days I don't let publishers change them), was my first crime novel, based on the career of 1930s Public Enemy Number One Wilbur Underhill. SHERLOCK HOLMES VS. DRACULA was my first book-length mystery, following two stories I published in Alfred Hitchcock's Mystery Magazine.

Jon: In 1980 you introduced the mystery genre to Amos Walker. And in the twenty plus years since he has come to be the definition of a hard-boiled detective. How much of Amos Walker reflects you?

Loren: I'm exactly like Walker: handsome, strong, courageous, and honest. Criminals blanch at the mention of my name and I shake women off my lapels like snow.

Jon: The Walker books seem to have a timeless quality about them. Do you think this is part of their appeal?

Loren: Possibly. I avoid topical and political references that don't age well. Jonathan Swift, writing in the 18th century, still has something to say to modern readers, while some books published during the abysmal period of the 1960s are excruciating to read today. I don't know if I can match Swift, but I certainly want my work to outlive me by more than a few decades.

Jon: Do you think there are similarities between mysteries and westerns?

Loren: Definitely. Both genres deal with a frontier, someone's attempt to tame it, and someone else's efforts to keep it wild. Conflicts are between archetypes, easily recognizable regardless of setting. It's worth noting that the only two uniquely American contributions to world literature are the western and the detective story.

Jon: Anyone who reads Amos Walker knows about your knowledge of cars. What kind of car do you drive, and if you could own any car from any time, what would it be?

Loren: I drive a 2000 GMC Sonoma four-wheel-drive pickup with extended cab, but in my head I'm driving a 12-cylinder Duesenberg; or for more practical parking purposes a 1949 Mercury--black, of course, with fender skirts--a marvel of aerodynamic engineering resembling Buck Rogers' spaceship.

Jon: What authors do you enjoy reading?

Loren: Robertson Davies, Ernest Hemingway, Edith Wharton, F. Scott Fitzgerald, Patricia Highsmith, Douglas C. Jones, Elmer Kelton, Willa Cather, Arthur Conan Doyle, Jack London, Elmore Leonard, Oscar Wilde, Raymond Chandler, Gustave Flaubert, Honore de Balzac, H. Rider Haggard, Lucia St. Clair Robson, P.G. Wodehouse, William Manchester, Flannery O'Connor, Rudyard Kipling, W. Somerset Maugham, George Macdonald Fraser, many others. If
you're curious about the fact that most of these authors seem to be dead, it's because they wrote their best work before the Beatles came to America.

This to me is the point at which western civilization began to decline.

Loren: By some standards; about 15,000 volumes. I collect modern first editions and research and reference books. The idea in the beginning was to cram my study with all of human knowledge, in the interest of total autonomy, but every time I begin a new project I run into an area of intelligence not to be found in my library. I understand computer technology is the closest thing to a source of universal information, but it includes the drawback of owning a computer. I'll stick with my books.

Jon: What other type of jobs have you had in the past?

Loren: Editing, reporting, and writing for newspapers. No honest jobs.

Jon: Do your books require a lot of research?

Loren: Yes. I'd estimate a year's research goes into each book, concurrent with what I'm writing at present. I'm blessed with a nearly photographic long-term memory, so the amount of cramming I have to do on each project diminishes in direct ratio to the amount of material I've written pertaining to that area. Once you know that Doc Holliday preferred colored dress shirts and that latent fingerprints evaporate with time, you're saved the trouble of looking up those details.

Jon: Writing as much as you do would take a lot of discipline I would imagine. Do you have a regular schedule you follow?

Loren: I'm not a born self-starter, a condition I share with most writers. Therefore I sentence myself to six hours per day at the typewriter, or however long it takes to reach my goal of five clean pages.

Jon: A nice selection of your earlier books are being re-released in trade paperbacks. With beautiful artwork I might add. Have you noticed a renewed interest in the earlier work?

Loren: Yes, particularly as regards my various series. When people discover one, they naturally want to read the earlier entries. At the moment I'm in the happy position of having all my published work back in print or about to be, so it's easier than ever for the diehards to track down my ouvre. I agree with you about the artwork. By and large I've been fortunate in the artists and designers who have collaborated on my covers. Some of these people have gone on to brilliant success in the world of art collecting.

Jon: Do you think the internet helps with sales? Do more people know about your books because of it and does it give people easier access to them?

Loren: It's advertising, a global billboard. It can't hurt, and it has made it easier for some readers to track down my harder-to-find work. My website (www.lorenestleman.com ; shameless plug) has increased my profile significantly.

Jon: Have you had any interest from Hollywood for any of your books? I think BILLY GASHADE would make a great miniseries.

Loren: Occasionally something is optioned, covering my mortgage for one month. If they ever get around to filming, I'll be able to pay it off. A producer of feature films flipped over BILLY GASHADE, but said it could only be done as a TV miniseries, and passed it along to a contact in television. I didn't expect to hear anything about it after that, and I wasn't disappointed. Two years ago, my agent in Hollywood congratulated me, saying EDSEL was "on the front burner" at Warner Brothers. Since then the option has run out and
he's retired. As far as Hollywood goes, I'm the anti-Elmore Leonard.

Jon: How would you describe a perfect weekend?

Loren: No work to do and a pile of good books within arm's reach.

Jon: Do you enjoy the public part of being a writer? Going to conventions, signings?

Loren: Some parts of it. Meeting readers and booksellers and getting together with other writers is a nice break from the solitary life. However, it exhausts me, whereas writing energizes me. No contest, if I were forced to choose. My worst day writing is still better than my best day on the job.

Jon: Is your taste in movies similar to your taste in books?

Loren: Yes, in that it's all over the map; although film noir is no. 1. I pioneered the concept of the home theater 15 years ago, building a movie room into my basement with a fifty-inch screen TV and a collection of movies on tape that runs around 1,300 titles at present. Now I've started on DVD. This access to film has been of enormous assistance with such books as THE ROCKY MOUNTAIN MOVING PICTURE AS-SOCIATION, about early Hollywood, and the Valentino series, about a film archivist who keeps getting mixed up in murder. I've also installed a VCR with a four-inch screen on my desk to monitor specific details. I broke it in while writing NEVER STREET.

Jon: Your books have wonderful titles. Does a lot of thought go into the title of a book?

Loren: A great deal. I always start with the title, although it may take several years before I think up a book to stick on the end of it. For me, the best titles evoke shadows and echoes, and I try very hard never to use one that someone has used before. In that, I've failed a couple of times, but not knowingly. I hold writers who pilfer other writers' titles in the same contempt I reserve for plagiarists. If they can't come up with one of their own, I suspect the sources of their characters and plots as well.

Jon: Writers spend a lot of time by themselves writing. How important is the support of your family?

Loren: They're sounding boards, marketing geniuses, and head-holders when nothing's going well. Deborah Morgan, my publicist (and wife; she's also an extremely accomplished writer), designed my website, concocts, arranges, and sends promotional items to thousands of readers and booksellers on an ever-expanding list, and has even been known to carry one of my books through airports with the cover exposed, to gather attention. If I weren't sleeping with her, I couldn't afford her.

Jon: Do you take inspiration from real life for any of your books?

Loren: Where else would I go?

Jon: If you were able to speak with a young Loren, what would you have said to him?

Loren: Avoid polyester.

Jon: I understand you've been asked to write a book about writing. Are you looking forward to this book?

Loren: At this point, I've written the introduction and three chapters, and Writer's Digest Books is happy with what it's seen. It's hard work-- I'd been away from journalism so long, I'd almost forgotten what it's like not to make things up and try to sell them to the reader--but very fulfilling. I see it as my chance to put my money where my mouth is and put down on paper the principles I've been spouting off on for thirty years. It will be an honest book, positive, a bit subversive, and I think helpful.

Jon: With the amount of writing that you do, do you write more than one book at a time or, do you concentrate on getting one done, then move to the next?

Loren: I'm writing the book on writing and a Peter Macklin novel simultaneously. It's the first time I've attempted to write two books at once, but the projects are so different I've found each to be a vacation from the other. I've often suspended work on a book to write a short story, but I think writing two novels at the same time almost guarantees two mediocre books as opposed to one strong one. Multi-tasking explains why so much sloppy work is being done in commerce.

Jon: What were the first DVD's that you bought?

Loren: 'Silverado' and 'Tombstone'._ The pattern was similar to when I bought my first VCR eighteen years ago; which incidentally is still operating, without ever having been cleaned professionally or visited a shop. At that time, I spent more on four westerns--'True Grit', 'The Shootist', 'El Dorado', and 'Big Jake'--'than I did on the VCR. Westerns cleanse and regenerate the creative faculties.

Jon: Between mystery conventions and Western conventions how many do you average a year?

Loren: Two or three. I've missed only one Western Writers of America convention in twenty years, usually attend the Bouchercon, and decide whether going to one of the smaller mystery conventions will cut too deeply into working time. I'm invited to a good many more than I'm able to attend.

Jon: What's the best way to get your attention?

Loren: Tap me on the shoulder.

Jon: What's the last book you read and what did you think of it?

Loren: 'Waiting for Winter', a late collection of short stories by John O'Hara. O'Hara's nearly forgotten now, and in his own lifetime he was hammered by critics for the sin of popularity, but this country never produced a more clear-eyed observer of American life through the microcosm of the small city. This collection, published in 1966, confronted some daring issues of sexuality that would only be nibbled at timidly a generation later, by younger writers who thought they'd discovered them. I can't remember the last time I read a collection from start to finish, without jumping around.
A riveting read.

Jon: What's the one thing that is always in your refrigerator?

Loren: Coke and/or Pepsi, preferably in glass bottles, otherwise in cans. I slam them the way Dylan Thomas slammed Irish whiskies.

Loren D. Estleman's Website :
www.lorenestleman.com

Loren D. Estleman's books

The Amos Walker Series:
Poison Blonde (2003)
Sinister Heights (2002)
A Smile on the Face of the Tiger (2000)
The Hours of the Virgin (1999)
The Witchfinder (1998)
Never Street (1997)

Sweet Women Lie (1990)
Silent Thunder (1989)
Downriver (1988)
Lady Yesterday (1987)
Every Brilliant Eye (1986)
Sugartown (1984)
The Glass Highway (1983)
The Midnight Man (1982)
Angel Eyes (1981)
Motor City Blue (1980)

Macklin:
Something Borrowed, Something Black (2002)
Any Man's Death (1986)
Roses Are Dead (1985)
Kill Zone (1984)

The Detroit Series:
Thunder City: A Novel of Detroit (1999)
Jitterbug (1998)
5 Stress (1996)
Edsel (1995)
King of the Corner (1992)
Motown (1991)
Whiskey River (1990)
Other books:
Peeper (1989)
Dracula vs. Sherlock Holmes (1978)
Dr. Jekyll and Mr. Holmes (1979)

Books of the American West:
BLACK POWDER, WHITE SMOKE (2002)
THE MASTER EXECUTIONER (2001)
THE ROCKY MOUNTAIN MOVING PICTURE ASSOCIATION(1999)
JOURNEY OF THE DEAD (1998)
BILLY GASHADE: AN AMERICAN EPIC (1997)
THE HIDER (1978)
SUDDEN COUNTRY (1991)
BLOODY SEASON (1988)
GUN MAN (1985)
THIS OLD BILL (1984)

MISTER ST. JOHN (1983)
THE WOLFER (1981)
ACES & EIGHTS (1981)
THE BEST WESTERN STORIES OF LOREN D. ESTLEMAN (1985)
PEOPLE WHO KILL (short stories)
The Wister Trace (1987)

Page Murdock series
PORT HAZARD(2003)
White Desert (2000)
City of Widows(1994)
The Stranglers(1999)
Murdock's Law
Stamping Ground (1980)
The High Rocks (1979)

Collaborations:
THE BLACK MOON (1989): with Robert J. Randisi, Ed Gorman, W.R.
Philbrick, and L.J. Washburn

LEGEND ( ): Estleman, Elmer Kelton, Judy Alter, James Reasoner, Jane
Candia Coleman, Ed Gorman, and Robert J. Randisi

Valetino - serial series short stories
"Greed"   EQMM   May 2002
"The Day Hollywood Stood Still"   EQMM   March 2001
"Picture Palace"   EQMM   July 2000
"The Man in the White Hat"   EQMM   May '99
"Director's Cut"   EQMM   December '98
"The Frankenstein Footage"   EQMM   July '98
"Dark Lady Down"   EQMM   March '98

Steve Hamilton

Steve Hamilton won the Edgar Award for best first novel with his novel A COLD DAY IN PARADISE. An outstanding book about an ex-cop who's escaped to the Upper Michigan of his youth to be left alone A COLD DAY IN PARADISE proved to be only the beginning. Alex McKnight is THE wounded hero in a generation of mysteries full of wounded heroes. With each book he recovers just a little more; being drawn back into the world by the mystery that unfolds before him.

Mr. Hamilton's sense of and ability to write setting has made his series of tomes featuring Alex McKnight THE must read regional series in a generation of mysteries full of well drawn regional mysteries. The climate is ever-present. The isolation of Paradise pulsates with its vivacity. The proud history of the people who've lived in the U.P. for generations resonates with every page.

The mysteries are all harrowing. You cannot read a Steve Hamilton book without being invested in the outcome. There is no such thing as "just a few pages before bed" in this series. Often there is a shared grief with the author. Often there is fear within the pages. always there is satisfaction at the end of the book. BLOOD IS THE SKY is one of the most compelling and haunting reads of 2003.

Hamilton has proven with his keyboard and writing skills that Noir is not just for the big city. Noir is hidden in cozy little towns .
-Ruth Jordan

Jon: In case some one has been locked in their home for the last four years, and hasn't read your books, how would you describe them?

Steve: Unconventional hard-boiled crime fiction, set in a small town on the shores of Lake Superior -- with a main character who has a lot of baggage, and who wants nothing to do with the private eye business. But he can't stop himself from helping people who really need him. So he ends up in a lot of trouble. How's that?

Jon: Alex has a very interesting background. How did you come up with his past, and is there any of Steve in Alex?

Steve: Not really.   After I tried to write my own version of the modern wise-cracking private eye, and totally failed, he was sort of just there, waiting for me. The first sense I had of him was that he felt like a failure, just like I was feeling that night. The baseball background, especially the part about being a catcher, seemed to fit his personality -- and, of course, he never played one day in the big leagues. After that, it just seemed natural that he'd become a police office. The death of his partner was the thing that kept haunting him, fourteen years later.

Jon: So far, Alex hasn't used a gun. Is this going to continue? Will it cause problems down the line?

Steve: The day his partner was killed, Alex had a gun in his hand. He didn't use it. Since then, he's had this thing about guns. He hates to even touch one. In the first book, he has to get over that, at least a little bit. But he'll never really want to carry a gun again unless he absolutely has to.

Will it cause him problems? Oh yes!

Jon: You write about Michigan and his surroundings in such a way that the reader really feels they have been there. Is this from personal experience or damn good research?

Steve: I grew up in the Detroit area, and we'd go up north every summer. Northern Michigan, especially the Upper Peninsula, seems so different from anywhere else in the country. As soon as you cross that bridge, time seems to slow down. And of course with Lake Superior always in the background -- the biggest, deepest, coldest lake in the world -- I thought it would be a great place to set a mystery.

Jon: Do you intend to keep writing about Alex McKnight for a while? Any plans to do stand alone novels?

Steve: Number four, NORTH OF NOWHERE, comes out next summer. I know the book after that will be a McKnight book, as well. I know I'll do something else some day, but not until the other kind of story (whatever it is) is just burning to get out. Stand-alones are doing very well these days, of course (Connelly, Lehane, Coben, etc.), but I don't want to do one just to try to

make a big score. I think it would show. You've gotta do things for the right reasons.

Jon: Laura Lippman said "Steve Hamilton already seems like a wily veteran to me". I think that she sums it up really well. Have you been writing a long time?

Steve: I sent a story into Ellery Queen Mystery Magazine when I was twelve years old. (No, it was not accepted.) I'm forty now, and the magazine just bought a story from me! In the twenty-eight years in between, I wrote through high school, wrote through college, promised myself I'd keep writing even though I was going off to work full-time at IBM, forgot that promise for about ten or twelve years, remembered the promise and joined a writer's group, sold a couple short stories, and then decided to try my
first book-length mystery. That book was A COLD DAY IN PARADISE. When it won the Edgar, I went up to the podium and said the same thing Tommy Lasorda said when he was inducted into the Baseball Hall of Fame: "Who are you people, and what are you doing in my

dream?"

Jon: What made you want to write?

Steve: I'm not sure there's a good answer to that question. I think, like most writers, I write because I have to. It's the only thing that makes me feel like I'm doing what I'm really supposed to be doing.

Jon: Do you have set writing time? Morning, night, weekends?

Steve: For me, there's only one choice. Nickie and Toni go to bed, and then I start writing around ten o'clock at night. I'll stay up until one or two in the morning.

Jon: Do you enjoy touring and/or meeting the readers?

Steve: I was so nervous the first few times, but now I just relax at these signings and have fun. I hardly ever read from the book, but I can stand up there and tell stories for an hour or so, no problem. It's still amazing to me that people would actually come to the store just to meet me. I don't think I'll ever take that for granted. Bottom line, though, that's one great hour and then twenty-three hours by myself, going to the next place, being away from my family. I wish I could just beam myself to the store, and then back home...

Jon: Do you think being a Father has an effect on your writing?

Steve: Dennis Lehane once told me that he didn't think he could have written 'Gone Baby Gone' if he had kids. I know I couldn't do it. Just the thought of one of my kids being in danger, even if it's just in my imagination as I'm writing fiction -- I don't know. If the story really demanded it, I suppose I could try. But it would be hard.

Jon: What authors do you enjoy reading when you get the chance?

Steve: I've mentioned Lehane and Connelly and Coben already. Who else? James Crumley, Lawrence Block, George Pelecanos, Laura Lippman, Elizabeth Cosin, Charles Knief, William Kent Krueger, Ian Rankin, Val McDermid. (I could go on and on.) Somebody I've just discovered is Denise Mina, from Glasgow. I
got to meet her in London this year and tell her how much I love her books. Of course, about twenty seconds after I meet her, I'm already-

showing her pictures of my kids. I'm hopeless.

Jon: If you were able to time travel to the past and talk with a teenage Steve, what would you tell him?

Steve: Hang in there. Keep day-dreaming. It'll all work out.

Jon: You have a job besides writing. What do you do for a living? And how do you manage to juggle a career, a successful writing career and having a family? Do you ever sleep!?!?

Steve: I still work for IBM, although I did take a leave of absence this summer. The people I work with, especially my manager, have been so incredibly supportive and flexible. The fact that I can stay up late writing and then come in late the next day, for example -- and work at home at least one day a week. So far, it's all worked out.

Jon: When you aren't working or writing, what do you do with your free time?

Steve: Not working, not writing, then it's spending time with my family... Okay, or golf. Every year, I play on this team with a bunch of Americans against some guys from England and Finland. We've played in Scotland and Ireland in the past, and this summer, we played in Spain. Life is rough, I know.

Jon: What kind of movies do you enjoy? How about music?

Steve: I enjoy real offbeat comedies, like anything from the Coen brothers. As you can imagine, I loved 'Fargo'. Music, let's see, I'll just tell you what I have in the tape box in my car: The Clash, The Smiths, The B-52's, Cocteau Twins, The Cure, Bach, and Vivaldi. So that's what... alternative rock and baroque classical.

Jon: So after reading your books I'm pretty sure I don't need to go outside in the winter! Do you like outdoor activities in the winter?

Steve: I grew up playing hockey every day, on the frozen lake behind my house. That or snowmobiling or skiing.

Jon: Baseball is a big part of who Alex is. Have you played baseball? And who's your favorite team?

Steve: I come from a baseball (and golf) family, and have played a lot, but never in the minor leagues. My team from birth has been the Detroit Tigers.
That's not going so well these days...

Jon: So is there anything about you that people would be surprised to know?

Steve: I'm not sure about this one. I guess if you only know me through the books, which happen to be violent (and cold), you might be a little surprised when you meet me in person. I'm the kind of person you could take home to meet your parents, put it that way.

Jon: Batman or Superman??? And why?

Steve: Batman. He's much more interesting. He has a real dark side.

Jon: Is there anything that really scares you?

Steve: The thought of anything ever happening to one of my kids.

Jon: I know I've told you this, and I would guess you hear it often; Your writing keeps getting better with each book. Do you as an author feel your are improving each time out?

Steve: I know that I'm trying. Of course I don't think anyone can make a big jump forward with every book. I think you're doing well if you make a jump, hold ground with the book after that, make another jump, hold ground again, etc. You know what I mean?

Jon: Has the way you read or what you read changed since you been published and are doing your own writing?

Steve: It's certainly changed the way I read crime fiction, although if it's really, really good, it can still be just like it was when I was twelve years old reading those Alfred Hitchcock paperbacks. The one tough thing these days is that I can't read a lot when I'm right in the middle of working on something myself. When I finally come up for air, I've got all these books waiting for me!

Jon: Can you tell me what's in store next for Alex?

Steve: He meets a woman in the current book, BLOOD IS THE SKY. So next up is what happens between them (and to them). It's a big change for Alex.

Jon: What question do you get asked more than any other?

Steve: It's usually some-thing about how with all the great-looking men writing mysteries these days, I still look the best when I put on a suit for the Edgar Banquet. It's

really embarrassing and I wish everyone would stop asking me about it. (And please, no more photographers! Somebody's gonna get tram-pled.)

Jon: What's your favorite album by The Clash?

Steve: Please, LONDON CALLING, of course.

Jon: What was the last live music show you saw and how was it?

Steve: It was actually a musical called COWGIRLS, about a classical string trio who accidentally get booked at a honky-tonk bar. Highly recommended.

Jon: What is the ONE thing that is always in your refrigerator?

Steve: 24-ounce bottles of Mountain Dew. How else am I gonna stay up so late every night?

Steve Hamilton's Website:
www.authorstevehamilton.com

Steve Hamilton's books :

A Cold Day In Paradise - 1999
Winter Of The Wolf Moon - 2000
The Hunting Wind - 2001
North Of Nowhere - 2002
Blood Is The Sky - 2003

Short Stories:
"The Nerve" appeared in EQMM Dec 2001

Charlaine Harris

Charlaine Harris- Graham Greene once said "I write Entertainments". Nobody does the modern Entertainment quite like this lady. One needs only to look at her protagonists to realize the lady's got it going on. There's the always coifed librarian Aurora Teagarden. Tragic heroine Lily Bard escaped her past by moving to Shakespeare . Her newest protagonist, Sookie Stackhouse arrived on the page as a waitress with a vampire boyfriend and a shape-changer boss. Harris's sense of humor comes through in the name of her heroines alone.
In all three series her plotting is always fast passed and has a sense of the wink of an eye like no other writer out there. As you root her protagonists on; cheering for their small victories, and shaking your head at their setbacks, time flies by. Often you finish her book before absorbing the full complexity of the lady's plot but when you do there's a feeling of marvel at the complexity of and messages sent by her latest offering. One of our most talented entertainers, Ms. Harris is "cozy with attitude" . - Ruth Jordan

Jon: So I guess the first thing I want to ask is, are you surprised by the success of the Southern Vampire series?

Charlaine: Yes, no, and you bet. I've had a long career in the mystery field, and to find such wide notice paid to something I tried for fun has been really exciting -- but sometimes baffling.

Jon: Any ideas for future titles? I would imagine that the possibilities are endless: DEAD BEAT, DEAD WEIGHT, DEAD LINE...

Charlaine: I am always in the market for a snappy phrase including "dead." I didn't set out to include this word in all the titles. It was my publisher's idea, to give the series a quick identity. The next one's going to be called DEAD TO THE WORLD.

Jon: Is there any one thing you've written that has generated more reader response than anything else?

Charlaine: Oh, sure. I have to say, two things. One is the install-ment in the Aurora Teagarden series called A FOOL AND HIS HONEY. More on that later. The other is the first Sookie Stack-house book, DEAD UNTIL DARK. That brought readers out of the woodwork.

Jon: So am I right in thinking that you have three different se-ries?

Charlaine: No. A couple of years ago, I lost my paperback deal with Dell for the Lily Bard books. The Lily books, set in Shake-speare, Arkansas, got me lots of critical notice but not big bucks. Without a paperback deal, it seemed impractical to me to con-tinue the series; especially since I felt I had written as much as I wanted to about the character. With the Aurora Teagarden books, I've fulfilled my last contract with St. Martin's with the Roe coming out in August, POPPY DONE TO DEATH. So, who knows? I have four more books to write, as of now, in the Sookie Stackhouse series.

Jon: I've heard a lot of authors say that they write books that they would want to read. Is this true of you?

Charlaine: It surely is.

Jon: How important is setting to your books?

Charlaine: Setting is very important in my books. I think the books don't work if you don't know your setting. If I read a book that could be taking place anywhere, from suburban Memphis to urban Los Angeles, I think that's a poorly written book.

Jon: In A FOOL AND HIS HONEY, you shook up your readers a bit with the ending. Is it safe to say that you got, and maybe still get, a lot of feedback for it?

Charlaine: And that's putting it mildly. FOOL is four years old, and I still get readers (some of them former readers!) who take me to task about that book. Maybe I should have had the character abducted by aliens instead of having him die?

But other fans are real happy I did it. I certainly never foresaw the firestorm that arose.

Jon: And why did you kill off Martin?

Charlaine: His jig was up. Actually, I'd planned on killing Martin for a long time. I didn't intend him to last through as many books as he did. But my editor at the time was a big Martin fan, and she wouldn't let me kill him. When the series went to another publisher, I immediately asked my new editor if I could write in his death, and she was all for it. Hey, he was never right for Roe, anyway.

Unfortunately, by sheer coincidence, there were three mystery writers who killed off heroines' significant others THAT YEAR. So some readers went into overload.

Jon: It's kind of funny that your books are labeled as cozies or 'woo-woo' type supernatural thrillers. I have to say that for books that are supposed to be cozy, they sure have some hard edges to them! And I mean that in a good way. Do you think having your work set into a certain category limits your readership?

Charlaine: Yes, I think it's true that having your books set into a category does limit your readership. That's why there are so many elements in the Sookie Stackhouse books; they sell to mystery, science fiction, horror, and romance readers. I'm always confused when I find them in the horror section, because I certainly don't think I'm scary. Even the Aurora Teagarden books, which aren't as overtly sexy as the Sookie books, are not all that cozy. But I find I'm not comfortable at all with coloring between the lines.

Jon: You seem to turn up at a lot of conventions. Do you enjoy the whole convention experience?

Charlaine: I enjoy seeing all my friends and, of course, it's a chance to meet booksellers, editors, and publishers whose paths I may not have crossed yet. I don't enjoy the expense and the lost work time, and sometimes I miss things my children are doing. From a self-promoting point of view, a convention panel is a great way to impress a room full of people who may never have considered buying your books before. I try to do about four conventions a year.

Jon: For people not familiar with them, what can you tell us about SWEET AND DEADLY and A SECRET RAGE, your first two books?

Charlaine: Both were stand-alones published by Houghton Mifflin. SWEET AND DEADLY, my first book published -- and also the first book I ever wrote -- is set in a small town in Mississippi, and the protagonist, Catherine Linton, is a young woman working at the local newspaper, who suspects her father and mother were murdered. Her father was the town doctor. I hate the title, which wasn't my idea.

A SECRET RAGE was kind of a cult novel for a time; it got endorsed by some prominent feminists. It's about a very beautiful woman who gets raped when she comes back to town where she attended college, and how she deals with it, and how she discovers who raped her.

Jon: When you started your different series, did you plan on them going on for as long as they have? Did you set things up for later, or discover that things get added to the history as you go?

Charlaine: I do throw a few things out in each book, threads that I can pick up later or discard, as I choose. Sometimes, that's quite unconscious on my part. Sometimes, it's deliberate, like setting up the mystery of the missing family in THREE BEDROOMS, ONE CORPSE, a mystery that would later be examined in THE JULIUS HOUSE. In this publishing climate, you never know when a book will be your last! So you can't leave too many loose ends.

Jon: Who does the cover art for the SOOKIE STACKHOUSE series? I think the covers are wonderful.

Charlaine:They are! I love them! And the artist is Lisa Desimini.

Jon: As long as I'm on the subject, what put the idea in your head for the Southern Vampire series? Were you just watching TV one night and thought "...wouldn't it be great if a vampire came on TV and announced that they were real?" I think the premise is terrific, but I'm curious where it came from.

Charlaine: I'd been reading vampire literature for years, especially the scene in one of Anne Rice's early books where Lestat enters the mother house of the Talamasca and introduces himself to one of the men who's investigating him   -- David, I think. I began to imagine what people would do if vampires lived among them, acknowledged. I thought about it, in idle moments, for a long time. Then Laurell's books came out, and of course she'd gotten there first. But I had a different idea about what it would be like, and decided that the time was right to write my book.

Jon: I'm guessing that you are picking up a lot of new readers because of the cross genre aspects. Would that be true?

Charlaine: That is SO true.

Jon: Do your kids read your books? I noticed in the dedication in CLUB DEAD that Timothy wanted his own book.

Charlaine: No, they don't read my books. Once the two boys were old enough, they didn't want to. And my daughter is a little young for Sookie, for sure. I'm just letting them do what they want about it. Maybe they don't want to know me that well.

Jon: When you sent out DEAD UNTIL DARK, did you have trouble finding a publisher? Because I'm guessing if you did, there are some people regretting they didn't want to publish it.

Charlaine: I sure hope so. I had never believed in a book so strongly, and I never had a book turned down so often. Of course, all the mystery editors turned it down because it was so strange, though some of them liked it a lot -- and some of them definitely didn't. My agent wouldn't even read me some of the letters, because he knew I'd get upset. Finally, an editor at Ace, John Morgan, fell in love with the book. All in all, I guess I wrote DEAD UNTIL DARK roughly three years before it finally was published in 2001.

Jon: Lily Bard is a body builder and also practices martial arts. It says on your website that you also do these things. Do you have anything else in common with Lily, or with your other characters for that matter?

Charlaine: Sure. All of characters have pieces of me in them, even the bad ones, I think. But none of them are wholly me. I haven't practiced martial arts, to my regret, in about three years; my sensei moved. Like Lily, I do lift weights, though the older I get the more painful it is. And like Lily, I'm a rape survivor. I read like Aurora does, I'm about the same social stratum as Aurora, and I love libraries the way she does. I hope that like Sookie, I have a rich inner life.

Jon: Are you a believer in a lot of research, or in just writing things in a believable manner?

Charlaine: Research is not my favorite thing because I am so easily sidetracked. It's not uncommon for me to spend hours when I should be writing just straying farther and farther from the main point. But I do enjoy learning odd things. Unfortunately, you can never use everything you learn, and you just have to hoard these little facts up to use when conversation gets boring. I do want what facts I use to be accurate, but I also know that if someone's come to me to learn how to embalm people or how to run a library, they're not going to achieve that.

Jon: How important are titles for you? It seems that you've taken great care in picking some great ones

Charlaine: I have friends who help me, and sometimes the cybercitizens of DorothyL chip in. I am proud of those I think of on my own, but my publisher, for example, came up with "CLUB DEAD."

Jon: Is it easier to keep a series fresh when you can take a break and write one of the others, in between books?

Charlaine: Probably. I'm still working that out.

Jon: What's the one thing always guaranteed to make you laugh?

Charlaine: The absurdities of daily life.

Jon: If you were doing an series on 'Survivor' with other mystery authors, who would you want on the island?

Charlaine: Hmmm. I'd want Lee Child, Barbara Seranella, Thomas Perry, and William Kent Krueger for their survivor skills; Steve Brewer, Janet Evanovich and Kate Munger to make me laugh; Denise Swanson for her psychological skills; and Dean James, Eve Sandstrom and Toni L.P. Kelner because I enjoy their company so much. I don't know how many people get to be on the island in 'Survivor', so I don't know if I could ask any more or not.

Jon: What's your favorite place and way to spend a weekend?

Charlaine: I'm boring. I like to be at home, which ᵀ haven't gotten to do much recently. I like to get a few things accomplished on Saturday morning, go out with my husband to dinner and a movie on Saturday night, go to church
Sunday morning, and veg out Sunday afternoon. Now that our kids are older (19, 15, 12) that increasingly likely to happen, but on the other hand, they're pretty social and there's a lot of fetching and carrying.

Jon: What's the one thing always in your refrigerator?

Charlaine: Milk.

Charlaine Harris' website:
www.charlaineharris.com

Charkaine Harris's books:
Sweet and Deadly (1981)
A Secret Rage (1984)

THE AURORA TEAGARDEN SERIES:
Real Murders (1990)
A Bone to Pick (1992)
Three Bedrooms, One Corpse (1994)
The Julius House (1995)
Dead Over Heels (1996)
A Fool And His Honey (1999)
Last Scene Alive (2002)
Poppy Done to Death (2003)

THE LILY BARD "SHAKESPEARE" SERIES:
Shakespeare's Landlord (1996)
Shakespeare's Champion (1997)
Shakespeare's Christmas (1998)
Shakespeare's Trollop (2000)
Shakespeare's Counselor (2001)

THE SOOKIE STACKHOUSE SERIES:
Dead Until Dark (2001)
Living Dead in Dallas (2002)
Club Dead (2003)

Vicki Hendricks

I want to tell you about Vicki Hendricks. In order to do that, I need to talk about the word "noir." It's a funny word. Sort of like "porn" in that it's difficult to define but I feel I know it when I see it. Noir.

Getting beyond the obvious, here's what noir means to me. It's a word I can use instead of "mystery" when I'm describing what I write -- usually at snooty academic conferences. This is relevant. Really. Like Vicki Hendricks, I also teach college-level writing. It's sometimes awkward having one foot in genre-land while the other is in academia. So I often feel a bit self-conscious when Professor Tweed of Ivy League University asks what sort of fiction I write. Noir. That's kinda smart, ain't it?

I don't know if Vicki Hendricks ever feels awkward around her professor-peers. Meet her for even a few moments and you'll realize she's a sunny, intelligent, interesting person. She jumps out of airplanes. She dives underwater. It's difficult to imagine Vicki Hendricks ever feeling awkward or self-conscious. So when we use the word noir in relation to Vicki Hendricks, it's not a trick or a cover or some kind of marketing gimmick. Novels like Iguana Love and Sky Blues are simply damn fine examples of noir.

But the more important fact of Vicki Hendricks is this: she's a skilled and talented writer, and no label (not even the mythical "noir") can contain her. My favorite Hendricks novel is Voluntary Madness. There are many novels I enjoy. Fewer that I recommend to friends. And a VERY few that I envy. When I finished Voluntary Madness, I sat back and said, "Damn. Why can't I write something like that?" Voluntary Madness is a work of literature. It's that simple. I hope her students are paying attention. They can learn a lot from Vicki Hendricks.

--- Victor Gischler (author of Gun Monkeys)

Jon: What is the coolest thing you could hear from a reader?

Vicki: What is the coolest thing a reader could say to me?

I think it's already happened, but I can't even make a choice between two. I really liked it when Barbara Parker told me she read MIAMI PURITY standing by the sink. She had picked it up for a cursory look and gotten so involved that she forgot to sit down. I'm sure that the event is slightly exaggerated, but nevertheless, I loved hearing that. I also enjoyed hearing that in the Borders near where I live, they kept having to pick the copies off the floor of the men's room. Seriously. And this was not the softcover edition with the woman wearing a bra; this was the hardcover with no pictures whatsoever. I consider that a triumph!

Jon: What other types of things have you done to put bread on the table besides writing novels?

Vicki: I spent many years studying literature and teaching English to avoid writing fiction because I didn't know how to do it. Luckily, that set me up with a paying job that allowed for the freedom of writing, instead of wasting my time trying, and encouragement to apply for acceptance to the creative writing program at Florida International University. I always mention that because I don't understand the negativity many people imply about this kind of program. I think it's either jealousy or they don't know enough to see the difference. I could have spent 20 years reading books on my own and following the trial and error method and still not written as well as I did after 4 years of learning technique from those wonderfully insightful writers. Nevertheless, I still make my living from teaching, and I continue to learn more about writing from the trial and error of my students and trying to explain to them how to improve their technique.

Jon: Do you pay much attention to reviews?

Vicki: I guess you could say that I read them closely, but I don't take them very seriously. I don't find many that I would have written myself, whether good or bad, although I generally enjoy the good ones much more! In many cases, reviewers focus on things that are not important to me or they interpret things according to emotion rather than reason. Sometimes they even get enough details wrong that I find it difficult to take anything they say seriously. For the most part, all my bad reviews have had a "moral outrage" somehow working against me, although it is generally disguised. This has happened twice with the Miami Herald.

Vicki Hendricks and Lauren Henderson

For example, in VOLUNTARY MADNESS the main character realizes with alarm that she's pregnant, but then reminds herself that her scheduled suicide will come long before the baby would ever be born, so it really doesn't matter. Now I can see why some people would find this reasoning appalling, but the woman reviewer referred to it as "boring"-- boring reasoning. Not even a logical adjective to apply. However, she based her whole review on that example.

Now, you can probably find many people who were disgusted with some of the scenes and characters in MADNESS, but truthfully, I'd bet my life that nobody found the book boring. I was angry that she would misrepresent my writing in order to hide the fact that it was a personal emotional issue for her. I can't imagine that anyone was fooled who read closely, but it bothers me that people come out of nowhere and don't even have to make any sense in order to be printed in the newspaper.

On the other hand, on occasion I've had sparkling reviews that didn't make complete sense either, though nothing as far off as that. For these reasons, I don't pay enough attention to reviews to base anything about my writing on them. Often I've had two reviews on the same book with completely contradictory pronouncements. On SKY BLUES, for example: not enough skydiving, too much skydiving; too much sex, not enough sex. Who could make any sense out of that?

Jon: Who did you study with at FIU?

Vicki: I studied with John Dufresne, who is not a mystery writer, but has three wonderful novels about, as he says, "life and death." Billy Bob Thornton is currently working on a screenplay with John for his first novel 'Louisiana Power and Light'. My personal mentor was Lynne Barrett, who writes short stories and is the most sensitive reader and articulate critic anyone could hope for. She has two collections out, currently one entitled 'The Secret Names of Woman', and has been published in all the major literary magazines in the country. Dan Wakefield, who is mostly writing non-fiction these days, has a history of novels, with some made into film, dating back to 'Starting Over' in the 60's. Les Standiford and James W. Hall are the two most well known in the fiction department at Florida Atlantic University, with their series of thrillers. Jim was my thesis advisor for a Master's in Fine Arts, Creative Writing, and MIAMI PURITY was my thesis. The defense was a hoot, probably an X rating.

Jon: Who are some of the authors who inspire you?

Vicki: Of course, there's James M. Cain, who inspired the whole animalistic passionate underpinnings of MIAMI PURITY. I found out after I'd written it that 'The Postman Always Rings Twice' also inspired Camus' The Stranger, so I figured I was in good company. I have also read everything that Harry Crews has written and his wild gritting writing has undoubtedly affected my psyche, if I dare to admit it. Larry Brown might be my favorite writer at present. His book 'Fay' has influenced me somewhat on the character I'm creating now in CRUEL POETRY, although I'm far enough along that I don't remember specific ideas that might have come from there. I have a CD of Annie Proulx's short story about the gay cowboys that I played over and over in my car for months a couple of years ago, until I could almost say the lines along with the reader, so I hope that some of her sensitivity toward character has penetrated my brain. There are so many others, but these are the few that come to mind right now.

Jon: When you write, do you just sit down and go at it, or do you wait for inspiration to hit?

Vicki: I can't wait for inspiration to hit, because it never does unless I sit down to write. This sounds ridiculous, but I'm mostly inspired by my own words. I usually start with the barest idea of a character or an event and then one sentence leads me to the next, and each action of a character leads me to understand that character better and know what the next action will be. I knew an artist who started a painting by wadding and twisting pieces of newspaper and dropping them down on a canvas. He would then spray over them however they lay, and after picking them up, begin to work from the shapes that had formed. Often they came out to be animals. Not knowing anything much about art, I don't know if this is ridiculous or not. I made fun of it in VOLUNTARY MADNESS by saying that somebody used dog shit shapes as inspiration, but that sounds like sort of an irreverent and fun idea anyway. I guess that's sort of what I do. I throw around words and then figure out what they might mean. Figuring out when they're better than dog shit is a major part of the process.

Jon: With that last sentence in mind, do you have other people read your work while it's in progress, or do you like to keep it to yourself till you have a finished draft?

Vicki: I nearly always wait until something is in the "final" draft before I let anyone read it. There have been a few exceptions, but I think I'm the best judge of the writing and whether something is working or not, and mostly what other people help with is to remind me if I've forgotten to think about something. I've come to the point where I don't feel the need for anyone else to see it, but eventually I show it to a few people. I don't have another writer to trade writing back and forth with, so I don't feel I can ask for a lot of time from others. The novel I'm working on now was a little different. A playwright friend of mine and I got together over lunch a couple of times and brainstormed some ideas for the characters and atmosphere, with the plan that I would write the novel and she would do the screenplay afterward. Since we were working together in a way, I sent her some pages a couple of times or called her and brainstormed, which made it more fun than being totally isolated. However, as I got farther into the novel and the vision was jelled, I found that outside input was distracting from where I was really headed and I told her to save her comments until the end. Now I'm nearly finished and I'll be glad to see what she says soon and take some of her suggestions.

Jon: I'd like to touch a bit on how you spend your free time. I know you sky dive, I heard that you spent some time dog sledding a few years ago. Is it safe to say you like outdoor activities, maybe with a hint of danger?

Vicki: I've been called a thrill seeker many times and have been interviewed in articles as such, where my writing was not even mentioned, unfortunately.

I've never actually felt that I was seeking thrills, however. I have enjoyed the beauty and tranquility of scuba diving for over 25 years, and I love the skydiving and dogsledding and swimming with the pink dolphins and piranhas in the Amazon--or sharks in South Africa--anything like that, but I would rather enjoy it all without the fear, if possible, as opposed to a few of the skydivers I know who like nothing better than a near fatal scare to get their blood moving. I did some reading on thrill seekers several years ago when my sister was considering doing a study on them for a Ph.D. in experimental psychology. It seems that I do have many of the characteristics used in the definition by Marvin Zuckerman, the leading authority. The chemical basis in the brain for this personality type has not been established, but the behaviors include skydiving and such, by people who are bored with normal life, whose curiosity overcomes fear. I guess I have to say is true in my case.

Other descriptive characteristics include liking adventure travel, fast driving, drugs and alcohol, spicy food, loud rock music, and a variety of sexual partners. I won't say which of these I embrace, but you can probably find people who could tell you. I've never had what people always ask about--the adrenaline rush, although I've had many symptoms of paralyzing fear in learning to skydive, including temporary partial loss of sight, hearing, and speech. But after sixty jumps or so, most of the fears normally lessen to the point that these activities make you feel wonderful. They recapture the feeling of fun that I remember from childhood. Currently, I'm recovering from shoulder surgery caused by a skydiving injury on exit from the plane a few months ago, and fear will return at some level for my first jump back, my 500th, but I can handle that in order to resume my normal weekend activity. I can't wait to have my fun back. There's nothing else like it.

Jon: I can see where overcoming fear and not letting it control you would be a major factor in doing things like this. And, quite honestly, I don't think I could overcome my fear of heights enough to jump out of a plane. Does the fear ever really go away, or is it something that you just learn to control?

Vicki: I'm not sure if there are things that I'm afraid of that I haven't overcome. Self knowledge is lacking. I don't BASE jump, for instance--jumping at low altitudes from cliffs or stationary objects--but I don't know if it's because I'm too afraid, or if I just don't see the value in it, because the main purpose is to create extreme risk. I enjoy skydiving from high altitudes because it feels like flying--it's extreme fun--there's no time to fly on a BASE jump.

Jon: And on the subject of danger, how did you get involved with Tart City?

Vicki: I think Tart City found me. I was writing unspecified dark and dirty stuff before Lauren, Stella, Sparkle and the others got together and invented the name and defined the style. I met Lauren when MIAMI PURITY came out in the UK in 1996. I was invited by a friend of hers--erotica writer, bookseller, and editor Maxim Jakobowski--to crash a costume party that Lauren was giving at her family's home in London. I was the only one not dressed as a cocktail, but she didn't mind, of course, and since then we've been good friends. She visited me in Florida, did a skydive herself, and hopes to do more. The group seems to like having me as a tart, since I take tartiness to the limit, writing generally darker and dirtier than the others. Perhaps I should have my own more sleazy American genre name, but the word "tart" allows me a little more respectability and it's nice to be included with such interesting women.

Jon: What are some of the more mundane things you do in your free time?

Vicki: Geeze. As a skydiver, scuba diver, dogsledder, gym rat, foodie, noir and erotica writer, I hardly have time for the mundane. I rarely cook or clean, unfortunately, although I fantasize about cooking and have a huge cookbook collection that I have read most of. I do teach classes daily, but I hope no one would label them mundane! Lately, I've moved, so I've spent a lot of time unpacking boxes--and I'm redecorat-

ing around my cat, choosing complimentary colors and animal print blankets and fake furs for her to sit on. I also chose an all tile floor so that I can get her a pet ferret in the near future. I guess that's pretty mundane.

Jon: I was told by someone (Karin Slaughter actually) that you should never throw away anything you write, because even bad writing can teach you something. Do you think this is true?

Vicki: I never throw anything away because I have so little time, that I'd rather rework something until it's good than totally dump it. One problem with learning to write is that you're never finished. Everytime you get to the end of a novel, you're a better writer than you were when you started, so then you have to begin over fixing. When you get to the end again, the same thing happens and on and on. You finally just get sick of it and hand it over, knowing that when you do your readings at the bookstores you'll be cringing and changing words as you go, and you'll come across techniques for the rest of your life that you wish you would have learned earlier. I agree that you learn from bad writing also. Over the years I've learned many things not to do from my students, so I'll never have to do them myself.

Jon: MIAMI PURITY is considered by many to be a Hardboiled classic. When you started the book, what were you setting out to write?

Vicki: I didn't realize MIAMI PURITY was so hard-boiled, but my reviewer for the NY Times, actually went to some trouble to make sure I was really a woman and not a man writing under a woman's name because it was so tough. Actually, when I started to write MIAMI PU-

RITY I was having a passionate affair with James M. Cain. He was dead, of course, but that never stopped me! A professor in the MFA program had just introduced me to his writing and I was totally obsessed, especially with 'The Postman Always Rings Twice' and 'Serenade'. I thought I would be writing "literary fiction" only, which is what I'd always read, but in Cain I found the highest form of literary technique with a knockdown plot besides. I had read a little Thompson and some of the classic detective novels, but those are crude next to Cain. His ability to condense the action and bring the story to life with the animal passion and emotion of his characters is unequaled to this day. Strangely, he has some real bloopers among his novels, so I don't recommend those. It seems to me he balances on such a fine line between the darkest truth and soap opera that occasionally he falls onto the wrong side. Maybe he was turning them out too fast for the movies--I don't know.

Anyway, for a class in creative writing I was assigned to write a third of a novel, using a model. I chose 'Postman', not only because I loved it, but it was only 120 pages in the paperback I had, so that meant I only had to write about 50 manuscript pages, as opposed to other classmates who chose novels such as 'Catch 22' and 'Lolita'. 'Postman' is in first person, has few characters, one main plot, and is mostly told in scenes, so this seemed to be on a small scale I could handle best. I finished the novel for my thesis and that was MIAMI PURITY. I remember calling it thing.wps on my computer because I didn't actually have the guts to say, even to myself, that I was attempting to write a novel. It seemed egotistical. I always told people I was working on a thing. Now if you mention you have novels published, people assume they're self-published anyway, so I don't have to be shy about it anymore!

Jon: What are you working on right now?

Vicki: I'm currently doing the rewriting on my longest, darkest novel -- CRUEL POETRY.

It's over 400 pages and is the first novel I've written with
multiple points of view, a prostitute of sorts and the man and woman obsessed with her. I've been working on it for almost four years now and still have a few months to go. It's taken me so long that I wonder if the psychological waves of the universe that seem to have some bearing on creativity have already been siphoned from and published by other

writers. For instance, I started reading Scott Phillips' 'The Ice Harves't this week and discovered that he has a major character named Renata, an unusual choice and the name of one of my narrators. Now I don't know whether to keep her name or change it. I worry that my plot is floating around in another book somewhere. Nevertheless, I think it's an interesting phenomenon, how ideas and techniques pop up independent of each other. I just don't like being late. I think this book is in pretty good shape already. I can tell it "worked," because the ending seemed to "fall off like ripe fruit," as Flannery O'Connor would say, and not like rotten fruit, which is always the fear until I get there.

There's more blood, sex, and drugs in this book than my others. I've always stuck to tidy murders before--especially the one inside a dry cleaning machine --and I worry that my research might be lacking on physiology, but it's always a challenge one way or another, and I'm enjoying all the personalities that have come to life or death. I haven't shown it to anyone yet, so that will be my next concern. Then on to another. I started rock climbing last summer, so I'm thinking I should include that in a novel, in order to round out the scuba and skydiving for

Laura Lippman, Vicki Hendricks and Lauren Henderson

a noir/adventure trilogy, but I'm not inspired so far.

Jon: What's the hardest part about moving?

Vicki: The hardest part about moving has to be writing. Even though the place I bought was pretty much ready to go, it seems that men were coming in and out at random moments on a daily basis starting at 8:30 am. I do all my writing in the morning before school, and it was difficult to concentrate on anything. I had this major book problem, due to the approximate 4,000 books I own, and had thrown out all my old bowed and swaying Wal-mart bookcases, so I was having one enormous heavy-duty bookcase built in. I've never bought new furniture before--my last sofa I had found by the dumpster, used it for five years, and returned it there for the next lucky scavenger, so I'm awaiting a new love seat and sofa with some excitement. However, generally, I choose adventuring over decorating.

Jon: What advice would you give to a sixteen year old Vicki Hendricks?

Vicki: This is difficult and interesting. I guess, knowing that I'm still alive now, I would say for myself at 16 to be bold and take more risks. I was a little wild as a teen, but too quiet and unaware of my abilities. I could have gone a lot further. In a way, I would be afraid to give any advice to myself because everything, good or bad, has contributed to what I consider now a really great life. Of course, there's always the desire for more time, travel, and the money to do it, but I still feel that I will get everything I want eventually. I'm tempted to say that I should have started writing earlier, (before my late thirties) but I probably didn't have anything interesting to write about and might have wasted years turning out drivel, instead of reading, traveling, and setting myself up securely so I could write later. I almost feel that I have somehow made choices all along with knowledge of the future that I don't realize I have, silly as that sounds.

It's difficult to get into specific examples without taking up pages, but choices made as whims often contribute to my life in unexpected ways. On the other hand, I'm the kind of person who has "happy" brain chemistry, so maybe I don't have such a wonderful life and I just don't know it! My emotional level is difficult to keep down for any period of time and perhaps I'm just rationalizing the grim" parts of my life as learning experiences that I wouldn't want to have missed. As a writer, most everything in life is useful as material, and I'm always comforted by the knowledge that whatever trouble I get myself into, people have short memories.

Jon: And, because I had to ask..... What inspired your story, 'Stormy, Mon Amour', in the Tart Noir Anthology?

Vicki: I love to talk about "Stormy." It's the only story I've written that had a clear inspirational moment that I can describe, although "ReBecca" was pure inspiration from beginning to end, as if I had lived a life as a Siamese twin. "Stormy" began with a trip to Islamorada in the Keys to swim with the dolphins--before I learned that it was a bad thing to do for the sake of the dolphins. My sister had made the trip a year earlier and told me to be sure to see Stormy, her favorite dolphin, who had swum and played with her exclusively the whole time she was in the water. I was taking a boyfriend along and told him about my sister's experience on the way. In the briefing before the swim, we were told how to proceed, and the woman guide mentioned that on occasion the dolphins became attracted to people, for example, Stormy, who had become a little sexually aggressive, resulting in his isolation from the swimmers in his private lagoon. This, of course, prompted an outburst of laughter from my date, who blurted out, "I knew it. Your sister ruined Stormy!" I doubt that she did, but the idea started me on my way to the story about the young Canadian woman who left her red-neck husband to pursue the love of a dolphin, father of her mermaid daughter. However, I became bogged down in the middle because I realized I needed a sex scene and had no idea of the details.

I put the story away for almost a year, until I coincidentally met Richard O'Barry, a dolphin rescuer and the author of 'Behind the Dolphin's Smile'. He was able to give me the necessary details to bring that scene alive, and he also told me other facts that enabled me to write the perfect climax when I reached that point. I had no idea where I was going and came to the epiphany at the same time my character did. I had to let the story go where I didn't want it to.

Jon: What's the one thing always in your refrigerator?

Vicki: You actually asked me what the one thing in your refrigerator is, and I have to say I don't have a clue! In case you meant my refrigerator, I have a lot of stuff in there at all times. Most of it is moldy or outdated, but my best items are pepper/fruit jellies and exotic sauces. I've collected these from my travels, and I have many jars in the cabinets still unopened because I'll never eat them since I can't buy them again. Violet petal jelly, baby eels in olive oil, and chocolate body frosting, among others, are quietly aging together on my shelf. I finally threw away a jar of Mexican mole that I had been moving to new apartments since the early 80's. You can now get it at Publix supermarket.

Vicki Hendrick's Books:

Miami Purity (1995)
Iguana Love (1999)
Voluntary Madness (2000)
Sky Blues (2002)

Laura Lippman

Laura Lippman- Laura Lippman's career in mystery fiction is unlike any other. An almost Cinderella story. Her first book was released by Avon Books as a paperback original just six years ago. Already she is recognized as one of Mystery's greatest talents.

BALTIMORE BLUES introduced readers to Tess Monaghan. An ex-reporter turned P.I. Tess knows the city of Baltimore. Her love for that city shines through even as she presents you with its many warts. The cases are as varied as Baltimore's neighborhoods. And there's an amazing evolution by the author from book to book. Lippman has honed her writing skills until the words are razor sharp. The publishing world has noticed. SUGAR HOUSE was Lippman's fifth book and released by Morrow as a hardcover. Lippman was introduced to even more readers and continued to raise her own standards. Her readers are the grateful recipients. Last year's IN A STRANGE PLACE is wonderful book. Taking Tess back to her very beginnings as a P.I. and presenting a growth of character, plotting, and suspense that cannot be denied. What more could we ask of this scribe?

Out now, EVERY SECRET THING. Baltimore is here but Tess is on vacation. It is a beautiful book. A horrifying tale of what women can do. In a year full of great to brilliant reading for mystery fans EVERY SECRET THING is one of the must reads. There is a trust in this novel presented by the author to the reader that is a rarity. It's gratifying. The morph sis is now complete. Lippman is a name for readers to know and writers to read. She can teach her peers how it should be done. We all get a piece of that glass slipper.
-Ruth Jordan

Jon: For those who haven't picked up any of your books yet, how would you describe them?

Laura: They're PI novels, plain and simple. Sometimes, I think they read a little bit as if they're PI novels written by JoAnna Trollope or Cathleen Schine after a one-night stand with Robert Crais or Robert Parker, but I'm flattering myself. They're PI novels. It's a tradition I love, and one in which I'm proud to work.

Jon: The books take place in Baltimore. It seems as though you know the city really well and it comes through in the writing. How important to the books is the city?

Laura: I know parts of Baltimore well, but it's an extremely complicated city. I'd be skeptical of anyone who had claimed to master all its cultures and subcultures, not to mention its history. It's like a really good song, a standard that a lot of people have covered over the years. Say, 'My Funny Valentine.' I have my version, and it's authentic, but it's not definitive.

Jon: How close did the TV show 'Homicide' come to capturing Baltimore?

Laura: Very well, in just the manner I described above.

Jon: And.... is it true that you used to work out at the same place as Kyle Secor (Bayliss on 'Homicide')?

Laura: Yes. Andre Braugher worked out there, too, and Clark Johnson. But Braugher was particularly notable, keeping up a running monologue about how much he hated exercise and how much he wanted a cigarette, even while he was running on the treadmill.

Jon: Are there many similarities between you and Tess Monaghan, besides you both having been reporters?

Laura: The verbal style is certainly similar. You know how some writers say that they give their characters the funny lines they think of too late? I have a bad habit of thinking of them and saying them. This has not been good for my journalism career..

Jon: In your books, Tess has a significant other. Do you get requests from fans concerning the relationship?

Laura: Not requests, but A LOT of opinions. I think that's inevitable, don't you? I really don't have a blueprint for Tess's love life. I'm just following along, waiting to see what happens.

Jon: Is it gratifying to move from paperback originals (PBO) to hardcovers?

Laura: Yes, because there are more reviews, more attention paid. But my primary goal is to be read, and I know a lot of fans can't purchase the books in hardcover. When I was publishing as a PBO, I could say to someone in a bookstore, "C'mon, you probably spent more on lunch yesterday."

Jon: What do you think of the new trend for authors to write stand-alone books? Do you have any plans to do so?

Laura: I'm for anything that lets writers stretch, in or out of their series. I also like to see writers reach bigger and bigger audiences, and stand-alones have allowed some of them to do just that. I might write one, but I have no plans to abandon Tess.

Jon: Are you published in foreign markets?

Laura: Yes, in the UK, Japan, France, Norway and Portugal.

Jon: I was told you have a very interesting Jimmy Breslin story. Is there any chance of you sharing it?

Laura: Are you sure it was Jimmy Breslin? Because the Mike Royko story is much, much better. Not to mention the Bob Greene...

I'll tell the Royko one here, and not just because he's dead and can't be libeled. When I was 19, three of my friends and I traipsed down to the Billy Goat Tavern in Chicago to celebrate the end of finals. Royko, a widower at the time, was at the bar. He became quite smitten with us. I was -- am -- a big-boned girl and he kept calling me "the one with the thighs." He also told us some wonderful stories about his career and noted that it was unusual to meet young girls who still blushed. Charlie Finley came in and bought us cheeseburgers. A drunken yuppie punched me in the stomach when I said something smart-ass. He was ejected from the bar. (See, I told you my mouth gets me into trouble.)

We thought the evening was a glowing success, down to and including the impromptu kiss Royko bestowed on one of my friends as we were leaving. ("I had a Pulitzer Prize winner's tongue in my mouth!") A few days later, Royko wrote a column saying he believed in keeping the drinking age at 21 because he was tired of tripping over "apple-

cheeked boozers" in his favorite bar.

Jon: You do some events with the gals over at Tart City. (Sparkle Hayter, Katy Munger, Lauren Henderson..) Are you one of the tarts, or more of an associate?

Laura: I'm the mascot, tagging at their heels, eager to be one of the gang but not quite tuff enough. (Sort of like Anybody in 'West Side Story.') They are very kind to me, encouraging my inner tart. The story I wrote for the Tart Noir anthology is very different than anything I've written to date and I credit their influence. But I do think I have a Tart sensibility. My first book, "Baltimore Blues," inverted a lot of PI stereotypes -- the women are strong, surrounded by slavish, adoring men who would do anything for them.

Jon: Harlan Coben said that you work a room better than anybody in the business. Do you enjoy doing signings and meeting readers?

Laura: Harlan said that? Hmmm, talk about the pot calling the kettle . . .

Pathologically outgoing. Most writers are shy. I'm not. I'm used to meeting people all the time through my work, sometimes in extremely painful or difficult circumstances. Talking to mystery fans and writers is easy, because we do have a common interest.

Jon: Harlan's comment was actually with regard to you winning the Agatha, Shamus, Anthony, and the Edgar in one year. (Way cool!) Do you attribute this to having crossed genre's or to a larger reader base? What do you think makes your series so much more accessible?

Laura: I don't think I managed to do that in one calendar year, for the record. At any rate, it would be folly for me to speculate. Fans and judges have been very supportive of my work and I'm grateful.

Jon: Who are some of your favorite new writers? And who would you consider your writing heroes?

Laura: Steve Hamilton already seems like a wily veteran to me, but I'll mention him here. I've read Karin Slaughter's new book and consider myself a fan/friend. Keith Snyder has been around longer than I have, but he's so young I consider him "new." I'm a big fan of Peter Robinson's work. Talk about cross-over appeal. Long-time cozy lovers and hardboiled aficionados would be comfortable with his work.

I was a fan of the Tarts before they were, officially, Tarts. As it happens, Katy Munger's first Casey Jones book and Lauren Henderson's first Sam Jones book got me through two separate crises in my life. My heroes include all the women who broke through first -- particularly Grafton, Paretsky and Muller.

Outside the crime genre, I read everything that Philip Roth writes. I'm a big champion of Richard Russo (not that he needs anyone to champion his work, but I've been telling people for years that he's the new, better John Irving.) I also was an early Michael Chabon fan. I love early McMurtry. And I love, love, love a book called 'Emma Who Saved My Life,' by Wilton Barnhardt.

Jon: When do you write? All the time, mornings, late at night? Outlines, from the hip?

Laura: It took me awhile to find a schedule, but since I began working on my third book, I've been a morning writer. I get up at 6am and work for two hours. I work on the weekends (although I usually give myself one day off) and I'll pull a few evening shifts toward the end. I'm a morning person, which is a hideous thing to be. No one likes morning people, not even other morning people.

I use outlines of a sort. I try to think it through beforehand, but I also know some things will become clear only after I'm in the thick of it. I begin each book with a challenge to myself. In BUTCHERS HILL, for example, I wanted to write about race because it's central to daily life in Baltimore. With IN A STRANGE CITY, I felt obligated to deal with Poe because he's the father of us all.

Jon: If you could go back in time and talk to Laura at 16 or 17, what advice would you give her?

Laura: Borrowing a line from Miss Trixie in 'Paper Moon', I'd tell her she had nice bone structure. I'd also tell her to stand up straight and to have a little more fun.

Jon: Aside from your writing, what occupies your time?

Laura: Baltimore. I really like to explore the city--go to new places, read the various historic plaques, drive around. I love to eat. And I'm a world-class eavesdropper. I sat at an outside restaurant the other night, listening to two suburban men indulge in what sounded like a very bad

David Mamet play, all about making the deal, etc., with a little side order of misogyny. ("Big breasts, pretty and smart--no one gets all three of those. Except, maybe, in Hollywood.") I wanted to wave my hand wildly at them and tell them I knew several women in Charm City who could hit that trifecta.

Jon: Do real events ever have a way of creeping into your books?

Laura: All the time. In fact, I think every book I've written has been inspired by a real event. CHARM CITY came from Baltimore's mania over getting a new football team. BURCHERS HILL was inspired by a real-life case. IN BIG TROUBLE was my way of going back and re-visiting a notorious Texas murder case. THE SUGAR HOUSE began with a newspaper story that caught my attention. IN A STRANGE CITY, about the "Poe Toaster's" annual visit to Poe's grave here, seemed almost pre-destined.

Even the unnamed seventh book has a real-life inspiration, although it won't be very obvious to those who read it. And I'm already thinking about a Tess book based on a story that I reported for the Sun, only to see it spiked.

Jon: What are some of your favorite movies? And what is some of your favorite music?

Laura: 'Citizen Kane' is my all-time favorite movie, bar none. I also love 'Miller's Crossing,' 'Manhunter,' 'Nashville,' '1900.' (I'm trying to name some more off-beat things here because, like so many people, I love the first two 'Godfather' films and 'Goodfellas' and 'Chinatown.') One of my favorite guilty pleasures is 'Crossing Delancey.' The one thing I really wished I owned on video are the two made-for-television movies about the Betty Broderick case. I could watch those every week.

As for music, my tastes are eclectic. Elvis Costello is my all-time favorite. I listen to a lot of jazz, primarily the great female vocalists, and I am very fond of the late cabaret singer Nancy Lamott. I adore the work of Stephen Sondheim. I like musicals in general. They make surprisingly great running tapes. I recently did five fast miles to 'Gypsy.'

Jon: Is there anything about you that people would be surprised to know? I mean like playing the accordion or something, nothing like, you don't pay taxes.

Laura: I can do an imitation of Ethel Merman singing 'Satisfaction.'
I'm a native Southerner, born in Atlanta. My family moved to Baltimore when I was 6, and the Lippman name comes from my father's paternal grandparents, who fled Germany in the early 20th century and settled in Alabama. But my family is really, really Southern -- I had two uncle Bubbas, and grandparents that we called Big Mama and Big Daddy.

I also had ancestors who were slave-holders, which is a difficult piece of family history to say the least. In a recent New York Times article on the subject of modern attitudes toward our slave-holding past, the writer noted that we all want to be from "innocent origins." I _know_ I'm not. Then again, I suspect most of us are not.

I carry in my datebook a piece of paper that my mother copied out for me, from the 1840 Census. Hardy Callaway Culver of Hancock County, Georgia, had 42 slaves, 31 "employed in agriculture." Culver was my great-great-great grandfather. I carry this piece of paper with me every day because I don't want to forget. I don't know what to do with the information, but I don't want to forget it.

Jon: How many drinks at Bouchercon to get you to do the Ethel Merman impression?

Laura: No one could afford it. Besides, inebriation is not enough. I've never done this for a large audience

Jon: Are you the same Laura Lippman who wrote 'Shakepeare's Henry V' and 'Urban Schools:The Challange of Location And Poverty'?

Laura: No, I'm not, but we're forever linked through the wonders of Amazon.com. It's a terribly common name.

Jon: Any thoughts on who in Hollywood would make a good Tess?

Laura: Not really. If that day comes, I hope only that she's tall. I know they'll make her really skinny, but it would be nice if she could be tall and broad-shouldered.

Jon: Do you want to keep reporting as you write, or would you like to be able to just write the books?

Laura: That's a very tricky question at this point in my life. It's not so much about money as it is about energy. Reporting is pretty vital to me. It keeps me connected to the world. A 40-hour-per-week day job may be less feasible as time goes on.

Jon: Your new book, EVERY SECRET THING, is your first with out Tess. Are you a little nervous?

Laura: I'm always nervous. I'm actually incredibly neurotic, but I hide it pretty well. I'm a big believer in developing worst-case scenarios, in order to cope. Even with the pre-pub reviews in, I'm a bit of wreck.

Jon: I read somewhere that you were hoping to have every other book feature Tess. What do you have in store for her in the next outing?

Laura: You've caught me in a mellow mood, in which I'm actually fond of the work-in-progress. I've given Tess a missing persons case -- an Orthodox Jewish furrier hires her to find his wife and three kids, who disappeared with no explanation. It allows Tess to confront her feelings about her own Jewish roots and a lot of Jewish stereotypes. And it allows me to continue mixing up POV, with about one-third of the book told by the mother, her oldest son, and the mysterious man who's on the run with them.

Jon: What is the thing most likely to distract you when you are working?

Laura: Since I've taken to working in Spoons, a local coffeehouse -- almost nothing. There's no Internet, no phone, and the staff is totally cool -- they throw a toasted bagel and a skim milk latte at me, then leave me alone. This morning, a fan came over and introduced himself, but that's the best possible distraction in the world. I find I can work

even on the rare Mothers-Day-Out morning in the coffeehouse, when up to eight toddlers are racing around, screaming.
That's what 20 years in newsrooms will do for you.

Jon: Is it true you are a huge Marx Brothers Fan?

Laura: Yep, but a much more humble one since a reader caught me in an error in IN A STRANGE CITY. I can name their films in order, however.

Jon: What book have you most recently read, and what did you think of it?

Laura: I just read 'Redemption Street' by Reed Coleman and thought it was terrific. And for complicated reasons, I started reading two novels at once -- 'San Remo Drive' by Leslie Epstein, and 'The Company You Keep' by Neil Gordon, and both promise to be pretty fabulous.

Jon: What is the one thing that is always in your refrigerator?

Laura: A Tupperware container with something way past its prime.

Laura Lippman's Website:
www.lauralippman.com

Laura Lippman's Books:
Charm City (1997)
Baltimore Blues (1997)
Butcher's Hill (1998)
In Big Trouble (1999)
Sugar House (2000)
In A Strange City (2001)
The Last Place (2002)
Every Secret Thing (2003)

Lise McClendon

I was first was introduced to Lise McClendon through an internet newsgroup. Prior to that, I hadn't heard of her work. Since I found her funny and witty on the newsgroup, I sought out some of her books and am glad that I did. She writes a tight, evenly paced story, and shows some keen insights. I'm certainly looking forward to future books from this author. We missed meeting at Bouchercon in 1999, but finally did meet in person at the convention in 2002. She is absolutely charming! Whenever I saw her, she was smiling, and seemed always to be in the thick of things.

I've really enjoyed Lise McClendon's books and the exploits of Alix--so, rather than listen to me babble on, I'll now let you read the interview and then take the plunge for yourself. I think you'll be glad you did. -- Jon Jordan

Jon: How would you describe your two series: Alix Thorssen, gallery owner, and P.I. Dorie Lennox?

Lise: My two series are different, both in style and tone, setting and time period. The Alix Thorssen books, set in contemporary Jackson Hole, Wyoming, are amateur sleuth mysteries featuring an art dealer. They're written in first person and are a little like the small-town traditional mysteries but breezier and a little harder edged. Even harder edged are the Dorie Lennox mysteries which the publisher is calling historical noir. They are set in late 30s/early 40s Kansas City, with a female private eye. They're written in 3rd person and Lennox's boss, an ex-pat Brit, gets some "interior time" as well.

Jon: I've heard that your latest book, SWEET AND LOWDOWN, will be published by St. Martins. Do you think being with a larger publisher might help break you out ?

Lise: SWEET AND LOWDOWN, the second in the Dorie Lennox series, will be published by St. Martin's Minotaur in July. The first, ONE O'CLOCK JUMP, was also published by SMP. I sure hope a bigger publisher can break me out!

Jon: What is it about Montana that makes you want to call it home?

Lise: I love Montana. I've lived all over the U.S.: California, Minnesota, Delaware, Nebraska, Wyoming, but sooner or later you want to set down roots. I love the mountains, the high plains when the rolling thunderclouds turn the sky purple, the blanket of snow in winter. Every place has its good and bad points but I like living in a medium-sized city in a rural state. I think it's the best of both worlds.

Jon: When you write, do you put your own characteristics into your characters?

Lise: I think it's impossible to write fiction without putting your own characteristics into your characters. Especially your main character. Since I've only been inside one head (mine) I really don't know what it's like inside other people's. (And maybe that's a good thing?) I can guess though and that's what fiction is all about, the things that make us human, our similarities, our frailties, our fears.

Jon: What made you want to do the first novel?

Lise: Insanity. Ambition. Naivete.

Jon: What other things have you done besides writing mystery?

Lise: Other books? I've written about four other novels that haven't seen the light of day. Mainstream novels, a couple medical thrillers. I'm trying now not to write too many books that never get published. But it was all helpful for me when I was writing those; writing novels takes lots of practice.

Jon: Does being a parent influence the way you write?

Lise: Being a parent is a big part of who I am so yes, it affects the way I write. I'm not sure how, but I'm sure there is an effect. Also as you go through life and people you know and love get sick, die, or are lost to you in a variety of awful and often final ways, you become a little more sensitive to the reality of what you write about. I think this really came out last fall after the terrorist attacks, with most mystery writers.

Jon: With the publishing industry being what it is, how important is self promotion?

Lise: Big question. If you figure this out, you could make a million bucks.

Jon: Do you like doing the signing tours and conventions?

Lise: I enjoy getting out and talking to people who read and write books, so from that standpoint doing signings and going to conventions is fun.

Most of my friends from my regular life don't understand writers and writing and it's a joy to find people who do. On the other hand, as Susan Isaacs told me, "it's our dirty little secret, we're happiest all alone in our room."

Jon: How do you approach your research? Is it hands-on or is more of a digging through books thing?

Lise: I try to do both general background research and hands-on, person-to-person research. The book and phone call stuff is easier and takes less time, but you have to do some on the scene research or your book will feel inauthentic.

Jon: You wrote the story for the indie film, 'The Hoodoo Artist'. Do you like being involved with films?

Lise: I helped produce and directed 'The Hoodoo Artist' too. It was a blast. I love movies and would love to do another short one of these days.

Jon: For the Dorie Lennox series, why did you pick the the WWII era? And, why Kansas City?

Lise: Sheesh you ask a lot of questions!!! Okay, Dorie Lennox. I lived in Kansas City for a couple years (forgot that on my list above) and always thought it would be an interesting place for a story. It has a rich history of wild living, a pure frontier story. But contemporary Kansas City is a bit boring to me. So I focused on the 20s and 30s when it was a wide open town like Chicago during Prohibition, with jazz joints, burlesque, gambling, and wild times. Lots of fodder for the crime writer. There's even a real murder in ONE O'CLOCK JUMP, from 1934, that I "solve."

Jon: What authors do you enjoy reading?

Lise: As mysteries go, I've been on a British kick for a couple years. I love Reginald Hill and Minette Walters, John Harvey, Frances Fyfield. I always read Sue Grafton, Katy Munger, Susan Isaacs, Michael Connelly, Elmore Leonard. Outside of mysteries I am a Jane Austen fan, and always Alice Hoffman.

Jon: Ok, it's many many years in the future, and you get to be at your own funeral. What is it that you hope people will be saying about you?

Lise: She loved her family with all her heart, and wrote some damn fine books. (Are you collecting epitaphs? Oooh, creepy!!!)

Jon: What kind of things do you like to do with your free time?

Lise: I'm afraid I have too many hobbies. I garden, ski, travel, walk, swim, have pets (bird, cat, dog, fish), collect stuff, and do laundry.

Jon: If there was a medical breakthrough that allowed you to eat anything you wanted, as often and as much as you would like, what would it be?

Lise: Ohmygod. Are you saying you have such a thing in the works??! Okay. It would be chocolate. Or lemon sorbet. No, it would be chocolate.

Jon: What's your favorite part of being an author? And what's the worst part?

Lise: The best thing about being an author is holding a book you've written in your hands, and having people tell you they enjoyed reading it. The worst thing is actually writing the damn thing! It's hard work.

Jon: Do you think it is important to 'play fair' with your readers and give them clues to solve the mystery along with the protagonist; or do you think the 'ride' is more important?

Lise: Absolutely, you must play fair with clues, even if it's not a complete clue, just a tiny itsy bitsy corner of a clue, it has to be there.

Jon: Is there anything that your fans don't know about you that would surprise them?

Lise: Probably everything would surprise them. Or bore them to tears. Do I have to say? Gulp. Nah, let 'em be surprised when they read it in National Enquirer.

Jon: What kind of movies do you enjoy?

Lise: I love all kinds of movies except scary ones. I don't like bloody or horror movies. Okay, I was bored stiff on a plane recently with 'Serendipity' because it was so corny. So no corny movies. I like movies that challenge you, like 'Memento' or 'Mullholland Drive', that you have to talk about afterward. I like non-corny romantic comedies, like 'French Kiss', and sagas like 'The English Patient'. I like beautiful lush movies that move me.

Jon: Who is your favorite comedian?

Lise: Tough one. Martin Short is the only comedian who has made me fall off my chair laughing, but I love Steve Martin and Woody Allen too. And George Carlin.

Jon: What are you working on now?

Lise: I'm working on a new book with new characters titled "BLACKBIRD, FLY." It's been sold to St. Martin's who will bring it out sometime in 2004 or early 2005. I pitched it as the first book in a series of linked stand-alones about five sisters who are all trained as lawyers. They make appearances in each other's books but each sister has her own "adventure." In this first book one sister is struggling with the sudden death of her husband. He leaves her very little money, although he is wealthy, except for a decrepit house in France. She and her son go to France to fix up the house to sell it. It's a book about secrets, about identity and middle age. Intrigue, of course, as well!

Jon: What advice would you give someone hoping to write a novel and get rich and famous?

Lise: My advice would be... good luck! Because you'll need it. Becoming rich and famous as a novelist is a crap shoot. Do you have the skills and charm and craft to write a best-selling novel? Nobody knows, not you, not your English teacher, not even the publisher who may (but probably won't) buy your novel! But if you must write a novel, this won't stop you. It's too much work, all that writing, to worry about what happens to it after you write it. Writing a novel will make you rich -- but not necessarily in monetary terms. You will -- hopefully -- develop a rich inner life, and that makes living much more pleasant. Famous? Not all it's cracked up to be. I think.

Jon: What is your approach to writing? Do you plot everything out ahead of time, or do you let the story take you where it wants to go? Do you write in spurts or everyday?

Lise: I have tried every approach to writing a novel -- spurts, every day, high page count per day, low page count per day, weeks off in the middle. My approach right now -- which only works for me, everyone should do what works for them -- is to write a complete plot outline, get it approved by my editor, and sell the book before I start. (I really like this part. I have written many novels, not a waste of time but still unsold novels, that sit in a drawer gathering dust.) This outline business makes it easier for me to have time away and come back and still remember where the hell I was headed. Because it's summer now and I have all this travel calling me -- fishing and camping in Montana, off to France for research, etc. A writer needs to get out and experience life as well as write about it.

Jon: If someone meeting you for the first time at a convention wants to make a good impression, what's the best way?

Lise: The best way to make a good impression on any writer is to say, eyes wide (on one knee optional but nice), "Oh my God, I love your books!!!" This tends to put a glow on anything else you might say, but try to avoid things like, "but why did you have Johnny die in Chapter Five, I loved him!" or "but where did you learn to do commas?!"

Jon: What's the one thing always in your refrigerator?

Lise: Don't laugh. Nonfat yogurt. I know, it's really really dull, but I love it!!

Lise McClendon's Website: www.lisemcclendon.com

Lise McClendon's Books:

The Bluejay Shaman (1994)
Painted Truth(1996)
Nordic Nights(1999)
Blue Wolf (2001)
One Oclock Jump (2001)
Sweet and Lowdown (2002)

Val McDermid

Val McDermid is, simply, the best. In a genre full of sub-genres McDermid has tackled them all. Her Lindsay Gordon series is a compelling series about the amateur detective. The Kate Brannigan series is certainly amongst the top ten of all female P.I. series written today.

With the Tony Hill-Carol Jordan series McDermid was one of the first fiction authors to explore the relationship between police and profilers. She does it as well or better than any of her contemporaries. The stand-alones are spoken of reverently by readers and critics alike. A PLACE OF EXECUTION won almost every mystery award the year of its release. KILLING THE SHADOWS is a novel so well written and thought provoking that THE NEW YORK TIMES declared her the best mystery author of our time. This year's THE DISTANT ECHO allowed McDermid to explore yet another aspect of what crime does to the individual in an amazing way.

The common thread in McDermid's many different styles is her genius. She writes with power. Character development, plot, setting, and contemporary themes are always deftly handled. Humor, sadness, fear, and relief are all done so well you will laugh and cry while reading her prose. And you'll think. McDermid's books are so deeply layered there's always more to think about.

The lady once said that she hoped she could contribute as much to the genre as Ruth Rendell. Only time can tell how much she'll accomplish. One has to believe at this point we'll all look back in awe.   -Ruth Jordan

Jon: For people who have heard your name, but who haven't read any of your books yet, how would you describe them?

Val: Eclectic? Because I write different kinds of book, different in style and tone as well as in content, it's not easy to slot them into a neat corner of the genre. The Tony Hill/Carol Jordan novels are dark psychological thrillers, the Kate Brannigan series features a smart-mouthed Manchester PI, the Lindsay Gordon novels are actually classic British mysteries with a somewhat radical contemporary twist, and the two stand-alone thrillers, A PLACE OF EXECUTION and KILLING THE SHADOWS are also quite different in flavour and tone from each other. I guess if you want to be harrowed, stick to Tony and Carol and KILLING THE SHADOWS, if you want atmosphere, go for A PLACE OF EXECUTION, if you like the PI genre try Brannigan, and if you're interested in an alternative take on the amateur sleuth, give Lindsay a go.

Jon: Will Kate Brannigan or Lindsey Gordon be showing up again in the future?

Val: I'm sneakily writing a Lindsay Gordon as we speak, provisionally titled HOSTAGE TO MURDER. It's set in Glasgow and St. Petersburg, and it'll be published in the US by Spinsters Ink, who have done the previous five in the series. I want Kate to come back, but it's a question of slotting her into the schedule. I certainly have a strong plot idea for the character, but the thrillers take so much time and energy...

Jon: How much has your experience as a journalist helped your fiction writing?

Val: Less than you'd think... I suppose it gave me an entree into other people's worlds that I wouldn't have seen otherwise. But the main thing I took away from journalism was a very prosaic attitude towards writing. When you're a news journalist, you can't wait for the muse to strike. You have to write the news when it happens, no matter what's going on in your personal life.

I learned pretty quickly that your heart can be breaking, the cat can be sick and the bathroom ceiling can be sitting in the bath tub, but you still have to write those 1500 words. So I treat what I do as a job. I sit down at the computer and I write, no matter what else is happening in my life.

Jon: Do you put any of yourself in to your books? Are there people who know you and see bits of Val while reading?

Val: You'd have to ask them that... Inevitably, who I am, what I believe and what I've experienced shapes what ends up on the page. But I don't think there's very much that's identifiably me in the books. Apart from the sense of humour. That's the one thing you can never make up.

Jon: You started writing with a protagonist who was a journalist, then moved to Private Eyes, and now you are writing about the forensic side of investigation. Is there a reason for the change?

Val: What can I say? I'm a Gemini, I get bored easily. Actually, the transition isn't nearly as clear as that, because I've written different kinds of books consecutively rather than writing one series then another. One of the reasons I love this genre is the opportunity it provides as a writer and as a reader to explore different styles and different approaches. Writing across the range means I never get bored, and I constantly have to push myself to get better.

Jon: What prompted you to write your non-fiction work, A SUITABLE JOB FOR A WOMAN?

Val: Too many drinks at a publishing party... No, really, that's the truth. I was talking to a non-fiction editor who asked me if there were really any women PIs, and I said, 'Dozens, darling.' Next day, she called me and said she'd like to commission the book. Now, how often does someone give you a wad of money to wander round the US and the UK talking to interesting women for four months? The only drawback was that at the end of all the fun, I actually had to write the damn thing. But I learned a lot in the process, and I have to confess that a few of the stories that never made it into the non-fiction book have ended up as subplots in the Brannigan novels.

Jon: Do you have any decision in the marketing of your books? Or book covers, touring, advertising?

Val: These days, I have a lot of input about the process of marketing. I see draft covers and my comments are taken seriously and acted on. We have meetings once a year with the sales and marketing and publicity people at Harper Collins in the UK to discuss the strategy for the next book. We talk about what went well and what didn't work on the last campaign and make changes accordingly. My US publishers also consult pretty extensively with me about promotion and publicity.

Jon: What is your favorite of the books you've written?

Val: Well, none of them matches up to my dream of how I wanted them to be. I have a very soft spot for CRACK DOWN, because I wrote it at a very happy time in my life and structurally, it had to conform to a very tight timeline, and I think it works very well. THE MERMAIDS SINGING was the book that changed everything for me, opened me up to a wider readership, and it gave me the confidence to keep pushing my range. But A PLACE OF EXECUTION is probably my personal favourite, because I'd wanted to write a book about the Derbyshire landscape for about twenty years before I finally came up with the right story. It gave me the perfect excuse to spend a lot of time wandering around one of my favourite pieces of countryside!

Jon: If you weren't writing for a living, what do you think you would be doing?

Val: I have no idea. I suspect I am unemployable.

Jon: I read that you were once attacked by a wrestler when you were a journalist. What brought that on?

Val: I was unaware when I knocked on his door that other papers had been chasing the same story I was after -- namely that this very butch 300lb wrestler's wife had left him for another woman. So I guess he was feeling pretty raw by the time I arrived on his doorstep. Which is no excuse for what happened. Anyway, he opened the door, I managed to say who I was and he just came at me, fists and feet flying. Not the most pleasant experience of my life. I always maintained I got somebody else's kicking, but that didn't make it hurt any the less.

Jon: Is there any chance of seeing something on the silver screen or television that says 'based on a book by Val McDermid' ? (..and if there already is, how did I miss it!!??)

Val: Next month, filming begins for a TV adaptation of THE MERMAIDS SINGING, THE WIRE IN THE BLOOD and a third film based on the characters of Tony Hill and Carol Jordan. Starring Robson Green, the three films, under the series title of 'Wire In The Blood', will be shown on the ITV network next spring. Everything else is in option at present apart from the Lindsay Gordon series. And I have a TV drama in development that is not based on any of the novels. It's not even a crime drama; it's a science-based film.

Jon: Are there any downsides to writing for a living?

Val: I'll tell you if I find them... Seriously, I love it. I love to write, I love going on the road because it takes me to places I'd never have seen otherwise. I love meeting people and I also love the solitude of working for myself. I guess the hardest part is delivering a new book and waiting for the reaction, but even that has its positive side, because I know that working on it with my editor is going to mean I end up with something better than I started with. Oh dear, that does sound very Pollyanna-ish, doesn't it?

Jon: Around people who know the mystery/crime genre, your name is spoken with a kind of reverence. Does this surprise you? Does it have an effect on the way you get treated by people?

Val: It astonishes me, frankly. I mean, there are a lot of people out there doing very good work in this genre, a lot of them profoundly underrated. I don't see myself as someone who should be on some kind of pedestal. Like many of my colleagues, I'm simply trying to write the best books I'm capable of and mostly I feel like I fall far short of my goals. I also feel profoundly grateful that I've had the success I have had, because, as I said, not everyone who deserves it makes that breakthrough. And to be honest, I haven't noticed too many people kissing my feet or spreading their jackets over puddles for me! I've always thought people found me reasonably approachable, and I wouldn't like to think that had changed because I've sold a few more books or won some awards.

But I guess publishers are a little nicer to me these days...

Jon: If you were able to talk to the 17 year old Val, what advice would you pass along? And would she listen?

Val: Of course she wouldn't listen... I guess I'd say something like,

"Don't listen to the people who say you can't. Oh, and when you meet that drop-dead gorgeous blonde on your 33rd birthday, WALK AWAY."

Jon: What do you like to do when you're not writing?

Val: Read, sleep, cook, go walking in the hills, spend time with friends.

Jon: What are some of your favorite books? Or favorite authors?

Val: Robert Louis Stevenson, Iain Banks, Margaret Atwood, Reginald Hill, Denise Mina, Ian Rankin, James Lee Burke, Sara Paretsky, Laurie King, Andrew Greig, Ruth Rendell, Jeanette Winterson... how long have we got?

Jon: How about Movies?

Val: 'The Big Sleep', 'The Sound of Music', 'Seven, Ran', 'The Big Clock', 'Dr Zhivago', 'Billy Elliott'. And for chasing the blues: 'Passport to Pimlico' and 'What's Up Doc'?

Jon: If you had a month with no deadlines, no commitments, what would you do with it?

Val: Three weeks in Tuscany with my partner and our son and a pile of books, a week in Moscow and St Petersburg with my Russian buddies and a couple of other close friends and a judicious amount of vodka...

Jon: Is it harder to break into the American market with your books? It seems that we Americans are really missing out on a lot good books and television.

Val: The American market is tough for Brits. Partly it's because you produce such a vast wealth of material yourselves. But partly it's because America does tend to be quite self-absorbed. Some American readers cherish a mythical picture of the UK and Europe, and they aren't comfortable with the more realistic picture painted by the best of contemporary British crime fiction. And of course, culturally, we are very different. Although superficially we have a lot in common with the US, because of the common language, we are far closer to Europe politically, socially, historically.

All of these factors combine to make it pretty hard for Brits to break out in your market. But thankfully, there are enough discerning readers out there to make it happen for some of us!

Jon: Is there anything about you that people would be surprised to learn?

Val: Yes, but I'm not going to tell you what it is!
Seriously, though... probably they'd be a little surprised to know what a quiet, domesticated soul I am when I'm not out there in public.

Jon: Any thoughts on electronic publishing? Or books on demand?

Val: I think it won't really take off till the electronic readers are lightweight, portable, cheap, resistant to sand and bathwater and as easy on the eyes as the printed page. But when that happens, and happen it will, I think they'll become very popular among people like me who want to take 14 books on holiday...

Books on demand seem to be working well as a way of making backlist accessible again to readers, and that's got to be a good thing, given how many series there are where the early books are unobtainable. But I'm very suspicious of sites that make available anything offered to them, without editorial moderation. Usually, there are good reasons why a publishing house hasn't accepted a novel. It may sound harsh, but there is no democracy of talent.

Jon: The television series, Wire In The Blood, is really terrific. Has been well received? And has it spurred new book sales?

Val: It's been a great critical and popular success wherever it's been shown. By one of those strange quirks of scheduling, it was shown first in Australia, and when we got the media reports, they were so amazing we thought our Australian distributors were making them up. I've certainly seen a direct connection to my sales figures, both on frontlist and backlist. For example, with THE DISTANT ECHO, my Australian sales literally doubled. And results have been similar elsewhere. It's been very gratifying, because really, the only reason writers ever agree to adaptation is in the hope it will bring us new readers.

Jon: Did you enjoy doing the cameo appearance?

Val: It was a lot of fun, mostly because Coastal run their shoots like a huge extended family. I certainly realised actors have a much more pampered life than writers. Lots of assistants running around with puffa jackets to keep us warm, folding chairs to stick under our bottoms between takes, endless hot drinks... And being referred to as 'the talent'. Very good for the ego.

Jon: You are involved in a project called The Brain Forest Appeal www.tithebarnschool.co.uk/. What exactly is it, and who does it help?

Val: Tithe Barn is a local primary school whose head teacher, Tim Buckley, is a man of great vision and he's assembled round him a team who are as committed as he is not only to making the school a centre of excellence but also to forging links with other schools around the world who are far less privileged than Tithe Barn. It's an amazing school -- you feel the buzz as soon as you walk in the door. The Brain Forest Appeal has been dedicated to funding a new building within the school to house new computer equipment and to facilitate Tim's programme of accelerated learning and philosophy for children. This in turn will improve their connections to other schools and allow them to offer more practical support in curriculum and other activities. The links they've built with other schools go far beyond the idea of pen pals round the world. For example, they are linked to a school in an impoverished South African township. Tithe Barn kids have raised money for various projects there, but the connection goes beyond that. Tim is currently in South Africa, spending part of his summer vacation running a series of workshops and seminars for head teachers in the townships.

Jon: Do you enjoy driving? You seem like a person who would really enjoy being in control of a well built car.

Val: A well built... oh, you said car! Yes, I enjoy driving, though it's less of a pleasure than it used to be on our crowded roads. Cars are my main self-indulgence -- I drive a black-on-black BMW 325ci convertible and 'it rocks', as you say on your side of the Atlantic. I learned to stunt drive last year in a Mini Cooper S, and that was an amazing experience, as was driving it at 145mph on a German autobahn...

Jon: What was the last book you read, and what did you think of it?

Val: Margaret Atwood's 'Oryx and Crake'. I've loved Atwood's writing for the last 30 years, and this sucked me in from the first page and kept me reading well past the point where my eyes were gritty and tired. She's a true storyteller, and the dystopic vision of this novel scared me witless. And her style is so apparently effortless -- art that conceals art.

Jon: Is there anything that you haven't done and hope to try someday? Maybe skydiving or something else no one would suspect?

Val: You think I'm going to tell you???
Actually, I do have a mad desire to go to Churchill and see the polar bears up close. But I'm going to wait till my boy's a bit older and do it with him.

Jon: If you needed to, would you be able to blackmail Ian Rankin with something? I don't need to know what it is.

Val: Yes. At least two things. But then, he has at least as much dirt on me, so I don't think it would work too well.

Jon: What's the one thing that is always in your refrigerator?

Val: Diet Coke.

Val McDermid's Website:
Www.valmcdermid.com

Val McDermid's books:

Hostage To Murder(2003)
The Distant Echo (2003)
The Last Temptation (2002)
Killing The Shadows (2000)
A Place of Execution (1999)
Star Struck (1998)
The Writing on the Wall (1994)
The Wire In The Blood (1997)
Booked For Murder (1996)
Blue Genes (1996)
The Mermaids Singing (1995)
Clean Break (1995)
A Suitable Job For A Woman (1995)
Crackdown (1994)
Kick Back (1994)

Union Jack (1993)
Dead Beat (1993)
Final Edition (1991)
Common Murder (1989)
Report for Murder (1987)

<u>Val McDermid's Short Stories:</u>

A Wife in a Million
A Traditional Christmas - Reader, I Murdered Him, Too, ed. Helen Windrath, 1995
A Breathtaking Experience
Driving a Hard Bargain - Perfectly Criminal, ed. Martin Edwards, 1996
Guilt (Trip)- No Alibi, ed. Maxim Jakubowski, 1995
The Writing on the Wall - 3rd Culprit, ed. Liza Cody, Michael Z. Lewin & Peter Lovesey, 1994
(*These first six were gathered in a limited edition chapbook called 'The Writing on the Wall'*)
Heartburn - Northern Blood II, ed. Martin Edwards 1995
Keeping on the Right Side of the Law - "http://www.valmcdermid. com" - 2003
When Larry met Allie - New English Library Book of Internet Stories, ed. Maxim Jakubowski, 2000
The Girl Who Killed Santa Claus - EQMM - January 2002
White Nights, Black Magic – 2002 - Crime in the City, is edited by Martin Edwards
The Wagon Mound - EQMM - Aug 2002
Metamorphosis - Tart Noir, ed. Stella Duffy & Lauren Henderson 2002
The Consolation Blonde
Homecoming (I wrote this for Endangered Species, the online short story anthology I'm editing for the Arts Council's Save Our Short Story campaign, so it hasn't been published yet. And it isn't a crime story (see www.saveourshortstory.org.uk)

Katy Munger

When I arrived at my first mystery convention, I barely knew anyone and was worried about having a lonely time. Fortune smiled: one of the first people I met was Katy Munger. She seemed to know most of the key figures in the world of crime writing, and all of them spoke of her with great fondness. Soon I was laughing at her hilarious wisecracks, and then trying to talk her out of confronting someone in the hotel bar who had impugned Tart Noir (the group of irreverent women writers she helped to found), and then we were in her rented convertible barreling down an Austin highway toward the honky-tonks downtown."

Some mystery writers can only fantasize about being like their protagonists, but reading Katy's work offers a direct pipeline into who she really is. Her P.I. Casey Jones, the first-person narrator of five excellent novels, is brash and brave, smart and wickedly funny (Don't read these books in public-people will stare as you laugh out loud). Underneath a rowdy exterior both writer and heroine share zero tolerance for hypocrisy or meanness of any kind, and both are generous champions of the underdogs of this world. Katy Munger has a heart as big as Texas-and the uncompromising talent to match it.-- Gabriel Cohen (author of Red Hook)

Jon: For people who haven't read your books yet (for whatever excuse they can come up with!), how would you describe your books?

Katy: They are entertainment, but entertainment based on a unique way of looking at the world (with humor and guts) and on a love of people who aren't afraid to be who they are, even when they're different. My books are funny on the surface, warm-hearted in the middle, and left-wing underneath. They feature a hardboiled, kick-ass female PI who really does not care what anyone thinks about her. The setting is Southern, but probably not the South foisted on you by bad tv. I balance them pretty equally between plotting, characterization and humor and I work hard to keep the pacing really moving at a rapid clip.

While my books contain guns, violence and sex, all that junk takes place off-stage, except for the chases. I love a good chase scene. The Casey books are sometimes accused of being feminist, but I have a lot of male fans who read my books and I appreciate them all. My male readers are real men, I'm sure, who are not threatened by a strong female. The big joke on the snobs in this world who won't read mysteries is that if you paid attention in high school and college you may even recognize hidden classic literature references throughout the Casey books, a sort of "Where's Waldo?" for literary intellectuals. It's probably also useful to add that I hate "funny" mysteries without a plot; I hate characters with no real heart to them; and I hate stupidity and ignorance, most of all. There, that should confuse everyone thoroughly. It's all a plot to make them buy one of my books.

Jon: It has been noticed that there are many similarities between you and Casey. In what big ways are you different? (...besides you not having a butt like a fridge)?

Katy: Thank you for appreciating my ass (if, indeed, not having it compared to a refrigerator can be called a compliment...). How do I differ from Casey?

Well, for one thing, I now outweigh the bitch and, for another, you won't see Casey wiping a 2-year old's butt, ever. That aside, I have a fouler mouth and fouler sense of humor than Casey, but felt the American reading public really was not ready for my potty mouth. Casey is also in much better shape than me at the moment, and so more confident of and prone to using her muscles and physical strength. Also, Casey gets to sleep around constantly; I don't. She has no regrets about short-term relationships (say, the 5-hour kind) and I was never quite able to pull that off, even in my heydey of being a slut. I am more politically active than Casey, but since I hate politics in mysteries, I keep it out of the books. And I don't dress quite so colorfully. Finally, Casey will never age. I will. At least I hope I will. Other than that, I'm afraid you're right. She's pretty much an alter ego. We both adore the underdog, adopt the disenfranchised, hate phonies and shoot off our mouths anywhere any time without much hesitation.

Jon: What is something about you that people would be surprised to know?

Katy: People would probably be surprised to know that in person I am a very happy person, not sarcastic at all and, in fact, full of love for other people to a corny degree. I even like sleazoids, whom I find charming in a misguided sort of way. In fact, I have been called "maniacally cheerful" and it's not an act. I was born that way and will die that way. It's all in the genes. (My daughter is the same way.)

Jon: How important is location in your books? If the location shifted would it change the feel of the books?

Katy: It is important that my books are set in the South, because Casey could only get away with a lot that she gets away with in the South (or, at least, get away with it safely). And a lot of the humor relies on the interplay between newcomers to the South and old-hands at it, as well as between men and women of a certain social pressure-cooker. I think changing the location would shift the feel. But interestingly enough (to me, anyway), Casey started out in New York City. She was a minor character in a book I wrote as Gallagher Gray,. And I had her working as a southern PI in NYC when I wrote the first Casey book for submission. The publisher asked me to move her out of NYC on the basis that books set in NYC sold poorly. I had just decided to move out of the Big Apple back home to North Carolina and was worried about keeping up the authenticity of the setting myself, so I took her with me. And she became a lot warmer, less mean, more defensive and more of an icon for being herself.

Jon: What do you read when you get the time to do so?

Katy: First of all, I read A LOT, whether I have the time or not. And I read mainly in my genre. I have no patience for all that psycho-babble crap masquerading as good literature right now so I stick to crime fiction and mysteries, plus funny little books like 'Mapp & Lucia', or anything by Joe Queenan. I love Joseph Wambaugh, Rex Stout, Ann Rule, just discovered Elizabeth George and am on an awards committee that requires me to read about 140 books this year by just about everyone in the business. Which means I am rapidly discovering some really good newer names, like Greg Rucka and Russel Atwood. So I am not one of those authors who never reads anyone else. That's a mistake. You can learn a tremendous amount reading someone else's books, whether they are good or bad. I also read Vanity Fair and the three major tabloids each week. Humans are so amazingly fallible, as these publications prove on every page.

Jon: Do you have strict working habits, or do you write when you are inspired?

Katy: I run a business full-time, write a column and review mysteries for The Washington Post, waste time on the Internet and am raising a 2-year old in addition to writing the Casey books -- meaning, I can not afford to wait for inspiration. I write when I can for as long as I can, usually first thing in the morning before my business clients start bothering me, or at night instead of watching television. Somehow it all works out. But even if my days were free and clear, I could not do more than three or four hours of writing fiction. It's just too exhausting. And you need to set aside time to get out among real people as well, or you lose your ability to get inside other people's heads and create strong characters. One thing that helps me work without "inspiration" is that I outline extensively before I begin a book. I always know where I am going, so it's easy to get started.

Jon: If Casey Jones took the leap to the big screen, who could you see in the role?

Katy: Kristen Johnson, the woman on 'Third Rock From The Sun' is definitely my #1 Casey choice. But I think Ellen Barkin could do a really good Casey if she wasn't afraid to beef up a bit, as could Holly Hunter, though she would REALLY have to add some size. If Clare Danes ages rapidly, she'd grow into the role. Sorry, Drew, but your voice will never make it as Casey. By the way, I'd rather see Casey come to the small screen, believe it or not, because the format is more compatible with my emphasis on continuing characters.

Jon: You have three books out now, and a fourth coming out soon. How long would you like to keep writing about Casey?

Katy: I am not anywhere near tired writing about her, so I would like to keep them coming for at least a total of ten books -- I've got story lines for them all -- and preferably indefinitely. Rex Stout did thirty or so in his Nero Wolfe series without a loss in quality, with a rare exception here and there, and there are enough characters in Casey's life to keep the plots interesting. It's not like Casey is perfect. She's got a lot of faults and watching these ebb and flow could make for a long and interesting series. Right now, I have a contract with Avon for a total of five. Whether or not it goes beyond that will probably depend on my sales for MONEY TO BURN and BAD TO THE BONE (due out June 2000).

Jon: When you go through a change in your life, does it affect Casey? For instance, having a baby, or moving to a new home.

Katy: Oh, yes. But never in the way I expect. When I had a baby, I got MORE hardboiled in my writing, as if my inner nature was struggling to maintain its balance between sentimental and cynical. But these changes tend to affect me at the beginning of a book only, which means they may shape the tone and plot but probably not the action and dialogue. Casey always finds her feet quickly as a character and moves forward on her own.

Jon: What are some of the things about the human race that bug you?

Katy: I loathe self-important people who are incapable of giving other people respect, or who have no concept that we are all about as significant as a June bug in the greater scheme of things. I feel sorry for people who hate people who are different from them; it's all based on fear and that's no way to live your life. I hate that we all seem to have such short attention spans these days, because the really good things in life tend to sneak up on you quietly and if you're living life at top-volume and full speed all the time it's very easy to miss them. I really hate that the minute someone has a good idea or new approach (whether in religion, for example, or psychology, or literature, or nutrition or what have you) half of America does its best to turn it into a money-making machine and soon drowns whatever new spark was created in a sea of mediocrity and greed.

I loathe our obsession with looks and the self-hate it creates. I can't stand that we fail to respect either our old people or our very young. I'm sorry that love has been turned into some sort of embarrassing, overly-analyzed experience now defined by Hallmark cards and bad made-for-television movies. No wonder people are becoming more and more afraid to take the wild ride and open up their hearts. I could go on, but you get the point. I want to live in a world where everyone can just be themselves, where it doesn't matter if they conform or are unique. I just want a world where people can find, and be, themselves.

Jon: I'm guessing you were a lot like they way you are now when you were in school. Did this cause problems?

Katy: Actually, in high school I was such a Goodie Two Shoes, I made myself sick and in college I was something of an, er, experimenter in higher substances, at least after that oh-so-difficult transitional freshman year when you can't decide whether to study or party. Partying always wins out. My excuse was that I could never write about life until I experienced it fully, an excuse used by 80% of the creative writing program majors. It caused no problems being this way. In fact, everyone else on the UNC-Chapel Hill campus was exactly the same way in the late 70's.

Jon: Will Casey ever get married again?

Katy: Over my dead body, but maybe to a dead body. But her ex-husband does rear his ugly head in the next book, BAD TO THE BONE.

Jon: Everybody has vices. Can you name one you should quit, and one you'll never give up?

Katy: I should probably quit ogling young rock-and-roll flesh. I'm old, I'm married, I'm overweight. Those days are gone. It's kinda pathetic at this point. But there's just something about those cute skinny little guys with their bad haircuts, delicate faces and knit shirts. Mmmm-mmmm-mmmmm. The one vice I'll never give up, by the way, is ogling young rock-and-roll flesh.

Jon: Can you give me any dirt on other authors? Please? (Optional of course!)

Katy: Of course I can. I mostly hang out in the bars at the writing conventions, so I get all the good dirt. I'll give you a Literary Babe Watch. Lise McClendon is a real charmer and a looker. She is also experienced at being hit on and capable of fending off two determined mashers at one time, even when drunk to the gills. Lauren Henderson is beyond hot, men faint when she wiggles her pierced eyebrows at them. Kate Flora looks like a delicate blonde yet is delightfully cutting, wonderfully crude when need be and nobody's fool. Nevada Barr only seems shy; she is capable of devastatingly funny comments but you have to be paying attention to catch them. Val McDermid is a wonderful person to orbit in the bar, she is loud and funny and raucous and to the point, always surrounded by a gaggle of friends. God bless her. Jerrilyn Farmer is as funny in person as in her books and nothing gets by her; her eyes are constantly moving as she notices absolutely everything happening in the room. C. J. Songer has incredibly beautiful hair, just a cascade of golden curls, and a wonderful California tan (and body) to go with it. Laura Lippman is tall, slender and quite elegant, with a somewhat shy demeanor that masks a deadly sense of humor. And Sparkle Hayter is as beautiful inside as she is outside, she is smart and determined and loyal to her friends.

Finally, on the babe front, watch out for Karin Slaughter, Morrow's big author for the spring. She's scary: smart, well-read and, as the book jacket will prove, a cross between Princess Di, Jodie Foster and well, herself. The bitch is also young.

I mustn't leave the male babes out, if I can get my tongue back in my mouth long enough to report. Greg Rucka looks very hot in his leather jacket and gold-rimmed glasses. Gary Phllips is smart and articulate and my #1 choice for hanging out with, whether at a poker game, restaurant or bar. His laugh is infectious, it's like rumbling thunder, there's no greater sound in the world. Keith Snyder has long dark hair and looks great in a pair of jeans. Best of all, he likes smart women, which mean he is not threatened and pretty damn smart himself. Kent Krueger could charm the birds from the trees, and, probably, the pants off them, too (if birds wore pants). He's wickedly funny. Cute, too. Parnell Hall has a mean jump shot and he's in great shape, so the poor fools on the opposing basketball team never have a chance. Steve Hamilton is wonderful, down-to-earth and devoted to his family, extremely modest and with a preference for staying out of the limelight, if possible. Which it won't be, if his first book is any indication. Jerry Healy is quite the twinkle-toes; the ladies love him, including me. The following gentlemen are not only extremely talented writers, but very nice, regular guys unencumbered by big egos: Michael Connelly, Dennis Lehane and Jeffrey Deaver.

There. That should satisfy your curiosity for a season, I hope. By next year, no one will be talking to me.

Jon: Do you ever take people you know and put them in a book? I always thought it would be great to write a book and come up with a reason to use an ex-girlfriend as a character who is a porn star. Just to piss her off.

Katy: Hmm.... I have tried that approach; I even started off putting an ex-boyfriend in one book with plans for revenge. But I have this uncontrollable tendency to only remember the best in people and the character turned deep on me. Most of my characters are amalgamations (admit it: this is the only time you have ever seen this word used, with the exception of the beginning of 'Parenthood'.) They come from my putting together two or three people I've met and rolling them up into one. I also make up characters out of my head and heart. Some probably sneak in through headlines, stories I've heard, my memory and imagination, strangers on the street, etc.

Jon: If you could go back and meet the 20year old Katy, what would you tell her?

Katy: "Girl, you don't have to keep drinking until the bottle is gone; you're not really fat at all, one day you'll find that you would kill to have this body back; what other people think really doesn't matter at all because you are the one who has to live with yourself; just relax and let it come, fate has a plan; and don't hide your light under the bushel, some people are just born plain loud."

Jon: You seem to get along well with everyone. I'm guessing you love meeting fans. Do you ever get gifts, and if so what is the strangest thing you've received?

Katy: I do get along with a lot of people because I just love meeting someone and figuring out what makes them unique and what makes them tick. I do receive gifts, and I guess the strangest thing I've ever received was the time a guy insisted I take the shirt off his back because I admired the color. He had nice pecs, by the way, but he didn't offer me those.

Jon: When you review books, do you pull any punches? Like not trashing a book you hate?

Katy: I tell my version of the truth when I review books, even if it is unfavorable. This sounds more honorable than it is. For one thing, I can't review books by friends because that is a conflict of interest. So it's not like I have to worry about hurting the feelings of someone I care about (or, more importantly, have to face again). Secondly, I usually receive a box of ten to twelve books and am allowed to select five or six to review in The Washington Post. If a book is really bad and by a mid-list author, I don't see the point of reviewing it. Continued obscurity seems punishment enough. But if the book is bad, and it's by a best-selling author, I think readers have a right to know not to waste their money.

I do feel bad about panning other people's books, however. After all, mine aren't perfect and much of reviewing boils down to a matter of taste. So I try not to be a smart ass about it. Sometimes I succeed. Some authors have been very gracious about my less than favorable reviews of their books, by the way, and I really appreciate their maturity. I think if you try to be fair, people recognize it. The worst sin a reviewer can make is panning someone else's book simply for a chance at showing off their own cleverness.

Jon: What are your five favorite movies?

Katy: That would be, in order of my very favorite on down: the re-cently-released 'American Beauty' -- a brilliant film -- followed by 'The Deerhunter', 'Gettysburg', 'The Right Stuff', 'The Big Lebowksi', 'American Graffiti', and a somewhat obscure film called 'Persuasion'. That's six, I know, and they'll probably change by next month, but I do love my movies. I worship Chow Wun Fat, by the way, and would meet him anywhere and anytime for a rumble.

Jon: A question that I'm sure comes up a lot -- any more Casey Jones books coming?

Katy: I sure hope so! I have one about one-third written, but my pub-lisher didn't offer me enough money to make it worthwhile to continue the series with them, especially given their dismal marketing track re-cord with the first five (as anyone who has ever seen the schizophrenic covers could guess). But it is very difficult to switch a series to a new house unless it is a blockbuster. My current plan with Casey is to finish the non-Casey book I am working on now, then finish Casey #6 so that it's exactly the way I want it to be without any pressure to tone her down. Then we'll try to find a new publisher or I'll bring it out myself if I decide it's better for me financially to do it that way.

Right now, I get emails from two or three readers a day so I have a huge database of reader addresses. I have no problem selling it directly off the web if no publisher is interested -- mostly, I just want Casey to continue, as I am definitely not done with her yet and book ideas for her keep insinuating themselves into my brain. As you know, my Casey books usually take on one form or more of bullshit per story.. and there sure are a lot of bullshitters in the world right now who could use a good asskicking from Casey.

Jon: What are you working on right now?

Katy: I am working on a very character-based novel involving a southern setting, a couple of crimes and a great deal of commentary on the way our society and media feed off sensationalism these days. It will probably weigh in at around 600 manuscript pages. I'm on page 450 as of today and I am so enjoying writing this book. I am doing it with no deadline pressure, entirely at my own pace and no marketing interference from a publisher. I've stripped the priorities down to just me, my characters and a blank screen every morning. What a wonderful feeling that is. I took a lot of time with the plot and outlined extensively and it's been nothing but fun since I started to write it. I expect to have a first draft done by September 2003, and a polished draft ready in early 2004 to send out. In some ways, I feel as if I am playing a big joke on everyone. People think I've disappeared or given up writing, and yet every day I get up and find myself in the middle of the best writing I have ever done and the most satisfying writing experience I've ever had. It's bliss.

Jon: Are you able to just sit down and work, or do you need to build up to it?

Katy: I don't sit down until I am ready to work, and so I don't need to build up to it. If I feel like skipping a day I do. I am inherently driven and fairly disciplined about my writing, so I can afford to trust my inner clock. I rarely let more than a few days go by without sitting down and working on one scene or another. I don't get writer's block because I think writer's block is really just your imagination telling you that it needs a rest -- and I respect my imagination when it tells me that. I give it a rest. Panicking because you don't write every day is completely counterproductive to producing a good book. You can't force your imagination without it showing.

Jon: Is there anything that truly scares you?

Katy: The growing willful stupidity of the American people terrifies me. Ignorance has become a badge of honor. When we start branding intellectuals as dangerous, elitest or somehow unworthy of being a part of our society, then we are in deep shit. I can't fathom what this says for our future. You won't find many of the happy moron crowd among readers, of course, but they are out there and they are legion.

Jon: What is something that is guaranteed to make you laugh?

Katy: I am so immature when it comes to humor. I love headlines that go wildly wrong ("7 Foot Doctors Sue Hospital") and typos or bad word choices that paint bizarre scenarios ("In honor of Easter, Mrs. Jones will come forth and lay an egg on the altar.") In addition, anything silly just slays me -- which is why I get along so well with 9-year olds. And I adore genteel, situation-based humor such as that found in books by P. G. Wodehouse or the 'Mapp & Lucia' series by E.F. Bensen. Come to think of it, I have a gay man's sense of humor, albeit an immature gay man's sense of humor.

Jon: What is the one thing that is always in your refrigerator?

Katy: That would be cold beer and sweet pickle relish, both Southern staples, you know.

Katy Munger's Website:
www.katymunger.com

Katy Munger's books:

Written as Gallagher Gray-The Hubbert & Lil series:

Hubbert & Lil: Partners In Crime(1991)
A Cast of Killers(1992)
 Death of a Dream Maker (1995)
A Motive for Murder(1996)

The Casey Jones Series:
Legwork (1997)
Out of Time (1998)
Money to Burn (1999)
 Bad to the Bone (2000)
Better Off Dead (2001)

Warren Murphy

I find Warren Murphy absolutely fascinating. He is funny, well read and outspoken. He reminds of a favorite Uncle that made my parents crazy by teaching us practical jokes. In truth, it was hard knowing when to stop asking questions because I love the answers so much.

His writing is every bit as entertaining as he is. He has a large body of work, and has won many awards for it. The Destroyer series is somewhere past 140 books. And beyond that he has written any number of different series. From the Digger series to the Adams Round Table books he has proven how well he knows his craft. This is a man who for me personifies the mystery genre and I think everyone should have at least a few of his books on their shelves.

I think what Warren says in this interview can say it better than I.
Jon

Jon: In addition to being a mystery writer, you've done some other interesting things. What are some of the other jobs you've had?

Warren: My first job ever was working on the Werner Brothers garbage truck in Secaucus, New Jersey. This was before the days of rear-end loaded garbage trucks and the pails -- which seemed generally to be filled with wet ashes -- had to be tossed up to the top of the truck to be emptied manually. This made me very strong and nasty, traits which have stood me in good stead over the years. I was a movie usher too. I saw Samson and Delilah 21 times. I never got over the fact that Victor Mature had a bigger bosom than Hedy Lamarr. I missed my big career opportunity--a job in the radio tube factory--after high school because I got lost in Brooklyn and couldn't find the factory. So instead, I wound up working as a copy boy in a daily newspaper office and then, before, during and after Korea, was a reporter, editor and possibly the fastest on-deadline rewrite man in history.

I drifted into politics, working for the notoriously-corrupt Democratic machine in Jersey City and Hudson County, running political campaigns and occasionally being deputy mayor. By the time everybody I worked for went to jail and I realized God wanted me to find new work. Dick Sapir -- then a local newsman -- and I had just gotten our first Destroyer novel sold (after waiting 8 years.) I chained Dick in my attic and we did the second one and then a lot more. Later, I returned to politics for a while to become a New Jersey State Meadowlands Commissioner -- (yes, I know where Jimmy Hoffa's buried.) All these years, I've never been far from my typewriter, whether in New York or Hollywood or wherever.

Jon: Most of us recognize your name from the Destroyer series, and we'll talk about that in a bit. What other things have you written? I know that you also did a series with two New York cops.

Warren: I write everything. I wrote a funny cop series, Razoni and Jackson, about a middleclass sensible black cop and his suicidal white partner. I wrote a private eye series called Digger which metamorphosed into the Trace series of books, about Devlin Tracy and his beautiful Eurasian live-in detective wannabe, Chico. I wrote the first book of a failed series, called LEONARDO'S LAW." And I did a lot of standalone books: RED MOON, CEILING OF HELL, HONOR AMONG THIEVES, JERICHO DAY, ATLANTIC CITY, THE SURE THING, SCORPIONS DANCE. I even wrote a horror novel called DESTINY'S CARNIVAL.

My ex-wife and partner, Molly Cochran, and I did a whole bunch of books: GRANDMASTER, HAND OF LAZARUS, TEMPLE DOGS, THE FOREVER KING, WORLD WITHOUT END and several novels under the name of Dev Stryker.

And of course, the Destroyer goes on and on and on. And I write occasional short stories for a writers' group I belong to called The Adams Roundtable: Mary Clark, Peter Straub, Larry Block, Susan Isaacs, Harlan Coben etc.

Jon: You were sued when you were sixteen years old. What was that all about?

Warren: In Jersey City, one of the best ways of getting publicity for a candidate is to sue someone or have them indicted. I was 16 years old and filling in on a rewrite desk late at night when I took a story by phone from our political writer, which I guess accused one political group of committing democracy. The next day, the forces of Mayor Frank ('I am the Law') Hague announced a libel suit against the paper, the reporter and me. They forgot it the day after election, but at 16, facing a million dollar judgment, I did have a dry mouth for a while.

Jon: You co-wrote the 'Eiger Sanction' screenplay with Rod Whitaker in 1975. It's a wonderful movie--was it a fun project to work on?

Warren: Working on the 'Eiger Sanction' spoiled me for Hollywood. Clint Eastwood called me out of the blue, because he had read some of my books, and after I hung up on him a few times, thinking it was somebody doing a lousy impersonation, he asked me to write the screenplay for Eiger. He was all very laid back and only later did I learn that his option for the book was on the verge of expiring. I had never written a screenplay before, so I got a book from the library on how to write one, and then I read the 'Eiger Sanction', and then I wrote the screenplay in eight days, and Clint took my first draft to camera. I was living in Las Vegas then and Clint was around once in a while, and he is a bright, funny guy, impossible to dislike. As I say, he was great to work with because he's not afraid to make a decision and, trust me, there's not a lot of that going on out in Lala Land, which I found out later, to my regret. I never met Trevanian/Rod Whitaker. What I know is that Clint put me in for solo writing credit on the movie and Whitaker appealed that decision to the writers' guild which wound up giving him credit too, even though Clint had chucked his screenplay into the waste basket. Then after suing to get credit for the movie, Trevanian later assailed the movie in one of his subsequent books. Which I thought was pretty cheesy. But, to each his own.

Jon: How many awards have you won over the years? I know there are a couple of Edgars and at least one Shamus award around your home.

Warren: I've won a dozen awards, I think: Edgars for GRANDMASTER and PIGS GET FAT, which was a book in the Trace series, and I've had a couple of other nominations. I won Shamuses from the Private Eye Writers of America for CEILING OF HELL and most recently, for a short story, called ANOTHER DAY, ANOTHER DOLLAR. And I've got a bunch of other special awards from PWA and other groups. The seven books in the Trace series wound up winning seven national awards, which is a pretty good percentage.

Jon: You have also written with your wife, Molly Cochran. What are some of the advantages to co-writing with a spouse?

Warren: About ten years ago, Molly and I co-wrote a piece for a Mystery Writers handbook which described the joys of working together. Then, after she quite justifiably threw me out, the book was being updated by MWA and so I wrote a new piece, saying "never work with a partner." So you pays your money and you takes your choice. The truth is I like working with partners -- at least, in part -- because I like to teach but a bad partnership is like the pain in a phantom limb: it just won't ever go away. (Anybody interested in same, however, is referred to 'Writing Mysteries,' published by MWA in 2002.)

Jon: How many Destroyer books are there so far?

Warren: The Destroyer, now published by Gold Eagle (Harlequin) is up to Book Number 131 and signed up for another dozen, although after Dick's death in 1987, I pretty much stopped writing them and contracted the series to publishers, who've done it with ghost writers. Some of the books have been awful but a surprisingly large number have been very good, thanks to good writers who've worked on the series, namely Will Murray and Jim Mullaney. Also, through my own website company, I've started to do Destroyer spinoffs -- a reprint of The Assassin's Handbook (from 1982), The Way of the Assassin, and soon, Assassin's Handbook II, (also known as Chiun's Big Book of Rainy-Day Fun.) The Destroyer's also been done by Marvel Comics; it's been a film and a TV pilot, and probably will be again...if Hollywood will stop stealing it long enough to let me use it for awhile myself.

Jon: Having worked for Hollywood, what was your take on the treatment your work got as "Remo Williams, the Adventure Begins"?

Warren: The movie was a near-miss which makes it all the more tragic, from my viewpoint. They did not skimp on production values and spent real money. However, Fred Ward as Remo was impossible; he was so freaking heavy that Dick and I referred to him as Lead Ward. But the real problem in the film was that nobody involved understood how a movie works. Great heroes, to exist, need great villains. Think of James Bond and you think of Dr. No, Goldfinger, and Blofeld, etc. Think of the Remo movie villain and what do you have? A guy who is selling cheap rifles to the government, which was a) just stupid and b) just silly left-wing crappo nonsense about the corrupt government and military, etc. Sometimes I think the producers were more interested in getting on Jane Fonda's A-invitation list than in doing the movie right. Dick and I told them about the script flaw but since they were all geniuses, they didn't bother listening. They also told us that they weren't going to do any martial arts because "it's chopsaki and nobody watches chopsaki." (Sometimes I wonder if they've seen 'Dragon' or 'Matrix' or 'Karate Kid' or any of the dozens of Destroyer martial arts ripoffs which have since come along.) Anyway, Dick and I wrote about our experiences in a subsequent Destroyer called FOOL'S GOLD The whole movie thing was a shame though; it could have been a franchise; instead it was a one-shot.

Jon: I'm guessing that you probably read mysteries as well as write them. Do you have any favorites, or anybody that you really enjoyed reading recently?

Warren: I'm a traditionalist. I read Agatha Christie. My all-time favorite is the J. J. Marric "Gideon of Scotland Yard" series. There are a lot of good contemporaries working too: Ed Gorman, Bob Randisi, Loren D. Estleman, Max Allan Collins, Bill Pronzini. Wonderful women writers abound...Sharyn McCrumb knocks me out; so does Joan Hess and Sue Grafton.

Among the new ones, Angela Zeman's going to be a big star. And I don't think I'd want to live in a world that didn't have books by Mary Higgins Clark and Larry Block -- (whose new book, "Small Town," is breathtaking.)

Let's face it; I'm a slut. I could give you thirty more names of people I read all the time. And, yes, I think Stephen King is the greatest writer of our age. Bar none.

Jon: With the different people involved with the Destroyer series: Hollywood rights, the publisher, Marvel, -- do you still maintain control of its destiny?

Warren: It has been a long and bumpy road but all the rights to The

Destroyer have finally reverted to me and my partner's estate. The only other gang with any kind of a hand in the mix is Gold Eagle (Harlequin) to whom I license the rights for producing four Destroyers a year. That contract's got a couple of years to go and probably won't be renewed.

Jon: Do you still do appearances at bookstores or conventions?

Warren: I was drunk for the last seven years and I quit doing bookstores and conventions because they were interfering with my bar-time. I'm over that now and I'm slowly getting back on tour. It's gratifying to learn that there are still some people who remember me. Earlier this month, I got a standing O when I did the keynote at the Maryland Writers Association conference and it brought tears to my eyes.

Jon: Out of all your work, do you have a favorite?

Warren: The thing one is supposed to say is "my next book." But that's glib and dogs it. I'm very proud of all the Destroyers Dick Sapir and I did together; we not only promulgated the most enduring myth in pop fiction -- the brash young westerner trained in the secret arts by an inscrutable old Oriental -- but I think we helped break series books out of the mire they were in by showing that they could be used for political comment and social satire -- and also to show that series characters need not remain static but can grow and change. That's heavy lifting, buddy. I think I did well with my Trace private eye series; seven books of quasi-autobiography and, as I said, they won seven national awards. My ex-wife, Molly Cochran, and I did some real good work too, especially GRANDMASTER and THE FOREVER KING. (But Mo did most of the work; I'm good at hanging around.) I'm also proud of the columns I wrote for Mystery Scene magazine when it was first getting started; I always told the truth even though it wound up getting me savaged by a lot of P.C. Nazis who tried to destroy my career. Screw 'em...I'm still here and all of them have retired to the Isle of Lesbos where they dance on the beach at night with the dirtbags who write the corrupt anonymous reviews in Publishers Weekly.

Jon: Are you finding the website to be helpful in getting news out to your fans?

Warren: Doing anything on a website is still very much a work in progress. But I have a lot more fan contacts now than I used to have and as

I begin doing Destroyer spinoffs, I think I might figure out how to make the web economically viable for writers. Check back with me in a year.

Jon: Knowing what you do now, is there anything would you have done differently? And what advice would you give new authors getting started?

Warren: Professionally, if I were starting over, I would use different pen names for different styles of books. Otherwise, if you work in a lot of genres, you can confuse your readers who are expecting one kind of work and getting another. The only one immune to that is Stephen King and, of course, his name alone trumps all other considerations. That would be one piece of advice.

Another would be to work a lot. You have to be awfully stupid to write a lot and not get any better.

And never give up.

Jon: What kind of things do you do to relax?

Warren: Over the years, chess and golf and gambling and math have all been hobbies of one kind or another. I love to teach. But mostly, to relax, I read and write.

Jon: Do you have any bad habits?

Warren: Au contraire; I have no good habits. I'm an emphysemic chain smoker; I drink too much; I have a foul temper. I don't exercise enough.

Well, maybe a couple of good habits: I don't lie and I keep my promises. I'm also very punctual. And I always put the seat down. Oh, as long as we're at it, I tithe my time to young writers. I have to tithe my time since I have no money. But tithing is in keeping with the wonderful tradition I've always noticed which has writers, no matter who they are, as always the most generous of people in helping newcomers. Maybe that comes from never forgetting how hard those early rejections were to deal with...and trying to help young writers to get through those rough patches with all their faculties intact.

Jon: If you could commit a crime with no consequences at all, what crime would you commit?

Warren: Why are you asking these tough questions? When do I get the stupid stuff, like what's always in your refrigerator? Anyway, I've already committed all the crimes I had on my wish list. Well, save one. I'd like to sneak into Hollywood and steal all the copies of The Destroyer that screenwriters have been ripping off for years, and then see what they do for an encore.

Jon: You mentioned political correctness. Do you think the whole PC thing has gone too far?

Warren: P.C. went too far the moment it raised its ugly head and I wrote about it back then in Mystery Scene. I knew we were in trouble when brainless Lauren Bacall started referring to herself as an "actor." Could "waiter" and "waitress" be left unattacked? So now we have, "Hello, I'm Gesualdo and I'll be your waitperson tonight." "Not in this freaking world, Gesualdo. Send me my regular waitron." And now we can't call sports teams The Braves or The Redskins, lest somebody's feelings be hurt. And don't dare use the perfectly-good word "niggardly" because some illiterate, who doesn't know how to use a dictionary, might take offense.

Today I was told of a woman's college which is taking all gender references -- "she" and "her" etc. -- out of their college catalogs, lest they hurt the feelings of some "transitionally-gendered" woman. Orwell was right: there are some things so stupid that only intellectuals could ever take them seriously.

Jon: According to your website you'll be teaching some classes on writing. Have you taught before? And, if so, do you enjoy it? Also, what kind of things can your students look forward to?

Warren: Yeah, I love to teach. And I've talked a lot at workshops and conventions and seminars; and at various colleges. And I try to give students and young writers the courage to keep working and to give them too a look at the nuts and bolts of writing, practical techniques for telling stories better. Artsy-fartsy theories, they can always get in literature classes; I try to teach them how to get the trucks out of the garage in the morning.

Jon: What was the genesis of Chiun? He's very unique in fiction in his role as a mentor/teacher.

Warren: Chiun started out in the early Destroyers as a Karate teacher, albeit one with an interesting backstory. At the time we wrote that first book, karate was a mysterious mystical art that few had heard of. But by the time we got published eight years later, everybody was doing karate. So clearly, we had to make Chiun into something more and out of that grew the real long-lived legend of the Masters of Sinanju, the sun source of all the world's martial arts. Dick Sapir once joked that Chiun, the world's greatest assassin, was modeled after a typical Jewish mother -- the only difference being, Dick said, that "Chiun kills cleaner." It was mostly my idea to make Chiun a sort of hustler-con man. Dick wrote most of the early legendary stuff. Physically, I modeled Chiun after a Japanese aikido master, very old, very frail and very deadly.

Jon: What's the most embarrassing thing you've ever witnessed?

Warren: I was once involved in the corruption trial of a politician who had been loudly proclaiming his innocence; and then one day, the feds came into court with $2 million that he had hidden in secret offshore bank accounts. That was a red-face-causing attention-getter.

Jon: What's been the happiest day of your life so far?

Warren: Five of them: the healthy births of my five kids.

Jon: What is something you've always wanted to try but never have?

Warren: I always wanted to write a stage play but when I've had the time, I've not had the energy, and vice versa. But one never know, do one?

Jon: Do you cook, or are you more of a take out kind of a guy?

Warren: I am a terrific cook, blessed with that kind of nit-picking, bus driver Type A mentality which guarantees that every single dish in a meal will be completed at exactly the right time. (This is no small feat.)

Jon: If you were to meet Chuin, would he like you?

Warren: One of the ongoing conceits of the Destroyer series is that Chiun, the hundred-year-old assassin star, reads the books and comments on them...in forewords, afterwards, by direct mail. "He" always publicly lambasted Dick Sapir and me as "two useless, fat drunken scribblers" who had gotten rich off his labors. (Chiun also regularly attacked our various publishers as "gangs of moronic criminals.") So, would Chiun like me? Yes. Because, first, I wouldn't tell him who I was, and second, I would grovel. He gets off on grovelling.

Jon: What's the one thing you dread doing?

Warren: Walking away...even though I know that discretion is the better part of valor.

Jon: What's the one thing always in your refrigerator?

Warren: A container of sour cream. I've had it for ten years now and I'm waiting to see what happens to it. Does it turn sweet?

Warren Murphey's Website:
www.warrenmurphy.com

Some of Warren Murphy's books include:

The Destroyer series
(Some of these were written with various co-authors)
Remo: The Adventure Begins
Inside Sinanju
The Assassin's Handbook (1982)
1-Created: The Destroyer (1971)
2-Death Check(1972)
3-Chinese Puzzle(1972)
4-Mafia Fix(1972)
5-Dr. Quake(1972)
6-Death Therapy (1972)
7-Union Bust (1973)
8-Summit Chase (1973)
9 -Murder's Shield (1973)
10-Terror Squad (1973)
11-Kill or Cure (1973)
12- Slave Safari (1973)
13-Acid Rock (1973)
14 -Judgment Day (1974)

15-Murder Ward (1974)
16- Oil Slick (1974)
17- Last War Dance (1974)
18-Funny Money (1975)
19-Holy Terror (1975)
20-Assassins Playoff (1975)
21-Deadly Seeds (1975)
22-Brain Drain (1976)
23-Child's Play (1976)
24-King's Curse (1976)
25-Sweet Dreams (1976)
26-In Enemy Hands (1976)
27-The Last Temple (1977)
28-Ship of Death (1977)
29-The Final Death (1977)
30-Mugger Blood (1977)
31-The Head Men (1977)
32-Killer Chromosomes (1978)
33-Voodoo Die (1978)
34-Chained Reaction (1978)
35- Last Call (1978)
36- Power Play (1979)
37-Bottom Line (1979)
38-Bay City Blast (1979)
39-Missing Link (1980)
40-Dangerous Games (1980)
41-Firing Line (1980)
42-Timberline (1980)
43-Midnight Man (1981)
44-Balance of Power (1981)
45-Spoils of War (1981)
46-Next of Kin (1981)
47-Dying Space (1982)
48-Profit Motive (1982)
49-Skin Deep (1982)
50-Killing Time (1982)
51-Shock Value (1983)
52-Fools Gold (1983)
53-Time Trial (1983)
54-Last Drop
55-Masters Challange
56-Encounter Group (1984)

57-Date with Death (1984)
58-Total Recall (1984)
59- The Arms Of Kali (1984)
60-The End of the Game (1985)
61-Lords Of The Earth (1985)
62-The Seventh Stone (1985)
63-The Sky is Falling (1985)
64-The Last Alchemist
65-Lost Yesterday
66 - Sue Me (1986)
67- Look Into My Eyes (1986)
68-An old-fashioned War (1987)
69-Blood Ties (1987)
70-The Eleventh Hour (1987)
71-Return Engagement (1987)
72-Sole Survivor
73-Line of Succession
74-Walking Wounded (1988)
75-Rain of Terror (1988)
76-The Final Crusade (1989)
77-Coin of the Realm (1989)
78-Blue Smoke and Mirrors (1989)
79-Shooting Schedule (1990)
80-Death Sentence (1990)
81-Hostile Takeover (1990)
82- Survival

with Molly Cochran
High Priest (1987)
The Temple Dogs (1989)
The Forever King (1992)
End Game (1994)- as Dev Stryker
Deathright (1999) as Dev Stryker
A Wilderness of Mirrors (2000) as Dev Stryker
World without End; A Novel of Atlantis (1996)

Razoni and Jackson:
City In Heat
Dead End Street
One Night Stand
Down And Dirty
Lynch Town

With the Adams Round Table Group:
Murder in Manhattan -Adams Round (1988)
A Body Is Found - Adams Round Table (1990)
Justice in Manhattan: The Adams Round Table (1994)
Murder on the Run - Adams Round Table(1998)
Murder Among Friends (2000)

Trace
7. Getting Up With Fleas
6. Too Old a Cat
5. 47 Miles of Rope
4. Once a Mutt(1985)
3. When Elephants Forget(1984)
2.Pigs Get Fat (1985)
1.Trace (1983)

Digger
1. Smoked Out (1982)
2. Fool's Flight (1982)
3. Dead Letter (1982)
4. Lucifer's Weekend (2003)
Novels
The Last Alchemist
The Red Moon (1982)
The Ceiling of Hell (1986)
The Sky Is Falling (1986)
The Last Alchemist (1988)
Leonardo's Law (1988)
Jericho Day (1989)
The Sure Thing (1989)
The Hand of Lazarus (1990)
Scorpion's Dance (1990)
Honor Among Thieves (1992)
Destiny's Carnival (1992)
High Priestess (with Richard Ben Sapir)(1994)
Murder Is My Business - Anthology-)Mickey Spillane & Max Allan
Collins, editors) *(1997)*

George Pelecanos

"You don't just feel them sweat. You sweat with them". Richard Katz on Pelecanos's characters.

So true. George Pelecanos is the genuine article. A few years back (ten) I described a book as "hard-boiled" and received some criticism. It seemed that the purists felt this particular book was "noir". Off to the Rara Avis list I went. If anybody knew hard-boiled it was these guys. I read or reread classic "hard-boiled" for three months. Hammett and Cain. A Thompson. Frustration was setting in. I knew these books were hard-boiled. Then came the next suggested read and everybody was excited. KING SUCKERMAN. This was my introduction to George Pelecanos. This was a standard I'd come to hold all contemporary novels up to when quantifying them as hard-boiled. It was also a standard Mr. Pelecanos would soon leave in the dust.

There are the characters that reverberate with life, flawed and bruised, dusting themselves off to fight yet another day. There is the city. Washington D.C. There's no Crystal City here. Instead we see the land of government housing, boys with either no fathers or Sunday visits to jail. For in our Nation's capitol there are few dreams. Day to day is hard and next week only a possibility. Pelecanos has captured this reality of Urban America like no other writer of our generation.

And then there is the content. Thrillers and mysteries that begin to break your heart on the second or third page. Books that leave you both shattered and rejuvenated when you set them down. So complex and layered is the fictional world of Pelecanos and his characters that as you dissect parts of the story, you continually find sub-plots that are more relevant and alive than most writer's books.

George Pelecanos is a man who is grateful to be doing what he is for a living. To express that gratitude to both readers and the publishing world he continues to hone his craft. Accomplishing the truly impossible, the man makes sure every book is better than the last. SOUL CIRCUS was such a complete reading experience I did not believe he could outdo it. I thought, "well this is it".

Lucky enough to get an Advance Reading Copy of next year's HARD REVO-LUTION I now feel I did the man a disservice. For once again George Pelecanos is going to take his readers to places they never wanted to go but will be so glad that they did.

Quite simply he is a modern master. -Ruth Jordan

Jon: Your work has been described in many ways. How would YOU describe it?

George: Crime fiction with an emphasis on character and naturalism. Charles Taylor of the NY Times called what I do "urban reportage." That's not bad, either.

Jon: I've heard rumors of King Suckerman being made into a movie. Is there any news on that?

Richard Katz and George Pelecanos

George: After several years of development, the rights have been returned to me.

Jon: I read somewhere that you initially set out to write just one novel. Things have obviously gone well enough for you to continue to write. Do you ever find yourself surprised to be making a living as a writer?

George: All the time. I don't want to say I'm lucky, because a whole lot of hard work got me here. But I do know how fortunate I am.

Jon: Your books have a real honesty to them. How much of this is because of your relationship with the city you live in?

George: I feel like I'm leaving a cultural and historical record of D.C., so I want it to be as accurate as possible. And I do love this town.

Jon: Do you think being a father affects your work?

Absolutely. My world view as changed considerably since I started raising kids. And because of that change--okay, call it a maturation--the books have gotten better.

Jon: What kind of jobs did you have before writing?

George: Cook, dishwasher, bartender, stereo and appliance salesman, shoe salesman, advertising director, retail manager, construction. I've pretty much done it all, and had a good time doing it. All the physical work in my past has helped me appreciate the gig I've got now. Which is why I can't stand being around writers who complain; yes, this can be an intense, mentally demanding way to make a living. But I'm well paid, and my back doesn't hurt at the end of the day.

Jon: Do you like doing the conventions and signings?

George: I like doing readings and signings, and I like to meet the people who read my books. The travel can be a drag, but once I'm off the plane, I'm into it. Because of what I do for a living, I've managed to see a great deal of this country and much of the world. Again, the word fortunate comes to mind.

Jon: I know that Hell To Pay has some of the same characters as Right as Rain , can you tell us anything else about it?

George: Strange and Quinn go even deeper into the inner city in this one. Like many of my recent books, Hell focuses on the exploitation of disadvantaged kids. Strange in particular goes through some serious changes here. I'm very happy with this one.

Jon: Will we see Nick again?

George: Nick Stefanos will be a significant character in a novel called Soul Circus, which I recently completed. It's the third in my urban western trilogy featuring Strange and Quinn, and will be published in 2003.

Jon: Who are some of your heroes?

George: Nobody famous. My heroes are the mentors, teachers, big brothers and sisters, and coaches who help at-risk kids in the cities. They generally go unnamed and their deeds are unsung. In the absence of any true government assistance, these people step up to the plate.

Jon: People sometimes feel that they know authors through reading their work. Is there anything about you that would surprise people?

George: Yes.

Jon: What would make a perfect weekend for you?

George: Each year, on the Saturday of Super Bowl weekend, my wife and I drive down to Maryland's eastern shore and get a room in an old hotel in a small riverside town. We spend the afternoon in a quiet bar and in the evening have a nice dinner. The next day we stop for crab soup in Kent Island, then head home, where I hang out with my kids and watch the football game. That to me is the perfect weekend.

Jon: What are some of your favorite movies?

George: I'm a sucker for just about any Western: Peckinpah, Leone, Ford. Don Siegel, Scorcese, Robert Aldrich, John Sturges, Kurosawa... do you see a pattern here?

Jon: You are very popular in the UK, and Europe. Why do you think that is?

George: My swarthy good looks?

Jon: Who are some of your favorite authors?

George: The novels that have haunted me most in the last couple of years were The Death of Sweet Mister, by Daniel Woodrell, and Ask the Dust, by John Fante. All the Kings Men remains my favorite American novel. The Burglar, by David Goodis, is my favorite crime novel. The Fred Exley trilogy. The Last Good Kiss, by James Crumley, has to be the finest detective novel written in my lifetime. We would be here all day if I started listing crime novelists I like, and even then I'd still piss some people off. Let's just say that I'm a fan.

Jon: Your books have a vividness to them that is similar to noir movies an books. Are you influenced by the classics?

George: I'm influenced by all the popular arts: movies, books, and music. I think most novelists of my generation, if they were honest, would tell you the same.

Jon: Do you think the internet has helped authors become more accessible to the readers? And, do you have a website?

George: http://www.georgepelecanos.com

It took me long time to come up with the name.

Jon: Drugs play a role in most of your work. Do you think its realistic for people to think that the problem of drugs can actually be stopped?

George: Drugs are a "problem" because they're illegal. Any American politician who presents a sane solution to the drug problem is a one-term politician. So the answer is No.

Jon: How do you approach the research for your books?

George: Each book is different. For this last one I hung out with ATF guys, rode with cops, and walked the neighborhoods I was writing about. Sat in bars and listened to people talk. For the period books I do some serious library-time and oral history work. For what I'm trying to do the key is to stay engaged; breathe the air and feel the dirt, if you know what I mean.

Jon: What's the hardest part of being an author?

George: Navigating the first one hundred pages of a manuscript. Convincing
yourself that you've done it before and you can do it again.

Jon: The comic fan in me wants to know, did you ever read comics, and if so what were your favorites?

George: War comics. You know, the WWII, Sergeant Rock stuff where the grunts are shooting the snipers out the trees. As the snipers fall they scream, "Aiyeeeee!" I'm not a big sci-fi or fantasy guy. I could never get my head around it, and still can't. I like some of the modern comics; the Preacher series is pretty cool.

Jon: If you were able to travel back in time and talk to your self as a teenager, what advice would you pass on?

George: Aside from some trouble I got into, I don't have too many regrets. All in all, I had big fun. That's what teenagers ought to do.

Jon: Curtis Hanson, the director of LA Confidential is going to direct Right As Rain. If it does well, is there a chance of the whole trilogy being filmed?

George: There's always that possibility. More likely, they'll draw key elements from all the Strange/Quinn books for the one film.

Jon: Are you careful with who you let option your books? Do you turn down any offers because you don't think it would turn out well?

George: Yes on both counts. You can't entirely control the end product, of course, but you can do damage control from the beginning by choosing wisely. On the Right as Rain deal, I was very fortunate. One of the producers is a woman I've known for a dozen years; she's a friend, and I trust her implicitly. Hanson is a world class director, but more importantly, he's an honorable man. I've also known the screenwriter, David Benioff, for many years. David's talented and a great guy. So I'm optimistic about the whole
endeavor.

Jon: Soul Circus has been out for a while now, and the Arcs of your next book are starting to show up. Is the next book in progress? And, are you planning the books after that?

George: Hard Revolution comes out in March of 2004. I'm just beginning to research the next book, which I will start writing this fall. As usual, I don't have a plot. But I've been getting some hellacious material lately on the street.

Jon: In the last few years your books have really started to sell very well.
Does this change your approach to writing, or does it mean you still write the same but more people are hip to it?

George: I effectively ended the Strange/Quinn books at the height of their
popularity; that ought to tell you something there. My ambition is to keep growing as a writer. Hopefully the audience will come along for the ride.

Jon: Did you enjoy doing the cameo in The Wire this season?

George: I happened to be on set one day when the Assistant Director realized we had not cast a prison guard needed for a scene we were about to shoot. He asked me to play the guard and I agreed. I went to the costume trailer, got fitted, and was shooting fifteen minutes later. That same day, novelist Richard Price was down from New York to play a part as a prison librarian, a role we had written for him. So it's pretty cool that we ended up in the same episode. I do feel that my performance is much more subtle than Price's, but maybe that's just me.

Jon: When people talk about your work they bring up things about social commentary, and urban realism. Do you set out to write about these things or are they just a part of the natural story telling process?

George: I write about my obsessions. I go out there and hang out and when I get passionate about what I see a book begins to form in my head.

Jon: What advice would you give to aspiring writers?

George: Read like a madman and live a fully examined life.

Jon: What's the one thing always in your refrigerator?

George: Kalamata olives and feta cheese. Cold beer for me and milk for my kids

George Pelecanos's website:
www.georgepelecanos.com

George Pelecanos's Books:

A Firing Offense (1992)
Nick's Trip (1993)
Shoedog (1994)
Down By The River Where
The Dead Men Go (1995)
The Big Blowdown (1996)
King Suckerman (1997)
The Sweet Forever(1998)
Shame The Devil (2000)
Right As Rain (2001)
Hell To Pay (2002)
Soul Circus (2003)
Hard Revolution (2004)

Manuel Ramos

When obsessively well-read mystery readers are left stunned by a book, you know something very special has happened. Manuel Ramos's stand-alone, Mooney's Road to Hell, succeeded in doing this with readers jaded by commercial schlock. Mr. Ramos has a clean yet rich style that leaves the mind sated and the soul stirred.

In Luis Móntez, Manuel Ramos has created a series lead of depth, human fallibility and resilience. He typifies hardboiled yet escapes formula. I am always left to marvel at Mr. Ramos's ability to write in such an evocative manner. This is done without extremes of good and evil featuring the noble hero triumphing over the clearly malevolent bad guy. Life isn't
that easy to define and neither are Ramos's characters. The line between winning and losing is just as blurred.

These books are character studies of humanness and treatise on the irony life deals us on a day to day basis. If you've been searching in vain for a new author to fall in love with, search no more. - Jennifer Jordan

Jon: What made you decide to start writing books in addition to practicing law?

Manuel: I wrote when I was a young kid, through high school and college. The writing came from all the reading I did. I think I read every book in the Florence, Colorado public library before my family moved to Colorado Springs when I was about 14. However, when I went to law school and then started on my professional career, the creative writing stopped--for 13 years. When the inevitable mid-life crisis hit, I returned to writing with a short story about a nameless, burned-out legal aid lawyer. That character eventually became Luis Móntez. I returned to writing because I   missed it. I get high on the creative process, but I do not understand it at all. I could never "teach" writing, no more than I could teach someone how to fall in love. It happens or it doesn't.

Jon: With your latest book, Moony's Road To Hell, you took a break from Luis Montez and created a new character. Why the change?

Manuel: It was time to try something else. I had different ideas floating around in my head and I wanted to put them together, but they didn't seem to fit with Luis Móntez. For example, I wrote Moony in the third person--big change for me and much more difficult than I expected. But Luis Móntez will always have to be written in the first person. Plus, I wanted to do something with the PI format. I was intrigued with a character who actually got paid to delve into the grime and violence of someone else's life--what kind of person is that? And then there's the noir aspect of the storyline--I crossed over into the dark side, and that needed very different characters.

Jon: Will we see Luis again? Is there a chance we might see Moony again, maybe an earlier case or something from his youth?

Manuel: Luis returns in the fall of 2003 with BROWN-ON-BROWN (UNM Press), a story that involves the ongoing   Colorado drought against the background of the rash of fires we suffered through in the last couple of years. The crime comes about because of a hundred years "water war" in Colorado's historic San Luis Valley. Luis is asked to defend the son of one of the patriarchs of the Valley. The son is accused of murder and arson but before Luis can really get into the case, all hell breaks loose, as they say, and Luis is off on one of his nostalgic, dangerous odysseys.

This one ends up at the Great Sand Dunes National Monument. The book has several new characters including Emilio, a hit man with a warped sense of humor, and Alicia, Luis's new love interest (a bartender, almost a natural for the guy.)

FYI, the first four Móntez books are going to be reprinted by Northwestern University Press. THE BALLAD OF ROCKY RUIZ and THE BALLAD OF GATO GUERRERO come out this fall in new paperback editions--new covers, new introductions, etc. THE LAST CLIENT OF LUIS MONTEZ and BLUES FOR THE BUFFALO are due next spring. I'm jazzed about this turn of events. Finally, the books will be readily available at realistic prices. As for Moony, I don't have any new story ideas yet, but there are some vignettes that I left out of Moony's Road that could grow into longer plots. To write that book, though, I will have to return to that dark, ruthless place in my head where Moony's world exists. Could happen.

Jon: When you decided to go ahead and start writing, why did you decide to write crime fiction?

Manuel: The main reason has to be that I'm a fan of crime fiction: mysteries, detective stories, police procedurals, hard-boiled dicks, amateurs, etc., I read them all and I have been reading them since the "teenage, formative years." THE BALLAD OF ROCKY RUIZ began as an exercise to find out more about the character I had created for a short story, who eventually became Luis Móntez, but it ended up as a mystery because of Luis's need to learn the truth about the murder of his best friend twenty years before the story's beginning. And one of the things that I recalled when I returned to writing was the way my grandfather used to insert a twist or surprise at the end of the stories he enjoyed telling to his numerous grandchildren. Mini-mysteries, almost, so that influenced me, too. Finally, the crime fiction context is a convenient way to write about life and people at the end of the twentieth century and beginning of the twenty-first century without engaging in diatribe or polemics--if one is so inclined and, quite often, I am.

Jon: Do you read mysteries and crime fiction? If so, who do you like to read?

Manuel: As I mentioned above, I read a little bit of everything. I focus on Chicano literature (because I dig it and because of a teaching gig I do on a part-time basis) and, of course, crime fiction. There are writers I return to, such as Paco Ignacio Taibo and Lawrence Block, but I go all over the board. I've dug into the classics (Chandler, Hammett, Cain) as well as the hot new folks. Here are the crime books I finished in the last several weeks (at least the ones I remember): 'The Burnt Orange Heresy', by Charles Willeford; 'Chinaman's Chance', Ross Thomas; 'The Diehard', Jon A. Jackson; 'The Shape of Water' and 'The Terra-Cotta Dog', Andrea Camilleri; 'Ask a Policeman', Rolando Hinojosa; 'Mystic River', Dennis Lehane; 'Daddy's Gone A-Hunting,' Robert Skinner; 'The

Big Heat', William McGivern; 'Inner City Blues', Paula Woods; and the 100 Bullets collections by Azzarello and Risso.

Jon: I've noticed that you included the 100 Bullets collections by Azzarello and Risso in the list of what you've been reading. Do you enjoy the graphic novel format?

Manuel: Yes. Provocative art, convoluted plots, crisp dialog, heavy atmosphere--the good ones have what I like.

Jon: How does your wife handle you spending your time writing? After ten years, I would imagine it is part of your life style and she is very supportive.

Manuel: My wife is great--my biggest fan and critic, and so busy herself (she's the CEO and general manager of a public radio station here in Denver) that she's probably relieved that she doesn't have to put up with me when I hide out at the computer.

Jon: You've mentioned the darker aspects of writing Moony. I would imagine, that when you are writing, things from the book stick in your head until after the book is done and gone. Could it also be true that writing would be a way to work out things that have been on your mind?

Manuel: Writing can be therapeutic--is that what you meant? It is a peaceful (but not always harmless) way to vent, get revenge, win the argument, whatever. However, although I know that happens, it is not a big motivation for me.

Jon: Your work is very character oriented. Has Luis taken on his own personality over the years? Have you become kind of a medium for him to channel through?

Manuel: I don't know about me being a medium, but I will say that Luis has taken on a life of his own, as much as a figment of my imagination can have a "life." I've heard many writers speak about their characters "taking over" a story--my wife scoffs at that kind of stuff. I think what happens is that we (writers) surprise ourselves. We dip into the dark pools of our subconscious without being aware of what we are doing, and for some it seems as though the character has led the way, instead of the writer.

Jon: Do you ever find a storyline changing as you write it? That is, becoming something different than you originally planned it to be?

Manuel: Oh yeah--often. Only rarely have I ended up where I thought I was going. But for a mystery, that's good, don't you think? If the writer is surprised, good chance the reader will be, too, No? I try to start with a concept and a character, and then go for the ride.

Jon: You've said that you are not Luis, but there are similarities, including the legal aid work. Why did you choose this path to follow with your law degree?

Manuel: Back in the day, way back, when I decided to go to law school, it was a political decision for me and many other young Chicanos/Chicanas graduating from college. We had been involved in a movement and we thought a law degree could help keep that movement going. We became public defenders, legal aid lawyers, or did other public interest work, and many of us became sole practitioners, like Luis. Doing legal aid work has been rewarding and about the only kind of law work with which I could feel comfortable.

Jon: Your path to writing books started with entering a contest. Was it hard to convince yourself to enter?

Manuel: No. Once I finished THE BALLAD OF ROCKY RUIZ, I

wanted everyone in the world to read it-- I still do. Entering that contest was one step to get others to read it. I encourage young writers to get their work out where it will be read and maybe commented on, and maybe even win some money or get published! How cool is that?

Jon: What kind of movies do you enjoy?

Manuel: I go on kicks--binges. I did a slew of contemporary Mexican movies recently but now I'm trying to collect DVDs of crime movies I've liked. So far, I've got 'Body Heat', 'The Big Sleep' (Bogart), 'The Maltese Falcon' (Bogart again), 'Reservoir Dogs', 'Pulp Fiction', 'Devil In a Blue Dress', 'L.A. Confidential', 'The Long Goodbye' (Altman's version), 'The Usual Suspects', and my wife just gave me 'The Road to Perdition" for my birthday. Next up, 'The Grifters' and 'Memento'.

Jon: What's the most rewarding part of writing? and what's the hardest part?

Manuel: The most rewarding is the reaction from a reader. The hardest part is dealing with the reaction from a reader.

Jon: What's your favorite way to spend a weekend?

Manuel: Seriously, I like to work around the house, and actually finish something, even if it's only tightening a screw on a door hinge, then go out with my wife and dance, dance, dance to a good Chicano band that plays tejano, oldies, r&b, and a little blues. Lately, I'm spending time with my first grandson (3 months old), and so that's been added to the agenda.

Jon: Do you do any non-fiction writing?

Manuel: I've written law-related articles and have published a book on Colorado landlord-tenant law that's now in its third edition. I also have written a bit on Chicano/Chicana crime fiction. One such article is on my website. Its title is "The Postman and the Mex: From Hard-boiled to Huevos Rancheros in Detective Fiction."

Jon: If you were to give advice to a thirteen year old Manuel, what would you tell him?

Manuel: Don't forget the Spanish.

Jon: Your covers are all very striking. Do you have any input on the art?

Manuel: I had some input on the cover of MOONY'S ROAD TO HELL, and that is my favorite. The art designer and I talked about the concept, the feel of the story, and she used some of my wife's photos of Mexican masks, and also a photo of one such mask made by my artist brother. I also came up with the cover art for the iUniverse edition of BLUES FOR THE BUFFALO. The art on that book is by a Denver artist, Carlos Fresquez, and it fits the story perfectly. Those covers are cool, I think.

I have problems with some of the St. Martin's cover art, especially the ones (THE LAST CLIENT OF LUIS MONTEZ and the paperback of THE BALLAD OF GATO GUERRERO) that have a man on the cover who is supposed to be Luis Montez, I guess. Those covers give me heartburn. They did a decent job on the hardback and paperback of THE BALLAD OF ROCKY RUIZ. Then there's the cover for the St. Martin's edition of BLUES FOR THE BUFFALO.

Some booksellers call it the "Michael Jackson cover." I'll leave it to you to figure out why.

I guess writers are supposed to be "above" being concerned about covers and jackets. But for a guy like me, not exactly a household name, one of the primary ways that someone who hasn't read any of my books is going to buy one of my books is by getting hooked by the cover and jacket blurb. So, those things become important. I'm pleased to be working with University of New Mexico Press, where the staff actually listens to and takes into consideration my suggestions.

Jon: Have you had any Hollywood interest in your work?

Manuel: THE LAST CLIENT OF LUIS MONTEZ was optioned by a producer, who wrote a script. That's as far as that has gone. Know any investors?

Jon: What's the one thing always in your refrigerator?

Manuel: A jar of Embasa Guerito Peppers (little yellow chiles).

Manuel Ramos' Website:
www.manuelramos.com

Manuel Ramos' Books

The Balled Of Rocky Ruiz (1993)
The Ballad Of Gato Guerrero (1994)
The Last Client Of Luis Montez (1996)
Blues For The Buffalo (1997)
Moony's Road To Hell (2002)
Brown On Brown (2003)

Ian Rankin

Photo by Paul Jordan

There can be only one. This is a theme running throughout the Highlander series. The myth states that the immortals must all fight one another until the last is alone in the world. In the real world the Scots don't think that way.

The year is 1987. The young author's name is Ian Rankin. He's been in University studying English Literature. He's written a little book called KNOTS AND CROSSES. Set in Edinburgh, the tome has been written, in part, because Mr. Rankin noted that the last internationally received Scottish novel was THE PRIME OF MISS JEAN BRODIE. His solution is an update of Jekyll and Hyde. He's breathed the first life into Crime Fiction's most fascinating character. We've traveled through foul play and skullduggery with John Rebus for sixteen years now. We've acquired scars with this loner policeman. We dread his retirement perhaps more than detective himself.

It's hard to say where the strength is in this series because there are no weaknesses. The characters are strong. The settings pulsate with life. The plots weave a spell on the reader. And always Mr. Rankin and Mr. Rebus work on the reader's psyche, taking us to places of darkness with a small glimmer of hope. Like Rebus we hold fast to that tiny light, dust ourselves off and wait impatiently for the next in the series.

In the real world Rankin's Rebus no longer stands alone as a testament to the contemporary Scot's novel. There's McDermid and Jardine and Mina to name a few. There's a lass by the name of Rowling. The world has received a gift well beyond the Rebus series from Mr. Rankin.

Favorite author? There can be only one. Mine is Ian Rankin.
-Ruth Jordan

Jon: For people who may live in a cave and not read any of your books yet, could you give a brief rundown of the series?

Ian: John Rebus is a police detective working in contemporary Edinburgh and exposing a side of that elegant city which tourists and visitors never see.

He's a loner, a fighter, not much of a lover. The job is his only salvation. The city itself is a central character in the series, and beyond that each book tries to focus on one part of modern-day Scotland, so that the series itself becomes a jigsaw, laying out where the country's going, and how it got to where it is.

Jon: Is there any of Ian Rankin in John Rebus?

Ian: A bit. The music; the loner; the drinking... But I'm nicer than him; maybe not quite so fucked up. Long time ago, he was a cipher merely, a way of telling my stories, then he started infecting me... now there's more of him in me than ever before. Addictive poison.

Jon: A lot of authors have had some strange jobs before they get published. What kind of things have you done before you were able to write full time?

Ian: Lots of weird jobs. I looked after pigs, but killed one by OD'ing it with alcohol. I collected tax from people, that was fun. I sang in a punk band, worked as a secretary in the National Folktale Centre in London; was a hi-fi /music journalist. I worked as an alcohol researcher (asking kids about their drinking habits). Lots of strange shit.

Jon: I really like the music references in the books. Is music a large part of who you are?

Ian: I'm listening to some new stuff right now, bought this afternoon: Arab Strap (Scottish band; you can't dance to them); Mogwai (Scottish band; you can't dance to them either). Also today bought secondhand CDs of Prefab Sprout and Hal Ketchum - I already have both albums on tape, but am a sucker for CDs. Music is the best of me. My wife hates my musical taste; so do most of my friends

Jon: Are you involved in the TV production of your books, or are you just an observer hoping it doesn't get too far off track?

Ian: I have nothing to do with the TV. The actor, John Hanna and I went out with the producer one night and got absolutely guttered. That's the extent of my involvement. I wish them well, I think it'll be great, but it's not my Rebus. My Rebus stays with me and inside me.

Jon: As a father who writes, I would guess that you get to spend more time with your kids than most fathers. Do you think   that people in general should try to spend more time with their kids?

Ian: I spend very little time with my kids: too busy touring or writing. They come home from school, I'm busy in my office. I should spend more time with them; everyone should spend more time with their kids. On the other hand, adults need space and time to themselves. That's why I like pubs: no kids...

Jon: You seem to be a very open and honest person. Is there any thing about you that people would be surprised to find out?

Ian: I have my little secrets; bad behaviour under the influence of bad influences. Jeez, we all need a few skeletons, especially the Protestants among us. Keep feeding that guilt, keep piling it on.

Jon: How much control do you have on the final books? Do you have any say in the artwork and the editing that is done?

Ian: I get a little bit of say on artwork, then the publisher usually ig-nores me. Actually, that's true in UK; in US, I only usually see finished artwork, so I have even less say. Editing... I trust my editor, am usually fairly amenable to change. I'm not a prima donna.

Jon: If you could go back in time and have a chat with a 18 year old Ian, what would you say?

Ian: I'd say get out more; I'd say cheer up; I'd say don't waste your time on poetry thinking it'll get you a harem... head straight for crime fiction. That's where the meat is.

Jon: I have found that authors are much more approachable than people in other parts of the entertainment industry. Why do you think this is?

Ian: Authors are human beings. Other media types are not. Actors play parts; they don't have to feel things; they're all surface (in many cases). Writers reach into their own souls and those of their characters. They feel. Musicians are in another sphere entirely, somewhere non-musos cannot wander into. Mind you, some writers I've come across, you wouldn't wipe your arse on them....

Jon: Raymond Chandler died before finishing his last Marlowe book. Robert Parker finished it, and then wrote another. Would you ever consider writing someone else's character?

Ian: I don't think so... unless the money on offer was vast. I certainly wouldn't want anyone finishing one of MY books.

Jon: Would you ever consider getting involved in the movie business?

Ian: I'd like to try a film or TV script (in fact, I'm about to embark on a TV drama, if my nerve holds). Thing is, it's writing by committee, and that's not the way I've ever written. Film execs want to know everything about the plot/story BEFORE you start writing, and essentially I make things up as I go along; I'm not organized enough to make it as a script writer. Plus all those rewrites... ugh!

Jon: Are you a practical joker?

Ian: Now and then. When some friends were away once, I stole a 'For Sale' sign and put it up next to their house as a homecoming gift. But practical jokes take effort, and these days I try to keep all effort to a minimum.

Photo by Paul Jordan

Jon: What would be a perfect weekend for you?

Ian: Perfect weekend: out on the bevvy (alcohol) with some pals, maybe hit some record shops, go see a football match, then sober up in the evening, a bath and a shave, and out for a meal with my wife. That's the Saturday. Sunday, I'd stay in bed late, and then assassinate the royal family.

Jon: What is the weirdest experience you ever had with a fan?

Ian: I've had a few. The 'fan' who painted the name WOLFMAN (name of one of my serial killers) at the scene of one of the murders. The fan who's a dentist and sent me check-lists of all the mentions of teeth in the Rebus books (she's a very nice lady, as it turns out, but I didn't know that then). Strange rambling letters from a German woman...

Jon: Are there any movies you have seen that have left a real lasting impression on you?

Ian: I don't know. Instead, here are some films I love: 'The Godfather', 'Goodfellas', 'The Big Chill', 'Toy Story', 'Singles', 'Terminator', 'Apocalypse Now', 'Blade Runner'.

Jon: Aside from writing and touring, what occupies your time?

Ian: Reading, listening to music, pub life. My two kids take up some time, too.

Jon: What are some of your pet peeves?

Ian: Noisy neighbours -- I imagine taking an AK-47 to them. Religious bigotry (as in Catholics v Protestants).

Jon: Do you ever start a book, and have something happen to change the direction from what you had planned?

Ian: Happens all the time. Like with the one I finished a couple of months back. Was going to be first book in a trilogy about Scottish parliament... but the guy who was going to be in all three books (making it a trilogy), well, I bumped him off on page 50. Didn't want to; the story made me do it. No idea who killed him or why.

Jon: With all the touring and traveling you do it must be hard to eat right. What's a typical meal on the road for you?

Ian: A typical tour meal for me might consist of a packet of potato chips, a couple of bars of chocolate, and several large glasses of wine. Of course, there are also posh dinners, laid on for booksellers and journalists. These usually take place at around 11pm, after a shattering day of travel and an evening talking/signing gig. On occasions such as these, I would normally eschew the chips and chocolate and proceed directly to an intravenous bottle or two of vino...

Jon: Is there anything that you regret having actually spent money on?

Ian: I regret spending money on most of Frank Zappa's later output. He tailed off more than a tad towards the end of his days.

Jon: If you were given the opportunity to write a comic book, which character would you like to write for?

Ian: I would probably want to create my own character: a private eye with special powers. My favourite comic book characters are Elektra, Faust, DR and Quinch...

Jon: The Rebus series is so popular that you must constantly be asked about how long you are going to write it, and what you're going to do with him next. What I'd like to know is what you'd like to write without Rebus. Any plans?

Ian: I have no concrete plans to write a non-Rebus book, but I know it'll happen one day. Maybe still a crime-tinged book; could be set in 18th century Edinburgh (lots of harlots, drunken poets, scum of the Earth... nothing much changes). Maybe a high-concept stand-alone novel, to get me a few of those Mike Connelly/Harlan Coben greenbacks!

Jon: Spending as much time as you do touring, and being "Ian Rankin-Author", does it get hard to find time to write and for that matter to just be Ian?

Ian: I get less and less time to write, which is very strange. Having said which, I'm slowing down, doing a book every 18 months-2 years rather than the 2-a-year I was writing in the early 1990s. I'd have plenty of time to write, if only I could find it in me to say 'no' to everything else (touring, TV appearances, interviews, charity work). Problem is: I like the 'everything else'... I do, however, find time to just be myself: I have a down to Earth partner, two kids who want daddy playing with them, and plenty of mates at the pub to whom I'm just another drinker who gets his round in, same as everyone. There's a cult of democracy in Scotland: no one's allowed to get above themselves. No room for egos.

Jon: Do you ever get ideas floating around in your head that just won't leave until you've put them down on paper?

Ian: If an idea bobs up to the surface of my brain, I need to get it written down pronto, before I lose it; same goes for lines of prose and dialogue. Just the other night, I got what could be the opening of the next Rebus. I got out of bed, switched on the light, and wrote that fucker down, then tucked it into my ideas file for later consumption.

Jon: What's the best way to get your attention?

Ian: The best way to get my attention is to say "Hey, Ian, what're you drinking?"

Jon: What do you think it is that makes Val McDermid such a wonderful person?

Ian: I think what makes Val such a wonderful person is a combination of her athletic good looks and her ability to say "Hey, Ian, what're you drinking?"

Jon: What is the one thing always in your refrigerator?

Ian: $200,000 worth of cocaine and a 9mm Beretta

Ian Rankin's Website:s
www.ianrankin.net

Ian Rankin's Books:

The Rebus Books
Knots And Crosses (1987)
Hide And Seek (1991)
Wolfman - AKA -Tooth And Nail (1992)
A Good Hanging And Other Stories (1992)
Strip Jack (1992)
The Black Book (1993)
Mortal Causes (1994)
Let It Bleed (1996)
Black And Blue (1997)
The Hanging Garden (1998)
Death Is Not The End (1998)
Dead Souls (1999)
Set In Darkness (2000)
The Falls (2001)
Resurrection Men (2002)
A Question Of Blood (2003)

Also:
The Flood (1986)

Westwind
Watchman (1998)
Herbert In Motion and other stories Short Stories (1997)
Beggars Banquet (Short Stories) (2002)

As Jack Harvey:
Witch Hunt (1993)
Bleeding Hearts (1994)
Blood Hunt (1995)

Peter Robinson

When I first read Peter Robinson I started a bit late, but I started at the beginning of the series. I was impressed by how well he wrote. The procedural aspects were wonderfully done and the characters interesting. As I made my way through his books I noticed a constant growth in the characters, a natural growth. As he keeps writing he just keeps getting better and better. He has a way of breathing life into his writing that should be mandatory reading for people thinking about writing mysteries. And with each new book he pushes himself and challenges his readers to keep up.

photo by Ann Chernow

Peter himself is a laid back and kind of quiet man. He seems to notice everything around him. He is also funny, charming and interesting. Listening to him talk about his writing you can feel his passion for it. And it comes through in his work, which is why he is one of my favorite authors. – Jon Jordan

Jon: Knowing that you have been interviewed quite a few times before, are there any questions that have been over done and that I shouldn't ask?

Peter: Only the thing about living in Toronto and writing about England. I grew up there. Period.

Jon: I think the biggest strength of the books are the characters. They are all fleshed out and real, even minor ones. As a reader I love a book that makes me want to follow the characters even after the book is done. Is there a trick to making this happen?

Peter: If there is, I don't know it. I try to both get inside their skins and watch them from the outside. Sometimes they seem to take on a life of their own, and it's like taking dictation, but not often enough! Banks certainly lets me know if I'm trying to make him act out of character.

Jon: Through the series we see Banks change a bit from book to book as he gets older. Does this reflect your own life at all?

Peter: Perhaps in some ways, but a lot more happens to him than happens to me. He's got more thoughtful and reflective as he's got older, and I suppose I have too. Moving into the 21st Century also encourages one to look back on the 20th Century, to try to make a sensible pattern of it, and that was one of the things I was doing with the '60s in CLOSE TO HOME. But Banks is still Banks, and I'm me.

Jon: Do you ever get into a book and find it taking you some place different than where you thought you were originally going?

Peter: Always. Partly because I don't know where I'm going. I don't outline. I let the characters and events take me places, and sometimes those places turn out to be dead ends. It's not a method I'd recommend. I always tell my students to know how their story ends before they begin writing it, but I don't practice that technique myself.

Jon: Music shows up in your books a lot. Do you listen to music when you write? And what kind of music do you like to listen to in general?

Peter: Yes, I do. Mostly when I'm writing it has to be instrumental music. Lyrics distract me. Sometimes jazz--Bill Evans, John Coltrane, Miles Davis, Milt Jackson--but mostly classical. Right now I have Bax's First Symphony on. Trouble is, I get so caught up in the story I don't even notice when the music's finished half the time. When traveling, I take my portable CD player and more often than not listen to classic rock--Stones, Beatles, Dylan, Dead, Led Zeppelin, Van Morrison, and some more modern stuff--Beth Orton, the White Stripes, the Strokes, System of a Down, David Grey, Radiohead.

Jon: What makes Toronto such a wonderful city?

Peter: It isn't at the moment. It's bloody cold and gray. Mostly, though, it's a relaxed kind of place with all the things you'd expect in a major city--foods from all around the world, opera, sports, concerts, bookshops, everything. We also have the lakefront, beaches and a long boardwalk. And it's very much a literary city. A lot of writers live here-- including fellow crime writers Giles Blunt, Howard Engel, Eric Wright and Alison Gordon.

Jon: In the interview with Michael Connelly, he wanted to know what question you wished he had asked, but he didn't want the answer. Can I have the answer?

Peter: "If you could go back to the beginning and change anything about Banks, what would you change?"

I'd have had him come from Leeds, where I grew up, rather from Peter-borough, which I'd never visited until I was researching CLOSE TO HOME!

Jon: What kind of things did you do before writing full time?

Peter: Mostly teaching and studying.

Jon: Being a writer, like any artistic person, you can probably get lost in your work at times. Is it important to have an understanding family?

Peter: It certainly helps. I like the place to myself, as much quiet as I can get--apart from the music--but that's not always possible. Whatever the situation, you have to work through it somehow. There's always a deadline whooshing by.

Jon: What's something you love to hear from readers?

Peter: How much they love the books and can't put them down.

Jon: Can you remember at what point you first wanted to write?

Peter: I was very young. Five or so. I used to write and illustrate my own stories in a large, hard-backed notebook, legal size. Mostly they were retellings of other stories, such as William Tell and Robin Hood.

Jon: What are your favorite beers?

Peter: I'm very fond of Theakston's Old Peculier, when you can get it on draught. Tetley's and Boddington's are usually quite reliable. I also just had my first pint of Guinness in Dublin, and that's something not to be missed. Nectar. But I'm no beer expert. I don't actually drink much of the stuff, to be honest. I drink more red wine.

Jon: In AFTERMATH the case that Banks is working on really takes a toll on him. Does writing a book like that take its toll on the writer also?

Peter: Well it does engender a nightmare or two. I sometimes wonder whether I give myself the night fears through what I write or whether I write what I do because I have night fears in the first place. It's that sensation where every little noise in the dark takes on sinister significance, and your heart's beating too fast and it won't slow down. You just want the dawn to come but it takes forever.

Jon: Who are some of your favorite writers? Is there an author you think everyone should read?

Peter: Chandler, perhaps, because he was one of the first to turn me on to crime writing, along with Simenon, Rendell and Sjowall and Wahloo. These days I don't get to read as much as I used to, but I enjoy Ian Rankin and Michael Connelly, Reginald Hill and Robert Barnard, Minette Walters and P.D. James, and have more recently discovered Henning Mankell. I also read non-fiction, especially history and biography, and I like novelists such as Graham Greene, Sebastian Faulks, Melvyn Bragg, Jane Urquart and Rohinston Mistry. Fine story-tellers, all.

Jon: How did you spend New Year's eve?

Peter: With a small group of friends eating sushi and drinking Champagne.

Jon: Is there anything about you that people would be surprised to learn?

Peter: That they had no secret shames.

Jon: What's the best time of the day?

Peter: Mid afternoon, when it's time to go to the pub.

Jon: Is there anything we will never see Inspector Banks do?

Peter: Harming a woman or a child.

Jon: What is guaranteed to always make you laugh?

Peter: Put on a Fawlty Towers or Black Adder episode.

Jon: What kind of things do you do to make touring a little easier?

Peter: I try to travel carry-on only and take off my belt, jacket, shoes and watch before walking through the screening machine. I also carry plenty of good books, CDs and DVDs. If the weather's good and I have a couple of hours to spare, I'll go for a long walk—although now my books come out in February this isn't such a good idea in the Midwest.

Jon: In AFTERMATH you opened the book in such a way that the reader knows who did the deed. The actual story is discovering the why and how. It was really a great read I thought because of this. What made you take this approach?

Peter: I've never really thought of myself as a writer of whodunits, though I'm aware that the identity of the killer remains a mystery until close to the end of some of my books. That's why it never really bothers me when people say they figured out whodunit. The stories are about character, conflicts and relationships, the effects of a crime on a community. Any "puzzle" is icing on the cake. AFTERMATH had to be told that way, but I think there's still enough suspense to keep readers interested and alert. One of my favourite books is Ruth Rendell's A JUDGEMENT IN STONE, which opens by explaining exactly what the crime was, who did it, why, and what happened to them afterwards. Yet you still can't put it down!

Jon: I would guess that the person Banks is right now is much different than when you wrote GALLOWS VIEW. Is the growth of the character planned, or is it more a natural progression that you happen to chronicle?

Peter: It's a natural progression. Banks's life is no more planned than the plot of each book is planned. One event grows from another, just as one novel emerges from another. A chance remark in CLOSE TO HOME might form the basis of the next novel, for example, as has happened before. Banks has aged through the series. Especially since his separation and divorce he has become more introverted, reclusive and melancholy. But the scotch and music remain constant pleasures.

Jon: Are you a good guitar player?

Peter: I learned the requisite three or four chords, and if I play them loudly enough, and with enough distortion to cover the fluffed notes, then I sound fine!

Jon: What do you think is the best advice you could give to an aspiring writer?

Peter: Write. Bum in chair, fingers on keyboard. I know it sounds obvious or facetious or whatever, but you wouldn't believe how many writing students I've had who fail to get anywhere not because they lack talent but because they lack application. Too many people want to be writers, but they don't actually want to write.

Jon: What's the one thing always in your refrigerator?

Peter: Leftovers.

Peter Robinson's website:
www.inspectorbanks.com

Peter Robinson's Books:

Gallows View (1987)
A Dedicated Man (1988)
A Necessary End (1989)
The Hanging Valley (1989)
Caedmon's Song (1990)
Past Reason Hated (1992)
Wednesday's Child
Final Account (1994)(UK title, Dry Bones that Dream)
No Cure for Love (1995)
Innocent Graves (1996)
Dead Right (1997)(US title, Blood at the Root)
Not Safe After Dark (1998)
In a Dry Season (1999)
Cold is the Grave (2000)
Aftermath (2001)
The Summer that Never Was (2003))(US title, Close to Home)

Short Stories:

"Fan Mail." First pub. in Cold Blood II, ed. Peter Sellers (Mosaic Press: Oakville, Canada, 1989). Reprinted in Canadian Mystery Stories, ed. Alberto Manguel (Oxford University Press: Toronto, Canada, 1991). Also reprinted in Ellery Queen's   Mystery Magazine (1996)

"Innocence." First pub. in Cold Blood III, ed. Peter Sellers (Mosaic Press: Oakville, Canada, 1990). Reprinted in The Year's Best Mystery and Suspense Stories, 1992, ed. Edward D. Hoch (Walker and Company: New York, 1992).
"Not Safe After Dark." Criminal Shorts, ed. Howard Engel and Eric Wright (Macmillan: Toronto, Canada, 1992).

"Anna Said..." Cold Blood IV, ed. Peter Sellers (Mosaic Press: Oakville, Canada, 1992). Reprinted in First Cases 2, ed. Robert J. Randisi (E.P. Dutton, 1996). An Inspector Banks story.

"Just My Luck." Bouchercon XXII Souvenir Programme Book, 1992.

"Lawn Sale." Cold Blood V, ed. Peter Sellers and John North (Mosaic Press: Oakville, Canada, 1994).

"The Good Partner." Ellery Queen's Mystery Magazine, March, 1994. An Inspector Banks story.

"Summer Rain." Ellery Queen's Mystery Magazine, December, 1994. An Inspector Banks story.

"Carrion."No Alibi, ed. Maxim Jakubowski (Ringpull: Manchester, 1995), also published in the Bouchercon 26 programme and in a signed, limited edition of No Alibi published by Scorpion Press, Gloucester, also in 1995.

"Some Land in Florida." Published in Ellery Queen's Mystery Magazine, Christmas issue, 1996.

"The Wrong Hands." Published in Ellery Queen's Mystery Magazine, April1998.

"The Two Ladies of Rose Cottage." Published in Malice Domestic 6, ed. Elizabeth Foxwell and Martin H. Greenberg (New York: Pocket Books, 1997.)

"Memory Lane." Published in Blue Lightning, edited by John Harvey, Slow Dancer Press (U.K.), 1998, p/b

"In Flanders Fields." Published in Not Safe After Dark, Crippen & Landru (U.S.A.), Oct. 1998.

"Murder in Utopia," in CRIME THROUGH TIME III, ed. Sharan Newman (Berkeley, July, 2000)

"Missing in Action," published in Ellery Queen's Mystery Magazine, November, 2000.

"April in Paris," published in LOVE AND DEATH, edited by Carolyn Hart (Berkley), February, 2001

S J Rozan

It would be hard to say which is more interesting the novels of SJ Rozan or the author herself. The Novels are set in New York, described lovingly as only a born and bred New Yorker could, and feature two of the most real characters in detective fiction. With each book, Bill Smith, a jaded, brooding fellow in his late thirties, and Lydia Chin, a twenty-something Chinese-American, evolve and develop as they are affected by the people encountered and complex moral issues tackled within the story. It is these things that help make it one of the freshest and vibrant series today.

Not to be outdone by these amazing stories, is the lady herself. An architect in her other life, Miz Rozan has also been a self defense instructor, a janitor, house painter and sold jewelry. She is witty, articulate and passionate about everything in her life, including basketball.. She has described herself as a" lousy, but dogged point guard". Don't you believe this for a second! I can tell you from first hand experience that, on the court, she can reduce 6 foot men to blubbering masses. On the court, as in her novels, this lady has got game! - Jeremy Lynch

Jon: How would you describe your books to some one who hasn't read them yet?

SJ: The Bill Smith books: hard-boiled, dark. The Lydia Chin books: a little less hard-edged. Both: deeply involved with place, concerned with moral issues.

Jon: The idea of switching the focus back and forth from Lydia and Bill is really a great one. What made you do that?

SJ: Having invented Lydia at first as a sidekick for Bill, it occurred to me I'd worked really hard to create someone who thought very differently from him and I'd be wasting her if I didn't take the opportunity to find out what it was she was thinking.

Jon: What made you want to write the first book?

SJ: I was working as an architect (my first profession) and I had a great job. It truly was a great job; but I wasn't happy. When I started to wonder why, a little voice in my head reminded me I'd always wanted to be a writer, and what I'd always wanted to write was crime.

Jon: In addition to being a writer, you are also an architect, what other jobs have you had?

SJ: Janitor, jewelry sales, house painting, book sales, bread baking, advertising copywriter (VERY briefly), self-defense instructor.

Jon: Have any of these other professions added your writing?

SJ: All of them. It's all material. And the people you meet...

Jon: What kind of research do you do? When I ran into you at Bouchercon you had just come back from shooting. That seems   pretty hands on!

SJ: I love research. I do as much as I can -- interviewing people; visiting factories, restaurant kitchens, sweatshops; walking streets; sitting in cafes; driving, reading, shooting. The more you know about a place or a world the better you can bring it alive.

Jon: Have you had any television or Hollywood interest in the books?

SJ: Some. They keep nibbling without biting, but we (my agent and I) keep tying flies.

Jon: Do you ever run into road blocks when you write? Something that just doesn't work? And what do you do about it?

SJ: I never know it doesn't work until I've written it. I once wrote a scene in which Bill Smith went to talk to a guy. After two pages of talking the guy's dog came into the room and, I wrote, "...looked from one of us to the other, wagging his tail and waiting for something to happen." As soon as I read what I'd written I thought, me, too, dog. And that was the end of that scene -- straight to the garbage file. So no, I've never had a block, but I've produced some seriously useless junk. But that's the stuff that primes the pump so the useful stuff can come out later.

Jon: I think your portrayal of New York is a key part of the books and your feel for the city is wonderful. Are you a native?

SJ: Born and brought up in the Bronx. I love this city and I especially want to show readers parts of it they don't usually see in books or movies -- the Bronx, Chinatown, Queens.

Jon: What's the coolest part of being a writer? How about downsides?

SJ: There is, to me, no thrill like the thrill of writing something I know is working. The downside is, if it's not working, there's no one in the room with you whom you can turn to and share the problem with (or blame it on).

Jon: What authors do you like to read?

SJ: John LeCarre, Margaret Atwood, Raymond Chandler, Ross Macdonald, P.D. James, Kazuo Ishiguro, Don Winslow, Keith Snyder.

Jon: Basketball. Better to watch or play?

SJ: I have more fun playing, but I watch better than I play.

Jon: What's the best advice you were ever given?

SJ: From Annie Dillard, THE WRITING LIFE: (Paraphrase): Never save anything for a better book or a better place in this book. Ideas bubble up from below like water in a well. If you don't take the ones off the top you don't get the next ones.

Jon: This is a little off the path, but I want to know. What's your favorite comic strip?

the UK, I'm now gearing up for the huge thrill of publication in the US which is one book behind. I find the whole process of checking proofs, looking at jacket designs - all of it- immensely exciting. Maybe I won't in a few years time, but at the moment I'm still pinching myself...

Jon: What other jobs have you had?

Mark: I'm also a stand-up comic and I was a jobbing actor, so it would be true to say that I've never done a proper day's work in my life. Hang on, I did work as a cleaner at a holiday camp one summer just before I went to University but I got scared after a few weeks and came home. I was working on the night shift with some very rough characters. One guy was a punk rocker who was trying to look like Sid Vicious from the Sex Pistols. He worked in the kitchens, and every day after he'd unloaded the meat he would put handfuls of fresh blood from the meat trays into his hair to get just the right amount of spikiness. He also had a padlock on a chain around his neck. It was a nice image, but unfortunately he'd lost the key and his neck was turning green. These were scary people. These were the sort of people who, because I had stayed at school beyond the age of fourteen, called me "professor"...

Jon: Does Thorne have any of you in him?

Mark: Well, he's around the same age and he likes a little of the same music, but aside from that, not really. He's definitely shorter than me! Sometimes if the character is musing about the state of London - the public transport, the health service, whatever, he may voice an opinion or two that I happen to share, but I don't see the point in just putting yourself on the page. It's fiction, not autobiography. I certainly have a much different life from Tom Thorne in domestic terms. Thorne is, to say the least, unsettled, but that of course goes with the territory. Cops have unhappy love lives and dark pasts in the same way that cowboys have six guns and Stetsons. I'm sure there are detectives who have perfectly blissful private lives and go home to their families every night and drink hot chocolate and watch television. I'm just not interested in reading about those characters and certainly not in writing about them.

Jon: Do your friends read this book and wonder about all this dark twisted stuff in your head?

Mark: Yes, there was a certain amount of that, a few odd looks. I think book, called, at least for now, ABSENT FRIENDS. A break from the series, not an end to it -- Smith and Chin will be back. Every now and then you need to clear your writing palate, as it were.

Jon: Looking back on your previous books, have you written anything that caused an exceptional amount of feedback?

SJ: No, but I'm expecting that from WINTER AND NIGHT, because it's about football, and you can't knock football in the US without hearing about it. Please note: I'm not down on football. I'm down on a certain type of adult and their approach to kids playing football. Okay?

Jon: So tell the world SJ, is there anything about you that would surprise people?

SJ: I doubt it. I'm really pretty straightforward. What you see is what's there.

Jon: Who is easier to write, Bill or Lydia?

SJ: Both the same. When I'm finishing a book in one voice, I can't wait to get to the other. His darkness can depress me and her optimism can be annoying.

Jon: Can you think of anything that you really regret having spent money on?

SJ: What an interesting question! Except for the occasional piece of clothing that one or the other of my sisters manages to talk me into, no, I don't think I can. Certainly nothing big, travel or anything like that.

Mark Billingham

Mark and I became friendly a couple of years ago when he came to interview me for Shots magazine about my books. As we talked, we realised a strange set of parallels in our lives. We're both huge Elvis Costello fans. Our favourite play is Trevor Griffiths' Comedians. Our wives both work in the entertainment business (TV director and theatre costume designer respectively). Our kids are the same age and same sex as each other. We were freeloading in the same flat at the same time during the Edinburgh festival in the Eighties, with the cast of a cubist interpretation of The Government Inspector (don't ask). We've both worked as stand up comics (although Mark has been much more successful at it than me). And, of course, we have a huge interest in crime fiction. As Elvis Costello said, 'In time we can turn these obsessions into careers.'

*And he has. Mark has had three books published now – **Sleepyhead**, **Scaredy Cat** and **Lazy Bones**. With them he has swiftly defined and cornered the market in North London serial killer noir, with hard bitten, cynical, loner cop, Tom Thorne, tracking down man (and woman)-created monsters in a world instantly recognisable as our own. Told with whiplash, diamond-hard prose, they're all deservedly critically and commercially acclaimed. If you haven't read them yet, do so straight away. You'll be in for a treat.- Martyn Waites (author of Born Under Punches)*

Jon: What can you tell us about your first book? Is it the start of a series?

Mark: Yes it is. SLEEPYHEAD is the first in a series of books featuring Detective Inspector Tom Thorne and a cast of supporting characters! In this first novel, Thorne is on the trail of a man who deliberately induces strokes in his victims and has left three women dead and a fourth in a coma. The police think that in leaving this woman alive, the killer has made his first mistake. The horrifying discovery Thorne makes early on is that it is the dead women that are the killer's mistakes. The fourth victim, Alison Willetts, is his one success. Alison lies in a hospital bed

SJ Rozan's Books:

China Trade (1994)
Concourse (1995)
Mandarin Plaid (1996)
No Colder Place (1997)
A Bitter Feast (1998)
Stone Quarry (1999)
Reflecting the Sky (2001)
Winter and Night (2002)
Absent Friends (2004)

Barbara Seranella

Stella Duffy and
Barbara Seranella

photo by Ann Chernow

I'm not quite sure how Barbara Seranella does it. NO HUMAN IN-VOLVED introduced readers to one of Mystery's most unique characters. Munch Mancini is a woman who had seen and done more by age twenty than most people do in a lifetime. And none of it was pretty. Addiction, prostitution, theft; all of these are a part of Munch. So too is a talent for making a car run and as the series progresses her mechanical skills provide our protagonist with a sense of self worth that allows her to beat her demons. Almost.

Munch hasn't remained the person in NO HUMAN INVOLVED. She'd be dead if she had. She has surrounded herself with people who care. She has taken steps towards a better life. Still, the past continues to, not nip at her heels, no, the past slashes her Achilles tendon in every book. And time and time again this gives readers someone to cheer for and a mystery to scratch their heads over.

I don't know how Ms. Seranella does it, but I'm very glad she does.
-Ruth Jordan

Jon: How would you describe Miranda 'Munch' Mancini?

 Barbara: She is pragmatic. She deals with her problems by being morally courageous, practical, and honest. All of these traits go through her own filter and might not meet society norms. Part of the advantage of being an ex-junkie, hooker, hell-raiser is that the small things don't get to her. She doesn't judge people for anything other that who they are now and what they are doing now.

Jon: Like Munch you actually worked in a service station. Were you also a mechanic? How about driving limos?

Barbara: I was an auto mechanic for twenty years. Technically, I still am since the knowledge didn't go away. I started working on cars when I was 15 and living in a hippie commune in the Haight. I quit officially in 1993 when I was 36 to pursue the writing life. I had my own limo company for four years. It was a horrible business and cost me much more than I ever made. But nothing bad ever happens to a writer. I'm using all those experiences now to get
Munch into situations.

Jon: Do you have a favorite among the books?

Barbara: I hate that question. It's like being asked if you have a favorite child. The book I'm most excited about is the one I've just written or the one I'm working on. In the process of editing and proofing, I have to read my own books so many times that I lose all objectivity. Every so often I go back and read an earlier book after letting it sit for a while and I always end up thinking (in all modesty), "Hey, this is pretty good."

Jon: I saw that your first published work was in Easy Rider magazine. I'm guessing that wasn't a real high paying gig. Does any one still call you Crazy Barbara?

Barbara: They actually sent me a check for $125 which was a small fortune to me in those days. No one calls me Crazy Barbara to my face. I have no idea what they whisper behind my back. I once spoke to an assembly of kids-at-risk at the high school I never went to because I dropped out. The first question from the audience was, "If you went to court today, would you be declared legally insane?" Another kid wanted to know if I had any diseases now. I found out later he had AIDS. The hardest question I got that day was, "If you were going to commit suicide, how would you do it?"

Jon: It says on your website that you may be the only member of Sisters In Crime who was actually ever a criminal. Is this something you can elaborate on?? Or would it be better to just say "that's   really interesting and move on?

Barbara: It's all public information anyway. By the time I was 22, I had been arrested 13 times. (This was in an article written about me in the LA Times. My husband read the article and turned to me aghast. "You were arrested 13 times?" I'm sure I mentioned it. Sometimes he doesn't pay attention) Anyway, I served over a month in Sybil Brand Institute for Women in L.A. because the judge wouldn't set bail until I got all my charges under all my different names cleared up. My dear father hired a lawyer and I was given three years probation and one year in prison, suspended.

Coincidentally, this is about the time I got clean and sober and so successfully completed the probation and didn't have to serve any more time.

Jon: What prompted you to start writing?

Barbara: I've always wanted to be a writer, ever since I was a little girl and first began to read. I met my husband in1991. He came in to be my boss at the gas station where I was wrenching. We fell in love. He didn't want me working on cars when I was forty. He felt it would be too hard on my body, and encouraged me to pursue my dream. Without his financial and emotional backing, Munch Mancini would probably never have happened. My back is giving me   problems now. So I probably lifted one transmission too many. Not to mention the aches you get from sitting hours hunched at a computer. I guess there's no way to escape the ravages of aging.

Jon: You've lead an interesting life so far: hippie commune, motorcycle clubs, becoming an auto mechanic. Do you think that this gives you an advantage in your writing?

Barbara: Certainly for the subject matter I write about. If I had lived a different life, I'd be writing about other things. Who knows? Maybe in that other life I would still be a practicing alcoholic. A housewife in the suburbs. Or I might have been ruined by a formal education.

Jon: I quit drinking back in '96. One of the first things I noticed when getting sober was the change in my sleep habits. Thus, more reading, and thank god for the internet! But it also allowed me to focus on things and concentrate like I haven't in years. Also, people seem really surprised that I'm so willing to talk about it. I figure that it's part of who I am. I don't want to repeat it, but it also got me to where I am now. Any similar experiences?

Barbara: The program dictates that we don't ignore our past or shut the door on it. We're only as sick as our secrets is another good cliche. Also, when we freely and honestly come forth, we reach others and hopefully help them. I think everyone has innate bullshit detectors and when you're not completely honest, it's picked up on. I know when I think someone is bullshitting, I'm turned off immediately and tend to stop paying attention. Personally, I love attention so I don't want that. Writers write because they have something to say.

Jon: How important do you think the side characters are to a series? In yours people like Mace St.John and Ellen seem to really fill out the books.

Barbara: It's always fun to create new and interesting characters. I love Mace St. John. Ellen is great because she's unpredictable, whereas Munch has to toe a certain line. In the book I'm working on now (Munch #7), Asia has a viewpoint and she's a cool little kid.

Jon: The glimpses back to Munch's hell raising days really add to the character. I think part of that is because they make what she has now more important. Do you think Miranda will ever totally conform and settle down, or will she always be a product of her past?

Barbara: In the next book, UNPAID DUES, which will be published by Scribner next year, we see a lot of Munch in the bad old days. The story line revolves around an incident that happened ten years previous (to the 1985 time setting of the series) with Munch and her cohorts. I wrote several scenes set in the mid-seventies showing Munch at the height of her despair and using. It's a very powerful and gritty book. The next one I'm working on (#7) brings back Asia's aunt (her father's sister) from book #2, NO OFFENSE INTENDED. Lisa has been away in the Witness Protection Program all this time. I only work on one book at a time. So I don't know what will happen next yet.

Jon: What kind of things fill your time when you aren't writing? I get the impression you and your husband like to golf.

Barbara: We live on a golf course. I like golf, maybe once or twice a month. I play tennis twice a week "in season." We have three dogs who we devote a lot of time to. I swim, walk, go to movies, and read, read, read. My husband thinks I read too much.

Jon: Are you a good golfer, or do you play strictly for love of the game?

Barbara: Ahem. So glad you asked. I play in the club's 9-holer group. Last year I won the club championship.

Jon: Have you had any interesting experiences while doing research?

Barbara: Oh gee, tons. I go to prisons, strip clubs, cement block manufacturers. Whatever. That's a whole other interview. As much as possible I like to go places and talk to people rather that getting my information from the internet. And of course ride-alongs are a lot of fun.

Jon: Do you write on a regular schedule, set hours each day, or more like binge writing?

Barbara: I leave the computer on all the time and sit down when the mood strikes me. Fortunately, it strikes often.

Jon: What do you think is the best looking Harley made? And, any plans to come to Milwaukee next summer for the 100 year anniversary?

Barbara: I'm torn between the Panhead and the Knucklehead. I always thought the Shovelhead was boring, and I got in a terrible accident and knocked out my teeth on a Sportster. Basically I like them chopped, lots of chrome, Springer front end, pull back handlebars, Black tank and fenders. If I had one super power, it would be Teleportation. Then I could go in the blink of an eye to all the places I'd like to. If they invent a transporter for home use by next year, I'll come to Milwaukee.

Jon: I think the realism of your characters is part of what makes your books a joy to read. It's easier to connect with a protagonist who isn't rich and driving a Porsche, and who's solving mysteries for fun... Is having the characters come off as real important?

Barbara: I think so. I want to believe the story I'm reading. I want to get lost in it. I don't want to feel the author is making the whole thing up or envision the writer at work at the computer.

Jon: Is there any subject you wouldn't write about? And why?

Barbara: Jeez. Never say never. I did start writing my last book about a dead kid and I couldn't handle it, so I changed the story line to having the murder victim clutching a life-size doll in death and that was just as interesting. It did take me 200 pages to figure out what part the doll played in the story. That's a cool aspect of the writing process. I become a detective. I have to make sense of the clues as they present themselves.

Jon: The mystery genre seems to attract very loyal fans. Aside from the Sci-Fi/fantasy readers I can't think of a group more loyal. And most of the authors are every bit fans as well. Why do you think that is? What is it about mysteries that hooks people?

Barbara: Well, first of all, we're all such darn nice, interesting, smart people. I think about this a lot actually. I think after reading good thriller/crime novels/ mysteries, you get jaded. Nothing raises the stakes like murder or life and death scenarios. Wondering if some college professor is going to leave his wife just doesn't hold the same punch.

Jon: What kind of music do you enjoy?

Barbara: Rock n Roll. 70s and 80s mostly.

Jon: Who are some of the authors you enjoy reading?

Barbara: Just read HELL TO PAY by George Pelecanos. Terrific book. Mike Connelly, S.J. Rozan, Dennis Lehane, Martha Lawrence, The Harry Potter Books, Harlan Coban, Martin Cruz Smith. I just finished

LITTLE AMERICA by Henry Brommel. Phenomenal use of language and setting. Again, a difficult question because I read so much and don't want to not mention many friends. These are just the first that come to mind because I read them most recently.

Jon: With all the events you attend, what is the coolest panel you've done?

Barbara: GM Ford moderated a great panel at Left Coast this last March in Portland, I also had a lot of fun with Martha Lawrence when Left Coast was in Tucson. And let us not forget sitting up there with Walter Mosley and Elmore Leonard in Denver. That was so amazing I kept checking my watch, which Walter teased me about.

Jon: I've heard that your books have been optioned for a possible TV show. What's the news on that front?

Barbara: I'm still waiting to hear. Two men are writing the pilot. They haven't asked me for any input. Last I heard they were shopping it to USA. Two years ago, before it was optioned by Studio USA, my agent tried to get HBO interested, but they passed because it was too dark. Can you imagine? I'd like to put that on the book jacket.

Jon: Any thoughts on writing something outside the series at some point?

Barbara: I feel like I should, but I'm very content to stay with Munch for now. I love sci-fi and the possibilities of creating universes where anything can happen. I don't really have a solid enough science background to write the things I like, but maybe some day I'll do something along those lines.

Jon: While writing is definitely an art form, it's also your job and the business you are in. Does the business end of things ever influence your writing?

Barbara: I fight that. I can only write the kind of books I write. Pandering to the taste of the majority is not something I'm capable of. I'm not in it for the money or fame, but I do need sales to keep being published. I try to give each book my best shot with promotion after it is published. I also try to write the best book I can every time out and hope that pays off in the long run.

Jon: When you are working what tends to be your worst distraction?

Barbara: Spider solitaire, a horrible mind-numbing addiction. Avoidance of attacking the blank page and having to figure out what happens next. Also, getting really good, exciting news can be as paralyzing as receiving horrible news. In the end, all life experiences are grist for the mill.

Jon: Over the course of the series, does the growth of the characters happen naturally , or is it planned out in advance?

Barbara: Sometimes I salt the mine with some unresolved issues that can come back and haunt the stories later. For instance, was Flower George really Munch's father or is there someone else out there who is going to pop up and claim the title? In the next book UNWILLING AC-COMPLICE coming out in May, 2004, there is a stolen ring with a blue stone that is never accounted for and might return in the future. These are all plot related tidbits.

As to character growth, I let them lead the way according to what happens to them in each book, what they learn, how their perceptions are altered. Munch's attitudes about cops and criminals and men are very extreme. The pendulum is still swinging there.

Jon: What's the one thing always in your refrigerator?

Barbara: Milk, ice water, Snapple, and non-alcoholic beer. Good question. The freezer always has chocolate.

Barbara Seranella's website:
www.barbaraseranella.com

Barbara Seranella's Books:
No Human Involved (1998)
No Offense Intended (1999)
Unwanted Company (2000)
Unfinished Business (2001)
No Man Standing (2002)
Unpaid Dues (2003)
Unwilling Accomplice (2004)

Charles Todd

Charles Todd with Jon & Ruth Jordan

I met Charles Todd back in 1999 while he was touring his latest book. A few months later I hung out with him quite a bit at Bouchercon here in Milwaukee. I find him to be an extremely likable person. He's a wonderful story teller and very funny. He was actually there when I met my wife Ruth. A few years went by before I saw him again. In the time between I heard speculations on what Charles Todd's real name might be (He writes under a pseudonym). In 2002 Charles revealed that the books are actually written by two people, himself and his mother, who goes by Caroline Todd.

In DC that year at Bouchercon seeing Charles was one of the highlights of the convention for me. To make it even more fun, we got to meet his Mother and Father. Having met them, it was easy to see why Charles is such a nice guy. His parents are great! If I ever get tired of being a Jordan I would ask them to adopt me.

My love for them as people aside, the books are wonderful. The series is set in England after World War One. They are written with such emotion and feeling that it is easy to get lost in the story being told. The characters are so real I kind of wonder if maybe the Todd family has a time machine hidden away somewhere.—Jon

Jon: Why the early 1900's and why England?

Charles: I was more interested in the psychology of murder than the science of it. A character who used his own wits, intuition and knowledge of people to solve a crime. No forensic lab second-guessing him. At the same time, 1919 gave me a modern mind-set that would be familiar to readers. Best of all worlds! I wanted to say that here's a man who has spent four years killing people and now he's come home to arrest people for killing people. An intriguing premise to work with. Having killed, do you understand the motivations better?? Instead I've discovered that he's more attuned to what drives people to murder and he listens to what is said to him. As for England, I think the village appealed to me. It is, in a sense, a "locked room" mystery.

Jon: Rutledge and his thinking process seems timeless. Do you think he would work as well in a different time period?

Charles: He is very close to us in his time and place, and he seems familiar to us, recognizable in his attitudes and clothing and means of getting around. If you were born before the Sixties, you knew his world. If you were born afterward, it seems historical but not stiff and dusty. If you've been to war in this century, you know what he went through and how it marked him. If you care about people, you understand the men and women he has to question. That's my definition of timeless. I don't know about other periods--the man himself, yes, but he'd be shaped differently inside. Different influences tend to do that.

Jon: You wrote the poetry for WINGS OF FIRE. Any desire to do a whole book of poetry?

Charles: When I tried to draw the reclusive and elusive woman behind the war poems, I suddenly realized that the reader had to know her through her work--and so did I. It was, after all, her voice. That's the sort of thing you get yourself into sometimes. I don't know if I'd ever do a whole volume. You'd have to find somebody crazy enough to ask me, and then I'd think about it.

Jon: How much research do you have to do for the books?

Charles: It never stops. It helps that I like history. And I'm notoriously fascinated by how things work. The big stuff is a little easier--the war, the background of the setting, how people thought--because of excellent primary sources. The hard part is the thing you never think about until you've got yourself in the middle of it. Ever cranked a car? Did they lick stamps in 1919? If there weren't any petrol stations, where did it come from? Did they have batteries for torches (flashlights) back then? What about the telephone or lighting or paved roads?

I'm always mentally taking notes when I hear anything that might be useful.

Jon: How disciplined is your writing? Do you write every morning, or when the mood is right, any kind of schedule?

Charles: I don't have a schedule. I have to feel in the mood. Then it drives me. I think the most important thing is to figure out when / how you do your best writing, and stick to that. Morning or midnight doesn't matter. Number of words doesn't matter. I write a scene until it burns out, then stop. Past that, it's not going to be any good anyway. So I may do chapters a day, or paragraphs. Or nothing. But my mind keeps going twenty-four hours while the work is in progress. That's the real secret.

Jon: If you could go back in time and talk to yourself at eighteen, what advice would you pass on?

Charles: That's hard! Nobody can see at 18 where they might be heading in life. So I'd probably say, Look, you think you're "there", that what you're doing and feeling right now is the "real world." It's only the start. The next ten years are the real world. After that, you're building on what you are, and what you've done, and what you've learned. So don't blow it before you've even given the next ten a chance. Then look back at 28 and tell me if I was wrong.

Jon: What else have you done besides writing books?

Charles: Gotten a good education. Traveled. Learned to do some things I wanted to do. Fished. Found out something about vintage cars and how to play golf. Found out that life is not always fair, and that there's no ref to blow the whistle when things go wrong. Learned that happiness is small things. Taught myself patience.

Jon: What authors do you enjoy reading?

Charles: I enjoy a good novel. It doesn't matter whether it was written by or about a woman or a man, as long as it's good. I liked Steve Hamilton's first novel and am looking forward to his next. I think Charles Knieff does a terrific suspense novel. I like Margaret Maron's Deborah Knott series, but if Deborah's Dad dies, I'll rethink that. He's one of the great characters. SJ Rozan has a hard edge and that's a change of pace. I wish I had more time to read. My parents were readers, my grandparents--there were always books available, and that's important, raising children.

Jon: You've had some great covers. Do you have any say in that? Or do you cross your fingers once you hand in the finished book?

Charles: You cross your fingers. That's the publisher's choice. But if you absolutely hate a jacket, and can give them a very good reason just as soon as you see the proof, they will listen. "Red isn't my favorite color" doesn't count. But I think St. Martin's has done a terrific job with mine. I think the English covers have been great too. I hope my luck holds.

Jon: Have you always written fiction, or did you just start recently?

Charles: I've always been good at expressing myself on paper--or computer. That seems to run in the family. So you can say I've been writing for years. Rutledge somehow came together on his own, he was just "there" one day, dug out of the subconscious or wherever such things grow. C. S. Forester called it finding barnacles on a sunken hull. I really liked A TEST OF WILLS--I just never realized that so many other people would like it too.

Jon: Do you enjoy meeting fans and other authors?

Charles: That's the best part of conventions and signings. It's important to hear your readers. And I'm still a fan myself. I've never been good with crowds, I'm not used to being a center of attention. I'm still trying to learn to deal with it.

Jon: Any thoughts on optioning the books for a movie?

Charles: The funny thing is, I know how some scenes could play out on the screen--that's how I write, it runs in my head like a film. The right director could take the mood and make it into something powerful. You'd have to find an actor who could bring Rutledge to life--the way Harrison Ford did with Jack Ryan. Fans write to me with suggestions about that. It's interesting to see who they cast.

Jon: Rutledge seems like a very old soul. Are people surprised when they see someone your age has written it?

Charles: People never ask about my age, they're more surprised to find that I'm not English. Actually Rutledge is typical of his time and place, just as John Rebus is typical of present-day Scotland or Morse works so well in present-day Oxford. Rutledge is educated, well read, thoughtful--like thousands of other Englishmen in 1919. He has the angst of his time (the war) and not the angst of 1999. Which probably makes him seem like a very old soul! Englishmen in his era would see him as typical of his class and background. And that's what I strive to write, because I owe it to the historical genre to make him fit his world.

Jon: Do you use an outline when you write, or do you find out what is going to happen as you go?

Charles: I can't outline. Even in high school I was the despair of my teachers. If I try, the story gets stiff and lifeless. The characters sort of drag around.

Charles and Caroline Todd

So I let them tell me what's going on. It doesn't mean I don't have control, only that I listen to them and try to see what they--if they were real people I knew--would do in such circumstances. That may be why so many people tell me that they find the characters very believable. One reviewer said that they moved her because she could see them so clearly.

Jon: What do you do to relax?

Charles: I watch TV. No, I think if you told me tomorrow that I'd have a week off and all the money I'd need to do my favorite thing, I'd go to a beach somewhere and watch the waves roll in. Most of the time I do what everybody else does: watch sports, take in a good movie, find a new restaurant, read a good book, wash the car, play a round of golf with friends, explore a place I've never been. And my family is important to me.

Jon: What kind of movies do you enjoy?

Charles: That's easy. Suspense. Mysteries. A REAL comedy. Something thought-provoking. I'm not into "meaningful". I generally go for the actor and the plot. I like Harrison Ford films, because they're fast paced and interesting. Steve Martin can be good--or terrible. Julia Roberts. I won't stay with a movie that bores me. I'll watch a great one more than once. The writing has to be good, and the acting has to live up to it.

Jon: What is the one thing that is always in your icebox?

Charles: Some ice. One of the cats likes ice in his water dish, and when I come in at night, that's the first thing I have to do. Even when I've been out of town for weeks, he doesn't let me forget.

Charles Todd Interview Part two
(This part was done two years after the first, with both Charles and Caroline Todd)

Jon: So a few things have changed since the last time we did this. Book number five has just come out. And we know that Charles Todd is in fact -- two people. So I guess the first question I have is, how did the idea to collaborate on the books come about?

Charles: With great hilarity....

Seriously, I thought Caroline was joking and I gave her a series of off the wall titles that we could play around with. Then I promptly forgot about it until I was stuck in a hotel room with nothing to do but watch re-runs on tv, and it seemed like something we ought to explore.

Caroline: I knew all along that we were going to do it, but I had to wait until he stopped laughing.

Jon: I have to say that seeing the two of you together at the nomination ceremony for the Anthony Awards kind of choked me up a little. Is it fun to do these things together?

Charles: It really is. Caroline has her fans, I have mine, and we are often off doing separate meetings or breakfasts, or whatever. The thing is, we don't live together, so when we do have a chance to visit like this, it's nice. My dad puts up with the two of us, but I think that he thinks we're both crazy. Taking after Caroline's side of the family tree, of course. But he works with us, driving the cars in England and taking a lot of photographs while we do research. He's a scientist, but enjoys reading mysteries too.

Jon: Are there advantages to working together with family?

Charles: Yes. We pretty much know each other's limits and that makes it easier. Also there's no sense of competition. We both care about Rutledge, and his needs are paramount. After five books, he's more real than ever, and I think that's what makes the whole thing work--we're more interested in him than ourselves.

Jon: So far, all the books have Rutledge being sent to small towns to investigate crimes. At some point will we get to see him do his thing in London?

Charles: He will occasionally do something in London, but in 1919 London was becoming more cosmopolitan, moving on towards the 'Twenties'. And that's a different ball game. We aren't particularly interested yet in getting ahead of ourselves. And in the closed room atmosphere of a village, we see more of the psychological interaction that makes the characters work so well.

Caroline: A village.. isn't a village.. isn't a village.. Each one is so different because of its history and its setting and individual development. There's more variety in writing about other parts of England than in sticking with London. Economic status divides London's population, but other things influence a villager's place in the scheme of its story.

Jon: At Bouchercon you told me about taking a family trip to England and doing research. Could you talk a little about that? It sounds wonderful.

Charles: It was wild. We had nine days because I work for a living and am always trying to save vacation time for conventions like Malice (Domestic) and Bouchercon. We began with meticulous planning, knowing what we wanted to do, where, and for how long. We got to Heathrow, and only Caroline's suitcase had arrived with us. Dad never got his and roughed it for nine days. We were so tired we set out the wrong way on the 'M' outside Heathrow, and it was two exits before we caught on. I got out my trusty GPS and started plotting the way to Kent, and we used that system the remainder of the trip. What we saw in Kent turned into the next book after WATCHERS OF TIME -- A FEARSOME DOUBT. We had great dinners in small country hotels.

Caroline: The English do know how to cook!!

Charles: But we picked up meat pies, cider, and bread and cheese for lunch, or ate in a pub. In between we were concentrating on all the things we had to photograph. We had a flat tire out in Norfolk on the narrowest of roads, and the only safe area to change it was in a mud puddle. We got to the town that was to become Osterley, and were fascinated by the great church there. It came into the story at that point. We tasted some Italian plum cognac in Colchester, and it gave a whole new meaning to jet lag. My dad's suitcase reached us in Eton, the night before we flew out. He looked great at dinner -- the only one with still-pressed clothes. But out of that short trip, we revisited some old and well-loved sights, climbed Tintangle again, found some new ideas and interesting places for later books, and we worked on WATCHERS and A FEARSOME DOUBT. Thirty-six rolls of film later...

Jon: Hamish MacLeod -- he's seems to be both a partner and a conscience to Rutledge. Where did this idea come from? How does the character of Hamish fit into the books?

Charles: We were interested in using The Great War as a backdrop to the story, and looking for ways to indicate that Rutledge had been a serving officer and how the war had affected him personally.

Suddenly we realized that we were looking at a man who had already addressed that problem in his own fashion. Hamish was his creation, not ours, and it seemed to be far more realistic than any superimposed idea on our part.

He's there in the books as Rutledge's conscience, his war wound. Here's a man who once hunted murderers--and now he considers himself one. It adds compassion and understanding and a far more personal view of the cases he investigates. He's not arrogant and he's not set apart from the people he has to question. He realizes that he's as human and vulnerable as they are.

Jon: The covers of your books are really stunning. Do you have much of a say in the cover choices?

Charles: No, but they show us the final design for any comments. Both of my editors have had the essence of the books in mind. Now they want to change the style of the jacket art a little. The books are enjoying such widespread readership that the feeling is it should reach even more people, some of whom might never pick up an historical cover. I can't wait to see what they come up with. Knowing Bantam, it will be in great taste.

Jon: Is reading something that you shared as a family? Are you both mystery fans?

Charles: My parents came from families that read all kinds of books: biography, history, literature, poetry--you name it. They also liked mysteries. I can remember Caroline reading aloud Sherlock Holmes and 'The Gold Bug' and other stories when I was very young.

We like suspense films, we watch mysteries on tv, we read more than we really have time for, and we have our favorites. But the more important thing is that we were read to when young, all of us, and it had a lasting effect. It's a family legacy, and something to pass on to every generation.

Jon: Who are some of your favorite authors?

Charles: (What -- you want to get us killed?!?)

Caroline: I like Tony Hillerman, Dorothy Dunnett, Frederick Forsyth and Jack Higgins. That's a varied group, but you see the influences. We read our contemporaries too. Margaret Maron's Judge Deborah Knott series, Nevada Barr's national park tales, Ian Rankin, Val McDermid, Steve Hamilton, Robin Hathaway, P.D. James, Elena Santangelo, S.J. Rozan, Parnell Hall...

I could sit here for half an hour talking about this. the exciting thing is to meet these people at conventions--to reach out and touch authors you admire. We also make an effort to try new writers, because you never have enough favorites.

Charles: I discovered a lot of new writers when I did the best first novel judging. speaking of favorites, Peter Lovesey was at Boucher-con, and he's a great guy. I remember watching his Sergeant Cribb series on Mystery. Little did I guess that I'd actually wind up knowing him as a person. I'd second Caroline's list an give you another half an hour.

Jon: When you began writing the first book, did you have any idea that it would be so wildly popular?

Charles: No. We weren't even going to send it in to an agent. Nobody would be interested, we weren't sure of that. Then we decided to send it to Ruth Cavin, just to find out if it was really a novel--we only wanted her to say something like, "I have enjoyed reading this manu-script, but--" and it would in a way give us a sense that we hadn't done too badly after all. Sort of that last flourish before putting the book away and looking for something else to work on together. I'd seen this neat video on building your own helicopter... but it's also why we just used the one name--didn't most collaborators?

Look at Emma Lathen or Maan Myers. And we intend to keep it that way, one name. Before you feel too sorry for Caroline, remember that Charles and Caroline have the same root. I told you she was clever.

Jon: How would you describe Rutledge?

Charles: I don't think we ever have. He's tall, to begin with, that's come out. And he has dark eyes, probably dark hair. The Celtic background, we think. He has an aquiline nose, like one of our ances-tors, and he has a compassionate nature. And when he smiles, and it touches eyes, you see something other than the thin haunted ex-soldier trying to survive. A glimpse into the man who lived before the war. Everyone tells us he's a very attractive man, and even sexy. But that wasn't what we were setting out to write. It's what others see in him.

More importantly, he cares about people and is interested in them. He can empathize while standing back to judge someone's involvement in a murder. He's attracted to interesting women, and that comes through sometimes in his relationships with them. Each one in her own way contributes to the healing process of losing his Jean. And a good show that he did. She wouldn't have made him happy.

Jon: With the publishing business being the way it is, most authors need to do at least some self-promotion. Does your
website help with this? What else do you do to spread the word?

Charles: Budgets are always tight for promotion, unless you've already sold 40 million copies. Then they try for 41. The publisher has ads out there for the series, and we were in the Sisters In Crime author's list in Publisher's Weekly this fall. Conventions are one of the best ways to reach readers, because it's so personal. And we get to as many as possible. We try to work with bookstores, because they support us and we sign boxes of books for them. They often hand sell us, and we appreciate that more than we can say. We answer all the messages from the website guest book, and it's interesting to see that there are many international readers as well as an American cross-section. The ages of readers is a cross-section too--we have everyone from high school students to people in their eighties. We do interviews when asked, because it's another way of reaching people. Keeps us busy!

Jon: When you plot out the books, do you think it's important to be fair with the reader and give them a chance to solve the mystery?

Charles: You have to be fair to the reader. All the clues are there, and it is just a question of how you put them together as to whether you figure out the murderer before the author does. A writer isn't trying to show he's / she's superior to everyone else, he's/ she's offering a challenge. Can you see what Rutledge sees? Can you judge people the way he does? How did you work out the ending? Anybody who buys and reads your novel deserves to be entertained, not annoyed.

Jon: Is Rutledge going to age in the series? Are we someday going to see him in his late fifties investigating or consulting?

Charles: If you have noticed, the books so far have covered nearly six months of his life after leaving the clinic. June was TEST OF
WILLS, July WINGS OF FIRE, etc. WATCHERS brings us to October. We used this system rather than the passage of years because   part of the story is how a man recovers his equilibrium, and the reader seems to want to share in that exploration, not to pick up the next novel and

learn it's now 1923 or whatever, Rutledge is completely healed and getting married in May. That works well with any types of characters, don't get me wrong. But here what is happening within this man is a gradual process of discovery.

All the same, if readers want him to go on, he's going to be there in his late fifties (looking quite distinguished with that graying dark hair) and probably still battling with Hamish. We've got November in the computer and a glimmer of an idea for December, so he's going to get to the 1920's before long.

Jon: Aside from the fact that I have to wait until next fall for the next book, what can you tell us about A FEARSOME DOUBT?

Charles: A FEARSOME DOUBT is something we thought would be interesting to try. It's November, Rutledge is having troubles with the Armistice celebrations that everybody is talking about--it has revived too many of his own memories of the war. He doesn't see himself as a hero welcomed home, he doesn't believe he belongs with the honorably wounded, and he's got too many dead on his own conscience after four years of fighting to stand and listen to political speeches about the meaning of dying for one's country. At this very difficult time, he's thrown into two investigations--one from his past, pre-war, pre-Hamish, and another present day one that inadvertently drags him back into an experience he had wiped out of his mind in the last day of the war. It's a challenge to write! If you can't wait, pick up the paperback of WATCHERS, when that comes out, and you'll find a preview of DOUBT.

Jon: Your series seems to have very wide appeal. I know people who read almost nothing but hard-boiled who love them, and the same is true of historical readers and cozy readers. Also, they seem to attract a broad age range. Why do you think this is?

Charles: At first we were completely unprepared for this. We expected to reach readers who wanted to walk through an interesting case with someone like Rutledge. Instead, there are thousands of people who are drawn to this man. Romantic Times has given us an award for SEARCH THE DARK, best historical for that year. Vietnam vets have told us that they see a lot of their own suffering in Rutledge's. We hear from readers who would never dream of getting hooked on this genre, telling us that they rushed out to buy the only Rutledge short story.

Someone form New York City told us that they understood their own emotions in the aftermath of September 11th because the novels had given them a different perspective of post-traumatic stress syndrome. Don't get me wrong-- all this is wonderful! But it is amazing as well.

Our guess would be that there'a a human quality to the story-- and to the characters, and to the emotions or fears -- that tear everybody apart. That must be what a reader finds first and stays with. History may not be his or her thing, but caring about the people is, whatever his or her favorite genre. that's what we like best in a book ourselves, and it must be something that we do well for that reason.

Jon: Any thoughts on doing kind of a flashback book, with a Rutledge on a case before the war?

Charles: Not really. We get into pre-war in some fashion in nearly every novel, so that there's a contrast, but A FEARSOME DOUBT comes closest to that idea. The Rutledge short stories are often set during the war when Hamish was alive. What intrigues us is a novel about the pre-war years that gives us a different flexibility in setting, action, and characters.

Caroline: What Charles refers to as my Dorothy Dunnett mode...

Charles: A non-Rutledge maybe, but certainly a mystery. And most certainly, a stand-alone, not a series. We'v learned so much about the war that we can't use in the Rutledge stories, and something is bound to happen.

Jon: Well, here's a question I usually can only get one perspective on. What was Charles like as a kid?

Caroline: Precocious, stubborn, too smart for word. Caring. And already marching to his own drummer. Stand him in a corner for being naughty, and he'd be making up games with the shadows on the wall. A slow temper. Some of the neatest ideas. Interesting guy, even at two. Of course, there are times when I could gladly kill him, you understand. But as he ages, like good brandy, he gets better.

Jon: Have you "tucker-ized" anyone in your books?

Charles: Not really because it's hard to force fit a character into a preexisting mold. But there are characteristics that show up sometimes and surprise us. A writer absorbs everything, and sooner or later it reappears. But you don't always see that until all at once you recognize a habit or a way of thinking. The question is-- is that character always the villain? No. We generously spread these things around.

Jon: When will I be able to buy a Rutledge Rain Coat?

Charles: I don't know. I can see a line of trench coats with his name on the label. Really cool stuff-- like those Hemingway fishing hats. What was that catalog that used to come in the mail? Peterson's? It had the kind of flair that goes with Rutledge and The Great War.

Jon: How important is a good editor?

Charles: How important is breathing? We've been lucky with two of the finest in the business, Ruth Cavin and Kate Miciak. When they speak, you listen. They have the knowledge and experience that a good writer needs to look even better. Both Kate and Ruth loved A TEST OF WILLS (Bantam did the softcover, St. Martin's the hardcover) and they understand where Rutledge is coming from. And we've decided that if we can ever kidnap half of Kate's very efficient staff, we could probably write two books a year.

Jon: Your next book, THE MURDER STONE, is out of the series. What's it about?

Charles: THE MURDER STONE is out of series, but not out of time and place--Autumn 1916, England, in the aftermath of the Battle of the Somme. But this is the civilian side of the story and the protagonist is a young woman. She's lost five cousins to the war, and now her grief-stricken grandfather, Francis Hatton, the man who raised them all, dies. When his obituary is printed in The Times, she finds she's inherited not only his estate but his enemies as well. Who cursed him? Did he kill the woman who went missing years before? What has the Murder Stone to do with the past? What happened to Francesca's family over the years, what destroyed all the males and now threatens the last of the Hattons, Francesca herself? It's psychological suspense with a twist.

Jon: Is the book for 2004 going to be another Rutledge?

Charles: Rutledge comes back in fine fettle in 2004, with A COLD

TREACHERY, the search for a child who may be a cold blooded murderer--or the victim of one. Rutledge also meets a woman he could care about. But Fate may decide otherwise.

Jon: You are reading for the Edgar committee, how many books does this mean you'll have read this year?

Charles: This year I'm chair of the Edgar Best First Committee. I hold in my hands the works of authors who may go on to be the next big block-buster--or who will slip into obscurity. It's terrific meeting them at the start of their careers, then following them to see how they prosper. The last time, when Steve Hamilton was chair, we had something like 96 novels. To date we've logged in about 45, and the late summer/fall/ winter novels haven't arrived yet. I really don't have time to read like this--but you find a way to do it.

Jon: What's the one thing always in your refrigerator?

Charles: You know what's in mine--ice cubes for a now 17 year old cat who wants to see icebergs floating in his water dish the minute I step in the door.

Caroline: You mean besides half gallons of chocolate ice cream? I think there's also a six year old lobster called George in the freezer. He was part of the celebration for publications of TEST OF WILLS, and we couldn't bear to eat him after somebody named him.

Charles Todd's website:
www.charlestodd.com

Charles Todd's Books:

A Test of Wills (1997)
Wings of Fire (1998)
Search the Dark (1999)
Legacy of the Dead (2000)
Watchers of Time (2001)
A Fearsome Doubt (2002)
The Murder Stone (2003)
A Cold Treachery (2004)

Brian Wiprud

There are a lot of success stories in the crime fiction world, but those are few and far between. Sadly, most people that have a dream to get published never achieve that goal. They work, they toil, they send their manuscripts to agents and editors who send back rejection after rejection. It's frustrating, it's disheartening. What's an aspiring writer to do?

That's why the story of Brian Wiprud is such a triumph. Because in the end, the stories he wants to write have reached an audience, gained a cult following, and won him a prized deal. I love stories that have happy endings, and there isn't a more deserving guy than Brian.

He's a man of many talents: manhole detective, fly fishing expert, collector of taxidermy, and knows how to make one mean mai tai. Oh yeah, and he's also the writer of some of the zaniest books you'll come across in the mystery section. For years, manuscripts accumulated in the drawer. His natural voice was the comic caper a la Westlake's Dortmunder, but time and time again, he'd get the same stock answer: "comic crime doesn't sell." And perhaps we would never have known about his gift for hilarious situations and madcap adventures had he not dived into the murky world of print-on-demand, which resulted in his first book, SLEEP WITH THE FISHES, appearing in select bookshops in the fall of 2001.

The word-of-mouth was pretty good, as it should have been. This was one funny tale, about a mobster named Sid Bifulco who'd jumped ship from the life and hoped to live quietly in a small Connecticut town, catching fishes and leading the simple life. Too bad things don't really work out that way. A dead body and a few crazy people and Sid's life turned totally upside down. And on it went. I laughed, I recommended it to friends, I laughed some more.

Then, the next year, heralded the arrival of PIPSQUEAK. Taxidermy, conspiracy theories...and a stuffed squirrel from a two-bit cable access show from the 1960s? The plot's nearly impossible to sum up, but the important part was that this book was non-stop laughter. And the buzz grew, and grew. Blurbs from the likes of Lee Child and Harlan Coben. Heady praise on message boards and mailing lists, at mystery conventions and independent bookshops. They stocked the book, it sold. The word-of-mouth was incredible. And by fate, dogged determination, or whatever, the book landed on the desk of a young editor at Bantam Dell. She loved it. Long story short? Look for the mass market edition of PIPSQUEAK in stores everywhere in the spring of 2004, with another book to follow.

If you haven't read any of Brian Wiprud's books, you're missing out one of the most unique voices to grace the pages of a crime novel. There's nobody quite like him, as you'll see in this interview, conducted just as PIPSQUEAK first saw the light of day. He's one of my favorite people, and his story really shows that there's room for all sorts in the publishing world – and memo to those agents and editors? Comic crime does sell after all.
--Sarah Weinman/August 2003

(Author's note - This interview was done in two parts, before and after Brian got his Lefty Award and Bantam contract)

Jon: Well, the first thing on my mind is the need to know how much of Brian Wiprud is in Garth Carson? Or is it the other way around?

Brian: There's a little bit of me in all my protagonists, which I think is unavoidable. I was almost named Garth, and perhaps a little more of me in Garth than in either Sid Bifulco or Russ Smonig from SLEEP WITH THE FISHES. The idea for the book stemmed from wanting to write a Nick and Nora Charles-type novel, and Angie and Garth are loosely -- very loosely -- based on Maggie and me. We collect taxidermy and thus frequent sundry antique stores hither and yon.

Jon: When you go to antique stores or thrift stores, do you sometimes find things that are just so cool you have to have it, and then wonder why no one else has picked it up? I know I've done this, and then I wonder if it's because my taste is just so weird.

Brian: Absolutely. But not just cool: hideous. Some things are so appallingly bad...the other week I saw a pair of brown paper mache elf statues, one playing a lyre, the other a flute, about two feet high, mounted in front of cheesy guilt mirrors. Elf taxidermy! And it was cheap at $48 for the pair! No, I didn't buy them, they belong in a different, scary collection, but I loved them.

Jon: In addition to just publishing your second novel, you've also written quite a few articles on a variety of subjects. Where have they been published, and what are they about?

Brian: I have two specialties other than writing: fly fishing and underground New York City. My publishing credits include articles on fly fishing for "American Angler", "Fly Fish America", "Mid Atlantic Fly Fishing Guide" and a host of others. My specialty within fly fishing are for some "off species" such as shad and pickerel, as opposed to more mainstream fish like trout and bass. Pretty esoteric stuff, to be honest. Articles on underground New York have appeared in "Mercators World" (a magazine for map enthusiasts,) the anthology "Concrete Jungle" and "Tribeca Trib."

Jon: Is there some where people could go to read these? (he asked knowingly...)

Brian: Most of these are available for browsing on my website.

Jon: You actually work in the New York City sewers? There has got to be some interesting stories you can tell about that.

Brian: My day job is as a utilities specialist, a consultant, which means I'm sort of a manhole detective. This entails trying to figure out, at a given location, exactly what utilities and other structures (like lost or abandoned tunnels) under the city streets. It can be very interesting, but like detective work requires a lot of research and grunt work, like long hours studying records, opening manholes and descending into sewers. I was called in post-9/11 to try and find a way into the World Trade Center complex through the subterranean infrastructure and find a means to search for people who might be trapped. Unfortunately, I was unable to find any access large enough to be useful.

Jon: What other kind of jobs have you had?

Brian: In hindsight, I'd say the most interesting would be projectionist. I used to mess with the audience. While the audience was waiting for the lights to go down in the theater, I'd turn them down just a little, and everybody slumped down in their seats all at once. Then I'd turn it back up a little and - whomp - up they all come again. I'd see how many times I could make them go up and down before someone started up the aisle to see what was going on. I also used to edit the films a little. There's a shutter on the projector so you can black it out, and I used to keep the   audience in the dark for the opening shot of "Honeysuckle Rose" (Willie Nelson, Dyan Cannon) so that all you could hear were cows mooing in the dark for the first ten seconds. An vast improvement. And "Herbie Goes Bananas" - alas, the last in a string of Love Bug movies - was much improved by my rearranging of the last, climactic scene. OK, actually, the film got a little mangled by accident, and I did some compulsory condensation of the final chase. But believe me, the sooner the audience was out of that movie the better. By accident, I once left out the entire second reel (out of three) of "The Main Event" and nobody noticed.

Jon: When you started the books, did you plan for them to be mysteries?

Brian: Is there any other kind of story? I once heard someone characterize literary fiction as a mystery with weak characters and a weaker plot.

Jon: PIPSQUEAK gets into the area of conspiracies. Are there any conspiracy theories out there that interest you? Are there some that are just good comic relief?

Brian: Conspiracies share certain qualities with cults that fascinate me. I mean, in order to tow the line in a conspiracy, to keep the operation secret, you have to buy into the guiding principle above all else, which means surrendering a big part of yourself. Lot to explore there. Cults and conspiracies both have comic elements for those of us on the outside because for the non-believers their cause can seem so ludicrous - fertile ground for misunderstandings, cross purposes and humor.

Jon: Garth and Angie have a very healthy relationship. What do you think is important to keep a relationship between two people going strong?

Brian: His and hers mayonnaise. You didn't really want a serious answer? Well, if you insist. I'd say a robust sense of humor and the ability to compromise.

Jon: So who uses what kind of mayo?

Brian: Mayonnaise is exactly what I won't compromise on. I use a lemon mayonnaise, made in Maine. Maggie is a traditionalist, a Hellmann's girl. That said, I should point out we share a jar of japolte mayo.

Jon: Garth drives a really cool car in Pipsqueak. We know this because of one of my favorite lines in the book, "When you drive with the top down, tin top motorists are Mr. Magoo to your James Bond". What do you drive?

Brian: Mine is a 1963 Mercury Comet convertible, red, white top, 6cyl three in the tree. You can see pictures of it on my website www.wiprud.com. Bought it about six years ago and never looked back. After years of driving heaps, I concluded life's too short to drive a boring car, much less something that isn't a convertible. The car Garth drives is a 1966 Lincoln convertible, the one with the suicide doors. I always wanted one of them, too. One day.

Jon: What gave you the inspiration for your first book, SLEEP WITH THE FISHES?

Brian: I was working with a contractor here in New York who was doing some exploratory digging for me in the street. Like a lot of contractors, he had an erstwhile wise guy demeanor. He had a boat, and on weekends would go fishing out in the bay. One Monday, I asked him how the fishing was over the weekend, and he said, "Me and Vinny whacked some doormats [flounder.]" That got me to thinking "What if..." there was a mobster who gave up whacking people for whacking fish?

Jon: You have a lot of references to things nostalgic, are you a nostalgic person?

Brian: Hardly. I'm not the kind of person who likes to chat about old times or to wish I lived back when. But I am what some would call old school, meaning I have an appreciation for the 40's, 50's and 60' styles.

Take cars. Contemporary cars? I can't tell them apart, they virtually look all the same to me. Rounded, bean shaped,
aerodynamic, hyper functional. Cars in the 50's and 60's had much more whimsical designs that appeal to me. I also have a large collection of thin ties, the only kind I wear.

Jon: I like that answer. So it's safe to say that you don't miss the times, but you miss the stuff?

Brian: I wouldn't say miss the stuff because I acquire what fits my style, where feasible, and can appreciate it even without owning it or having it be the style of my time. And I think I appreciate the stuff more because it's now rare.

Jon: Who are some of the authors you like to read?

Brian: I'm absolutely insane for Fraser's "Flashman" novels, which I only discovered a couple years back. In mysteries, in the humor sub-genre? Westlake, Evanovich, Coben, Fitzhugh. Outside of that it's Lee Child and Steve Hamilton.

Jon: I'm guessing from your website that you are a bit of an outdoorsman. Is that how you spend a lot of your free time?

Brian: Inordinate amounts of time April to October tromping around in rubber waders through rivers, creeks and marshes, chasing fish with a fly rod. Or rowing miles and miles to far flung spots, hauling the boat over beaver dams and rowing some more. I also do a fair amount of outdoor photography, especially of birds and fish. You want to find a cuckoo or a pileated woodpecker nest, you have to get way back in that swamp. People always think about fishing as being relaxing, but for me it's akin to an "Xtreme" sport.

Jon: And let's see if I read this correctly, you have "Brooklyn's largest collection of taxidermy" in your home?

Brian: That's a fact. Everything from a curassow to a kangaroo rug. If you include skulls, we probably have over a hundred pieces in an apartment that's about 750 square feet. It's cozy.

Jon: I'll bet you get some interesting reactions when people come over for the first time. Has anyone every freaked out and had to leave?

Brian: Our contention is that taxidermy is art, and a collection is a sum of it's parts. An art collector can collect velvet paintings of clowns even as a taxidermy collector could collect amphibians playing guitars. Some art can be creepy, whether made of paint, clowns, or frogs. People have been apprehensive and then found that our collection --but almost universally-- find it quite stunning. We've never had anybody freak out, but then again we don't know any PETA enthusiasts.

Jon: If a movie were made of your life, who would play you, and who could you see as Maggie?

Brian: A film of my life? Pretty lousy screenplay with no villains. So let's start with a villain for my life, say Larry Block. And let's throw in a sidekick for me - Paul Rubens. Bruce Campbell can play me, and Maggie says Lucy Lawless would be good for her.

Jon: Is it difficult living with a 23 pound cat?

Brian: You mean that black and white ottoman in the living room is a cat?

Jon: What will we see from you next, a sequel to SLEEP WITH THE FISHES, or PIPSQUEAK, or something new? ...and could you write a little faster please?

Brian: DIRT NAP is next, and is the sequel to SLEEP WITH THE FISHES. A private hunting and fishing club hires Sid to solve their poaching problem, and the cure may be worse than the disease. The sequel is considerably longer than the first, and thus the complexity level goes up, making it more difficult to finish. I have the rough draft, but have a lot of tweaking to do. Unlike PIPSQUEAK, writing in third person is a lot more difficult for me because I have to jump in and out of a bunch of people's heads, and the timeline has to be kept straight of who is doing what when, and exactly what their motivation is. Like SLEEP WITH THE FISHES, DIRT NAP is full of mix-ups that require no small amount of fine-tuning the characters to make hit on all cylinders. Any publisher out there that wants me to work at this full-time and make it all happen faster, you know where to reach me.

Jon: What would you consider a must for a complete music collection?

Brian: My jukebox includes surf music, mambo, soundtracks, swing, rockabilly, some lounge and alternative country. For brevity's sake, I'm going to whittle it down to ten albums, which is still a woefully deficient collection:

"Havana 3 AM" Perez Prado
"Night Beat" Tito Puente
"Viva Los Straitjackets" Los Straitjackets
"Ramonesmania" Ramones
"Beethoven's Nine Symphonies" Cleveland Philharmonic
"The Good, The Bad and the Ugly Soundtrack" Ennio Morricone
"Full Western Dress" Derailers
"Dance All Night" Room Full Of Blues
"In Like Flint Soundtrack" Jerry Goldsmith
"Dirty Boogie"
Brian Setzer Orchestra

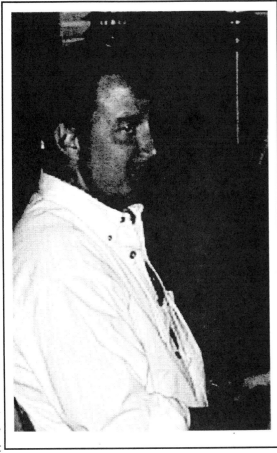

Jon: When are you at your happiest?

Brian: Maggie keeps the happy meter pretty high, but the needle swings into the red zone when I find the really clever conclusion to the book I'm writing, or when I'm having a really special and exhausting day of fly fishing.

Jon: What's the toughest thing about the writing process?

Brian: Not procrastinating.

Jon: With the Lefty award under your belt, and a contract

with one of the big boys of publishing, has the way you approach your writing changed?

Brian: My approach to writing has changed in a number of ways. For one, I now write what my publisher wants me to write. In this case it's the continuation of the PIPSQUEAK series, which is fine by me. I have an editor now and deadlines that have to be met, which keeps me from goofing off as often as I might have been tempted to do otherwise. It's all a part of having a publisher and all positive. I'm also composing on a lap top now so I can optimize my writing time.

Jon: What is the book your working on now titled, and what is it about?

Brian: As you know, I have two series. One was started by SLEEP WITH THE FISHES, and is about a mobster who retires to a rural community where his past keeps catching up with him. The other is the PIPSQUEAK series about Garth Carson, a taxidermy broker in Manhattan.

Before the Bantam Dell deal, I was hard at work on GRANITE HAT, the third Sid Bifulco book. I had just finished the manuscript for DIRT NAP, the second in the Sid Bifulco series. Both books have been shelved for now.

So I'm now back to working on the prequel to PIPSQUEAK, for which I had a partial manuscript already. The working title is FIFTY DOLLAR MOOSEHEAD. You should know that PIPSQUEAK had a number of alternative titles, and right up to the very end it was entitled "Bin of Squirrels." The second Garth Carson book covers the first two times Garth got in hot water and the early days with Otto. In the mix is the illegal trade in bear gallbladders (animal chop shops) and a certain extremely rare Asian bovid called a vortung.

It's kind of frustrating that DIRT NAP has to wait, but launching the PIPSQUEAK series with Bantam Dell obviously takes precedence. Anyway, I've got no shortage of novels to work on.

Jon: If you could ad something to your own bio, without actually having to back it up, what would it be?

Brian: "Test Pah-let." ...There was a demon that lived in the thin air. They said anyone who challenged him would die. Their controls would freeze up, their plane would buffet wildly and they would disintegrate. The demon lived at Mach 1 on the meter.

Jon: Why should everyone make a point of seeing The Derailers play live?

Brian: Don't postpone joy.

Jon: When PIPSQUEAK comes out in Hardcover, are you going to do a signing tour?

Brian: PIPSQUEAK is coming out as a mass market paperback June 1, 2004, and thus a signing tour is unlikely.

Jon: And what is the schedule for the books?

Brian: FIFTY DOLLAR MOOSEHEAD is supposed to come out less than a year after PIPSQUEAK.

Jon: What are a few things in your life that you just won't compromise on?

Brian: That depends on whether you're talking about writing or life in general. As for my writing, Bantam Dell's editorial comments haven't required any compromises, and my editor and I are in sync so I don't foresee any problems. But I can see how an author might be asked to dumb down or "formulize" his work. You know, like insert a pet gerbil to make a character more likeable, add a crippled child for empathy, and change the character "Billy" to "Gramps" in order to capture the AARP demographic. I would have a very hard time compromising on that kind of stuff.

As for life in general, I won't compromise on sour mash whiskey or crab cakes.

Jon: My wife, my sister, and I decided that you must be one of the most mellow people we've met. What's your secret?

Brian: Mellow? Perhaps by comparison with your immediate family, but I think there are a number of people who would take exception with that characterization. If I seem mellow, a skeptic's Weltanschauung peppered liberally with humor is probably to blame.

Jon: What is the one thing always in your refrigerator?

Brian: The refrigerator: Martini glasses. The freezer: Little Smokies.

Brian's website:
www.wiprud.com

Brian Wiprud's books:
Sleeping With The Fishes
Pipsqueak

Photo by: Jennifer Jordan

JON JORDAN COULD BEST BE DESCRIBED AS AN OBSESSIVE COMPULSIVE CRIME FICTION READER, BUYER, COLLECTOR AND FAN. HIS LOVE OF MYSTERY LED HIM TO THE NEXT LEVEL. QUESTIONS. NOW, WHEN NOT READING, JON IS ASKING. AND PEOPLE, NAMELY MYSTERY AUTHORS, ARE ANSWERING.

JON LIVES A MOSTLY NOCTURNAL EXISTENCE IN MILWAUKEE, WISCONSIN WITH HIS VERY PATIENT WIFE RUTH AND A BEVY OF PSYCHOTIC CATS.

Printed by

DIGITAL GRAPHICS
OFFSET & DIGITAL PRINTING